The Ultimate Flower Gardener's Guide

The Ultimate Flower Gardener's Guide

How to Combine
Shape, Color, and Texture
to Create the
Garden of Your Dreams

Jenny Rose Carey

TIMBER PRESS • Portland, Oregon

Frontispiece: *Rudbeckia fulgida* var. *sullivantii* 'Goldsturm'
Page 6: Orange dahlia with verbena, crocosmia, and nasturtium.
Copyright © 2022 by Jenny Rose Carey. All rights reserved.
Garden and photography credits appear on page 349.

Published in 2022 by Timber Press, Inc.
The Haseltine Building
133 S.W. Second Avenue, Suite 450
Portland, Oregon 97204-3527
timberpress.com

Printed in China on paper from responsible sources

Text and cover design by Sarah Crumb

ISBN 978-1-64326-038-9

Catalog records for this book are available from the Library of Congress
and the British Library.

::::::::::::::::::::::::::::::::

I dedicate this book to my gardening mentors and friends,
who have freely shared their knowledge and love of flowers with me
over the decades, and to my children, nieces, and grandson,
the next generations of flower lovers. May you experience the beauty, joy,
and fulfillment that growing your own flower garden can bring.

::::::::::::::::::::::::::::::::

Contents

Preface

Starting and tending a flower garden is a personal affair. Each of us has our own life experiences and preferences that we bring to it. Even if we have never put a shovel in the ground ourselves, we love flowers because they are a part of our celebrations and daily life. We have been given bunches of flowers or seen them in gardens, but we may not have thought much about how to grow them.

Every place that I have lived I have grown flowers. I started gardening as a child in my parents' cottage garden in England, then in small plots as a young adult, and now here at Northview, my Pennsylvania garden on the East Coast of the United States. Over the course of my gardening life, I have planted thousands of different flowers and found favorites that I grow every year and others that reappear every now and then.

If you are interested in starting your own flower garden, don't be afraid—just have a go. Everyone has to start somewhere. Making a personal garden is a wonderfully creative process. It involves finding flowers that you love, learning how to put them together, and getting them to flourish. Unlike other creative arts like cooking, where a meal is made and then immediately consumed, making your garden is a continuing process. The flowers are your ingredients, and they are mixed together and assembled into a beautiful concoction of your own making. This is not the end, though, because your flowers are alive and continue to grow and change. You will also refine your flower garden palette over the course of this growing season and the next.

Gardeners live concurrently in the past, present, and future. Walking around my garden with friends, I might reminisce: "Oh, you should have seen the flowers last week. They were so gorgeous"; or exclaim about a flower in bloom: "Wow, look at the beautiful color and shape"; or muse about the future: "I definitely have to have more of that flower next year." Relishing past successes and learning from your failures has always been a valuable part of gardening. You find out which flowers you really love and which ones grow well for you. It is also important to savor the garden as it is right now. Visit it every day to see what has changed since yesterday. Revel in the sights, smells, and sounds of your garden. Steal a moment of peace and quiet among your flowers as a break from the hustle and bustle. Lastly, think about the future. Gardening teaches us to be optimists. We plant seeds and bulbs that look brown and wrinkled and expect them to grow. We wait, not always patiently, for something to happen. Our minds race on to the full-blown flower and how beautiful it will look. Oh, what a glorious sight your flower garden will be!

Your flower garden should be beautiful to you. These apricot parrot tulips in hues of white, pink, coral, and green bring me joy.

opposite Outside my front door I love to grow some of my favorite flowers, like foxgloves.

Introduction

Flowers! Just thinking about the word makes me happy. Spending time among and between flowers is even better. There is nothing like walking out of your door on a beautiful morning and seeing a patch of gorgeous blooms that you chose yourself. You are instantly drawn to check on their progress to see whether there are petals peeking out of buds for you to scrutinize. Other flowers may be in full bloom, revealing the subtle details that fascinate you and the buzzing insects that enjoy them. It is an appealing and engaging scene, which begins with your first dream of a future garden. You can turn the dream into a reality with some inspiration and guidance. Immerse yourself in the world of flowers! Be inquisitive, think about what you like, and learn as you go along. Each step forward on your flower gardening journey will help you improve your garden and make it more to your liking.

Flower gardens are as individual as the blooms that grow there and the gardeners who cultivate them. The flowers that are available to grow in our gardens have been assembled from all around the world for centuries. They have been selected for their beauty, their usefulness, or just because people loved them and passed them on to others. Additional flowers have come into our gardens from plant breeding. Deliberate selection and hybridization—crossing one flower with another—has given us increased floral diversity.

Individual flowers are the building blocks of your design. Each one is a beautiful jewel in its own right but is far better in combinations that sparkle and adorn your garden. Combining flowers is the artistic side of flower gardening. It involves careful observation and appreciation of the specific sensory qualities of individual plants. Observation is also key to the scientific side of flower gardening. By closely examining potential flowers and learning how to grow them according to their needs, you will create a successful and beautiful garden. Luckily, plants have a will to grow if they are given decent conditions. Much of gardening is learned by doing. Come on a floral exploration with me as we look into the fascinating world of garden flowers.

opposite (clockwise from top left) Three beautiful blue flowers: Siberian iris, camas, and delphinium.

11

Getting the Most from This Book

In the first chapter, you will learn to look carefully at individual flowers, start a wish list, and understand the benefits of combining flowers not only by color but by shape and presence. Next comes an overview of a gardener's typical year, with plant types, tasks and activities, and standout flowers for each season.

The third chapter is the plant palette, which lists nearly two hundred genera of beautiful flowers for your garden and includes their shape, role, and position in the flower bed along with selected species and cultivars. All flowers mentioned in the book are treated here in the palette, giving you quick but detailed information to inform your design process.

In the fourth chapter you will lay the groundwork and think about location, where to find inspiration, and how you will design your flower beds. Finally, the last chapter gives you practical advice on planning and planting techniques as well as maintenance practices to keep your plants happy and healthy.

By the end of this book, you will have the knowledge and inspiration to design and install the flower bed of your dreams. And I hope it won't be your last!

opposite A cottage-style mixed herbaceous bed in my garden with poppy, rose campion, betony, and verbascum.

Your Garden of Flowers

A Look at Shape, Role, Presence, and Color

Your flower garden is your creation. It should be packed with the flowers that you love to interact with, look after, cut for your house, and photograph. When we start gardening, we often assemble a random assortment of flowers that appeal to us. This unplanned collection of plants can be made into a beautiful-looking flower bed if you understand how to coordinate them. Though every flower is unique and the range of available flowering plants is incredibly diverse, they can all be divided into groups that share » certain visual and functional characteristics. Once you recognize these groups, you can mix and match them to create a beautiful flower garden design. Flowering plants are the ingredients of your garden, and the way you combine them is your recipe. As in cooking, you can take the same ingredients in different quantities and assemble them in different ways to make distinct creations.

Your Flower Wish List

I love flowers. To keep track of the ones I might like to grow, I have a wish list on which I write down plants I see in books or magazines that I want to look up later. I add in flowers that catch my eye when I visit other gardens, and it's no surprise that the wish list has become rather extensive!

We all have personal preferences, so your wish list will likely be different from mine. One gardener can't live without their blowsy dahlias in pastel pink, but another wouldn't grow them.

However you record your flower wish list, make sure it is portable. You will want it with you as you visit gardens and plant nurseries. If you already have favorite flowers, they should be first on your list—they are the ones you would really miss if they were absent. Add other flowers that tug on your heartstrings because of good memories or other personal meaning. Continue to fill your list with plants that you have always wanted to grow. If you don't already have strong favorites but you love flowers generally, keep exploring and you will find the ones that fill your soul with joy. Reflect on gardens from your childhood and gardeners who motivated you to begin growing flowers. This may bring up some important memory flowers that you might want to have in your garden. It might take a while to perfect your own style, and you may come up with some strange combinations along the way. Each change becomes part of your experimental approach to flower gardening.

previous (clockwise from top left) A trio of a white dahlia, white daffodil, and white holly.

below This semi-double pale pink peony is just my style.

from left I love to grow pot marigolds because they remind me of my earliest gardening experiences with my mother.

My wish list has a plethora of pink and purple flowers for every season, like those in this fall combination of border phlox, New England aster, tall verbena, and hybrid flowering tobacco.

Record anything about the flower that might be helpful later, including the date and place where you saw it, what it looked like, and why you were attracted to it. Other useful details are approximate plant height, the shape and color of the flower, anything about the leaves that you noticed, and what flowers were nearby. Take photos to remind yourself. Your flower wish list will likely continue to grow even after you start or expand your garden. It is a way to remember beautiful flowers you have seen and can help you learn plant names.

Pink Macedonian scabious and lavender make a great summer combination for a dry area.

As you develop your flower garden, you will further refine this list and find out what plants you absolutely love and must have. Some of the plants you are excited to grow may turn out to be duds—you may end up not liking the way they look with other flowers in your garden, or they may look puny or just die. Not all plants are winners in every garden. You will improve your selection every year as your flower garden grows. Once you have a start on your flowery wish list, it is time to think about how you could grow them together in a garden.

PLANT TYPES FOR YOUR FLOWERY GARDEN

Flowers are grouped according to the length of their life. The longest-lived plants in a flower bed are perennials, some of which may live for decades, depending on the type of plant and how it is grown. Herbaceous perennials die down to the ground in winter and reemerge from their roots the following growing year. They are a long-term investment and the

To extend your flowering season, pack your beds with perennials, annuals, and bulbs like silver sage, love-in-a-mist, and allium.

backbone of your flowery border. Perennials tend to bloom at a set time each year. The length of time they are in flower varies by species, and some may rebloom if cut back after their first flush. Many perennials get bigger and better year by year. Annual plants have colorful flowers that continue their show for a long period during one growing season and then die after setting seed. Biennials start to grow leaves in one gardening year and bloom in the next. Flowering bulbs and tender perennials add to the floral profusion.

It is possible to grow just one of these plant groups in a bed, but if your goal is a seriously flowery border that blooms for months, it is best to grow most or all of them. Perennials, biennials, bulbs, and annuals, when grown together in one garden space, are described as a mixed herbaceous planting. It is possible to add woody flowering shrubs and trees in or around your flower garden, but they are not necessary for a full flowery look. Be aware that woody plants have extensive root systems, and they may grow large and shade the area around them.

How Flowers are Named

Throughout the history of gardening, people have grown the same plant under various lyrical and descriptive common names. Most plants today have traditional names that originated in their native ranges. As plants were transported from country to country, common names proliferated, leading to confusion among gardeners when they tried to communicate with each other. Latin is the language of plant classification instituted by European botanists and spread throughout the world alongside colonialism. We choose to use Latin names to ensure we are talking about the same flower. Don't let using or learning Latin plant names be a barrier to entry into flower gardening. Some people love the challenge of learning the names and treat it like taking on a new foreign language. To others it has no relevance, and the names don't stick. This is not going to make or break your ability to be a good flower gardener!

Viola tricolor, Johnny-jump-up, has a descriptive Latin species name, *tricolor*, that means it has three colors in its flowers.

The botanical Latin names listed in catalogs, on seed packets, and on plant tags have two parts. The first name is the genus and is always capitalized. Think of that as your last name. A genus (plural "genera") contains a group of different yet closely related plant species. The second name is like your first name. It distinguishes you from the rest of your relations. The plants within a genus are distinguished by this second name, which is called the specific epithet or species

Centaurea macroceph-ala has a bigger flower head than others in the genus (*macrocephala* can be translated as "large head").

placed into groups. Analysis of their genetic codes has since revealed that not all plants that look alike are closely related. This has led to some groups of plants being renamed and moved into other genera. Much to the consternation and confusion of gardeners, some of the familiar flower names used for decades have been altered. For example, Russian sage, which had been known as *Perovskia atriplicifolia*, is now reclassified as *Salvia yangii*. I have used the most up-to-date names for this book, but some may change again.

Following the genus and species of some flowers is an additional name in quotation marks. This is the cultivar name, and it is usually not in Latin. Cultivars are cultivated varieties of a species, which vary in size, color, or other characteristics that make them distinct from the straight species and other cultivars. For example, if you were looking for a peony, you could select a cultivar according to its height, season of bloom, flower color, shape, and fragrance. Though the two peony cultivars 'Sarah Bernhardt' and 'Krinkled White' are the same genus and species, they look very different in the garden. Knowing cultivar names allows you to select precisely the flower you want, and knowing the names of flowers in general will help you talk about them with other gardeners, shop for them, and find out the conditions that they need to grow.

name and is written in lowercase. The species name might describe a characteristic aspect of that plant. Maybe it tells you the color of the flower or the size of the plant. For instance, in the botanical name *Viola tricolor*, known commonly as Johnny-jump-up or heartsease, the species name refers to the fact that its flowers have three colors. Before genetic research was available, plants that looked similar were

Flower and Inflorescence Shapes

One consideration as you ponder the design of your flower garden is the overall shape of flowers both up close and from a distance. Some solitary flowers are large enough and have enough presence to be seen from a few feet away, while others are too small to be differentiated from a distance. As you design your bed, pay attention to the shapes of individual blooms as well as the clustered flower heads called inflorescences.

The shape of an inflorescence is influenced by the form of the individual flowers it is made up of as well as the way they are held and arranged. Some inflorescences have an obvious overall shape, while others are indistinct and hazy. As you investigate the shapes of flowers, think about how they would look placed near to each other in your flower bed. Each flower and inflorescence shape adds something to the complete garden picture, bringing interest, movement, drama, and visual variety. When flowers are combined thoughtfully, they contribute to the beauty of your design.

PEEKING INTO A FLOWER

The purpose of every bloom is to attract pollinators to take pollen from one flower to another, facilitating seed production for the plant. Flowers are beautiful assemblages of tiny parts, each with a specific role to play. Some protect the flower as it grows, and others attract the pollinator. Additional bits of the flower make the pollen and egg and safeguard the seed as it grows. One of the best ways to get to know a flower is to watch it open. Choose one plant to observe over the course of a few days, and tie a bit of string around a stem to remind you which one you are looking at.

Starting on the outside, the green sepals protect the flower when it is in bud, waiting for the right conditions and time of year to open up. As the flower bud opens, the sepals crack apart, then bend back or fall away to reveal the petals, usually the first thing we notice about a flower as well as the most attractive. The number, shape, size, texture, and color of petals are characteristic of each flower, and they are positioned in a circle within the sepals. Some flowers have modified or fused sepals or petals, so it may not be obvious which is which. Flowers are designed to be highly visible not to humans but to passing pollinators. They can attract attention by

Observing flowers up close provides unexpected surprises, like the purple and orange stamens of this nettle-leaved mullein.

from left As you observe flowers, you will notice that each species has its own unique arrangement of floral parts. The stamens of this hibiscus surround its fuzzy five-parted stigma.

Large-scale blooms like this lily 'Black Beauty' provide easy viewing of the inner workings of flowers.

being large, bold, brightly colored, or held on tall, whippy stems that wiggle in the breeze like a waving flag. Their message to a passing pollinator is "Stop here, we are open for business."

The ring of structures inside the petals are the pollen-containing stamens. At the top is an enlarged part called the anther, which holds the pollen. Each anther is on a filament, a flexible stalk holding the anther at the correct angle for pollen to attach to pollinators feeding from the flower. Anthers are colored by pollen, which is often orange, yellow, cream, or brown but may be white, magenta, pink, red, green, black, or occasionally blue. Some insects eat the pollen, which is rich in protein and fat, and others feed it to their young. Another food source for pollinators is the sugary nectar hidden within nectaries deep in the center of the flower. Elaborate mechanisms exist to prevent insects from robbing the plant of its nectar without taking pollen with them to the next flower, though some bees have worked out ways of boring through the outside of the petal to suck it out without entering the flower.

Safely tucked at the middle of the flower are the female parts. At the top is the stigma, where pollen from another flower gets caught. If the pollen is compatible, it fertilizes the female egg in the ovary, and a seed begins to form. The fertilized seed then grows, sheltered and protected in place. All the structures that were used to attract the pollinator are then useless to the flower, and the petals and anthers drop off or shrivel up. The energy from the plant is redirected from attracting pollinators to producing seed.

To see the smaller-scale parts of the flower, you can take close-up photographs or use a magnifying glass. If you have no flowers, try watching time-lapse videos of flowers opening. An easy way to look at flowers closely is to cut a flowering stem, put it in a vase, and study it with good light so that you can clearly see the specific flower parts. If you like, you can draw the bloom in detail. Start with a pencil and paper and draw the outlines of each flower section. Concentrate on the numbers and relative sizes of each. This comprehensive exploration can improve your observational abilities, and the sketch becomes a record of one of your garden flowers.

THE SHAPE OF INDIVIDUAL FLOWERS

As you inspect blooms up close, you can count the number of petals and also look at the shape of the flower as a whole. The petal numbers, sizes, and overall form affect how they look in the flower bed. The larger the flower, the more impact it has from a distance. Even small, distinctly shaped flowers can contribute to the appearance of the garden. There are so many individual flower shapes that they are hard to categorize. The following are some of the most commonly encountered fundamental shapes, which may appear on their own or as part of a flower head.

Bowls and Cups

These open-faced flowers are simple to see into and study. They share a basic shape of a bowl or cup: deepest in the middle with sides that slope up to the edges. The petals form the bowl and are often equally spaced and symmetrical when viewed from above. They are easy-access flowers that are available to lots of different pollinators. Large bowl- or cup-shaped flowers like tulips, poppies, or single peonies stand out in a garden bed, while smaller ones like crocus and hardy geranium mix well with others.

from left Some hardy geraniums have bowl-shaped flowers.

Single breadseed poppies hold their petals in the shape of a bowl.

from left *Fritillaria acmopetala* has a pronounced bell-shaped flower.

Campanula incurva lives up to its common name of bellflower.

Bells

A bell-shaped flower is cupped with a kick-out flare at the opening, resembling its namesake, and is a distinct, rather cute shape that is recognizable from a distance. Bells usually dangle down, though some angle off to the side or are upright. If the bell is hanging down, pollinators need to be able to cling to the flower surface and crawl in from the bottom. The pendulous shape is a benefit to the flower, as it keeps the floral parts dry in rain and snow. They may be clustered together along vertical stems or carried singly. Examples include bellflower (*Campanula*, Latin for "little bells"), fritillary, Sicilian honey garlic, and hyacinth.

Tubes

These flowers have fused petals joined together in a tube that varies in diameter from plant to plant. Some tubes, like foxgloves, are wide enough to admit bumblebees. Others are narrow and elongated, with nectar hidden deep within the flower and only accessible by birds with long bills or by butterflies. Some tubular flowers, like flowering tobacco, have a flat face, while others may flare out or curve back on themselves. Check out the tubular flowers of red hot poker, beardtongue, obedient plant, and tuberose.

from left Flowering tobacco has dangling tube-shaped flowers.

Wide, tube-shaped flowers of common foxglove 'Sutton's Apricot' are well suited to bumblebees.

Trumpets

Dramatically shaped trumpets are calling out for pollinators. A flared opening and a nice wide entrance to the flower indicates an easy place to land and an obvious nectar source. Some trumpet flowers have petals that are separate, and others are fused. The shape of the face can vary from a round or ruffled outline to a star shape, adding noticeably different forms to the flower bed. Trumpet-shaped flowers may be fragrant, like some lilies, so the pollinators come buzzing. The traditional yellow daffodil has a back ring of petals and then a trumpet in the front that protects the reproductive parts. Look for daylilies, crocosmias, petunias, and surprise lilies.

from left *Iris dardanus* has a perfect iris-shaped form, with three upright petals called standards and three downward sloping ones called falls.

Viewed from above, the three-parted symmetry of an iris flower becomes obvious. This is 'Banbury Beauty', a Pacific Coast Hybrid.

Iris-Shaped

Irises have a shape that is easy to distinguish, as they are unlike any other in the garden. Everything in the flower is in threes, including three petals that hang down and three that stand up. The iris shape is so distinctive that it has been used for emblems and heraldry for hundreds of years. Think of French fleur-de-lis in tapestries and other decorative arts. Irises are useful in the garden because their recognizable shape contrasts well with other flowers, and you can have them in bloom for many months of the year. Try rock garden iris for early spring, followed by Dutch iris, bearded iris, and Japanese water iris.

Bilaterally Symmetrical

If you could fold this flower form in half from top to bottom, every part would line up with its opposite. These flowers have two equal halves across a vertical axis and are described as bilaterally symmetrical. Pea-shaped flowers like blue false indigo and many herbal flowers, such as mint, sage, rosemary, and basil, fall into this category. They are fabulous flowers for pollinators because they are easy to land on. Other bilaterally symmetrical flowers like snapdragons require a large bee to spring open the closed mouth of the flower by landing on the bottom lip and wriggling its way inside.

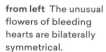

from left The unusual flowers of bleeding hearts are bilaterally symmetrical.

Larkspur is another example of a bilaterally symmetrical flower.

from left Pink evening primrose, *Oenothera speciosa*, have obvious four-petaled flowers.

Honesty and closely related flowers are all four-petaled.

Four-Petaled

This floral shape consists of four petals arranged at right angles to each other like a cross. They are often petite flowers that are grouped in a cluster. Most of them bloom in the springtime and are often fragrant. You could grow basket-of-gold, wallflower, sea kale, candytuft, or sweet alyssum. Look for this shape if you let your broccoli or cabbage go to flower.

from left Snow-in-summer is a wonderful tiny, five-petaled flower.

Poached-egg flowers consist of five petals.

Five-Petaled

These simple flowers have five obvious petals that make a pentagon or star-like shape. The petals may be pointed, toothed, or rounded and tend to be on a small scale. Examples include campion, catchfly, pinks, flax, and Egyptian starcluster.

from left Double versions of some flowers, like this white double daffodil, make them hard to recognize.

This double-flowered poppy has so many petals it is difficult to see into the center.

Double Flowers

As you look at possible flowers to grow, you will see that some have extra rings of petals. These are called double flowers. They are exciting to look at in the garden, as they have a full and blowsy appearance. The flowers may be semi-double, with only one extra ring of petals, or fully double, with a center that is congested with petals. Some double flowers don't make pollen or set seed, so they are especially long blooming in the garden. A side effect of this is that they may not be useful pollinator plants. Many flower shapes have been bred to produce double-flowered cultivars: double iris, hyacinth, pinks, or peony, for example.

THE SHAPE OF FLOWER INFLORESCENCES

As you approach a bed from a distance, the first thing you see are the shapes of the biggest, boldest flowers and strongly geometric inflorescences like vertical flower spikes, flat-topped horizontal flower heads, and ball shapes. Other less prominent shapes become obvious as you step nearer to the bed and peruse the flowers more closely. A garden that contains predominantly one floral shape can lack interest, so check your wish list and look at the flower shapes of the prospective plants. Including diverse shapes makes your composition exciting and dynamic, while repetition of some shapes brings the bed together as a whole.

Vertical: Spikes and Spires

Like mini Eiffel Towers, upright flower stalks, known as spikes or spires, pierce through the general mounded look of the border. They are a real dramatic asset in the flower garden. They grab the attention of flying pollinators because their flowers are held up in the air and easily accessible.

Spikes and spires have individual flowers attached to the upright stem. The flowers may be tubular or cup shaped, depending on the species. The

from left The vertical flower spikes of this bicolor lupine stand out in the flower bed.

The large-scale spiked inflorescences of blazing star have more of a vertical impact than the smaller-scale anise hyssop behind it.

inflorescences are often slender and take up a small horizontal footprint. These can be grown near the front or middle of the bed because you can see past them to the flowers behind. Carefully placed groups or single vertical flowers can act like punctuation marks in the garden. Using too many in your composition lessens their impact, so place them strategically. Some of the best small-scale vertical accents for early and mid-spring are grape hyacinths and hyacinths. Later there are the joys of foxgloves, lupines, mulleins, and salvias, followed by red hot pokers, perennial lobelia, and blazing stars.

Some flower spikes open from the bottom to the top and keep on growing. Others open in sequence going down the stem. It doesn't affect their presence in the garden, but it is another fascinating thing to notice. One category of vertically held inflorescences are tiered whorls where flowers encircle upright stems, with gaps in between. An example is Jerusalem sage, which adds a fun shape when planted in an otherwise low flower bed. Another group of vertical plants has wider inflorescences that resemble plumes. Their fuzzy, flame-shaped appearance is less sleek than other vertical flowers. Some of these plume-shaped plants, like celosia, amaranth, and goldenrod, have multiple side shoots that add to their sturdy presence in the garden.

from left The dense horizontal flower heads of this yarrow 'Gold Plate' stand out among other shapes in a flower bed.

The floaty yellow umbels of bronze fennel have a gentle horizontal presence in a bed.

Horizontal: Flat Tops and Umbels

Flower heads that look flat when viewed from the side provide an easy landing pad for pollinators, and their clear horizontal lines guide your eye along a bed, complementing the vertical lines of spire shapes.

Loosely structured flat-topped inflorescences called umbels are held on tiny stalks that look like the spokes of a bicycle wheel or an umbrella. Their distinct form looks lacy, adding a wonderful frilly appearance to the flower bed. Try herbs like fennel and dill or cold-hardy annuals like white lace flowers or lady's lace. Other flat tops like yarrow and sedum have closely packed flowers that give a solid appearance. These flower heads catch the light from the sun when it is overhead, brightening up the garden. Horizontal flowers add instant interest to a seasonal composition.

Spherical: Balls and Globes

Ball or sphere shapes are some of the most beloved in the garden, especially when borne on long stems that rise above the leaves below. A slight breeze can catch the large heads and set them moving like an upside-down pendulum. Symmetrical spheres are a great geometric shape that contrasts well with nebulous, fluffy flowers and are a great addition to a flower bed that lacks pizzazz.

There is something intriguing about these perfectly round spheres, and I love to include at least one in each season, preferably both a short and a tall one. Alliums are the classic ball-shaped flower of spring into summer. By planting a range of allium species and cultivars, you can have them in bloom for months. In summer, use eye-catching perennial globe thistle and sea holly. Globe amaranth and pompon dahlias end the growing year.

Hemispherical: Buttons and Daisies

Buttons and daisies are vaguely rounded shapes that are easy to combine in a border with spiky, plumed, and mounded flowers. They are one of the most instantly recognizable flower shapes, and they bring a smile to people's faces. The top view is often circular, and the side view can be nearly flat, slightly domed, or with an obvious central cone.

Daisies and their relatives are sometimes described as composite flowers because their flower heads are composed of many smaller florets. True daisies have two types: the outer ray florets that look like petals and the inner disc ones that form the center. Button-like flowers are also composed of many florets densely packed into a hemisphere.

There are abundant button and daisy flowers you could grow in your garden. They are so cheerful that it is tempting to fill your beds to the brim with them. They range in size from towering annual sunflowers down to Shasta daisies for mid-border and miniature pincushion flowers near the front. Some flowers in this group are held on flexible stems that add welcome motion to the bed. Their blooms appear to float among and between their solid neighbors, morphing and

from left Daisy-shaped flowers like this purple coneflower look hemispherical from the side.

Scabious, like this *Scabiosa graminifolia*, have button-like hemispherical flowers.

changing as the wind blows. Summer through fall is the prime time for buttons and daisies. There are annuals that are simple to grow from seed, like marigolds, cosmos, and zinnias. Add in longer-lived floriferous perennials like coneflowers and rudbeckias. For excitement in the bed, be sure you select daisy-shaped flowers with different colors and sizes.

Amorphous: Clusters and Clouds

Clusters and clouds are easy to mix into a flower bed because they have numerous flowers held above their foliage. The size and density of the cluster varies by species. Some are packed into a solid-looking group with a distinct outline, like

from left White gaura holds its flowers on tall, tousled stems.

Border phlox has irregular domed clusters of flowers.

border phlox. Others, like baby's breath or Russian sage, are hazy and diffuse, giving a soft, airy, cloud-like impression. Add these to your bed to loosen up a static grouping where all the flowers are obvious, rigid shapes.

Each flower shape brings a different look to the garden. By integrating solitary flowers and inflorescences from several groups in each season, you elevate your border from ho-hum to sensational.

Flower Roles in the Garden

Another way to design for seasonal charm and excitement is to look at the visual roles flowering plants play in the garden. You can categorize their blooms by size, presence, and what they contribute to the complete garden picture.

BOLD BEAUTIES

These flowers have a wow factor. Their spectacular presence catches the eye and beckons you into the garden. Bold beauties are the stars of their season. Without these standout flowers, a border can appear to be dull. When our eyes scan a bed or border, our brains instinctively find patterns and locate focal points. If the whole bed is made of flowers of similar scale and shape, the garden may seem monotonous.

Bold beauties' flowers tend to be large relative to their neighbors, and they are borne on imposing plants. Their individual flowers or inflorescences may also be noticeable due to

a distinctive geometric shape. The final component of a flower's boldness factor is its color. The strongest, zingiest colors seem to pop, while other, softer colors recede. They are bold enough that we can quickly recognize them when glancing at a flower bed.

from left Choose some bold flowers for your garden in every season, like this pink double peony.

Large, unusual-shaped dahlias in intense colors, like this cactus-shaped 'Doris Knight', steal the show in fall.

Bold flowers may be clustered for impact, either because of how they grow naturally or because you have planted them in close proximity. Include a bold beauty for each season to create continued drama in your flower garden. I love large fritillaries and glorious tulips in mid-spring, which have flower stalks that pop up among and between clumps of perennial plants. The next bold beauties are peonies, foxtail lilies, and Oriental poppies for later spring into early summer, followed by lilies in the height of summer. In late summer and fall, large-scale dahlias stand out from the crowd because the plants cover themselves in flowers when they are in bloom.

SUPPORTING CAST

Not every flower can be the star of the show. Supporting flowers don't steal the limelight from the bold beauties; instead, they enhance them. The flowers may be less intensely colored and medium to small in scale. If all the flowers in a bed were the same size and shape, you would not be able to distinguish them from afar, and the composition would be dreary. Supporting flowers fulfill a range of functions in the garden.

Background plants are the tallest part of the supporting cast and may be perennials or annuals. They are planted behind the bold beauties to provide a backdrop. You may choose a combination of tall plants to give height or use one plant and repeat it to give uniformity to your background. Tall plants take a while to grow during spring and early summer, providing a nice leafy setting for flowers in front of them before producing their own flowers later in the gardening year. They add fullness to the bed and can be used as a screen to block unwanted views. I like to use Joe-Pye weed, queen-of-the-prairie, hollyhocks, and New England asters. Some people are wary of using large herbaceous plants in a small garden, but you may lose visual drama if you stick exclusively to low-growing plants. If you are concerned about overwhelming your space, choose something that grows just a little higher than the bold beauties and the other plants in the bed.

Mid-border delights are the intermediate-height flowers that fill most of the space in the bed between the short front-edging plants and the background plants. Most of the flowers you will select for your garden fall into this category. They tend to have good foliage presence in addition to their flowers. The flowers are smaller than bold beauties but will still be noticeable from a slight distance. From afar, they might appear to form a wash or haze of color. I love to add plenty of flowers like daffodils and columbines in spring, yarrow and hardy salvias in early summer, followed by coneflowers, butterfly weed, and hummingbird

Tall plants like the vertically flowered Culver's root and the dome-shaped clusters of Joe-Pye weed make a great background for a flower bed.

mints in high summer, and then turtleheads with mounding asters in the fall. There is boundless choice in flower shape, color, and plant form so you can express your preferences and personal style.

Weavers and mixers are usually part of mid-border groupings, but they can grow toward the front and the back. They play a special role in enhancing the cohesiveness of the whole garden picture. These mixing flowers can be planted in groups or scattered among and between the larger, more distinctive plants. The most successful flower beds include some of these plants in each season repeated throughout the planting area. Their recurring colors or forms are the glue that holds the flower bed together as one.

Mixers may have sprawling stems and small-scale flowers that make them well suited to mingle with others in the flower bed. Most gardeners tend to leave them off their initial wish lists because they are oohing and aahing over bold beauties. However, they play an essential role in coordinating the bed. In my own garden I really enjoy hardy geraniums, Bowman's root, baby's breath, and gaura. Self-sown plants can also fulfill this role. Each individual self-sown annual or biennial plant doesn't take up much space, but if they are scattered throughout your border, they will have a significant harmonizing presence.

Choose a variety of flower shapes in your chosen color palette for the middle of your bed, like this grouping of white lace flower, perennial salvia, purple ball-shaped allium, and dame's rocket at Pennsylvania Horticultural Society's garden at Meadowbrook Farm.

Some plants, like this pink hardy geranium, sprawl through and between neighboring plants, like this sedum.

from left For the front of a bed, choose a tiny treasure like creeping thyme and a front-border treat like a short hardy geranium.

I like small plants so much that I have created raised beds to show them off. This one features tiny treasures like pinks and snow-in-summer.

Tiny treasures and **front-border treats** are sometimes-forgotten additions to a flower bed, but they add tremendous appeal. Their petite stature and little flowers mean that the plants should be grouped together for impact. Like weaving and mixing plants, their repetition can have a unifying effect on the flower bed. At the front of a bed, they give a delightful finished look to the edge. They can be planted in a straight or zig-zag line or in repeated clumps. In a formal flower bed, the plants can be kept trimmed for a neat appearance. In a more informal garden, they may spill over the edge and soften the front. If you garden in containers, tiny treasures are essential, whatever your style.

Little flowers can also be grown in a rock garden, a trough, or other raised bed that brings them closer to eye height. I have a particular fondness for little plants and have dedicated a bed just to display my favorite tiny treasures. Site these small plants by a bench or path where you will be able to see them clearly and enjoy every cute detail of their flowers. Keep larger plants trimmed so they do not flop over and smother the small ones. Whether on their own or at the front of a border, I particularly enjoy Grecian windflower, Johnny-jump-up, and forget-me-not for spring, and low-growing bellflowers, flossflower, creeping thyme, and prostrate heath asters for later.

Plant Presence: Size, Form, and Foliage

With the focus on flowers, it is easy to lose track of the plants themselves. If your goal is to have a full, fresh-looking bed for most of the gardening year, it is important to consider each plant's presence. This is a combination of the plant's form, overall dimensions, leaf size, texture, color, and shape, as well as the time of year it is in full growth. Foliage is vital in a bed, though it rarely has the sensational effect that flowers bring to the garden composition. Plants with great foliage are always an asset, and they provide a backdrop that enhances the flowers' presentation.

One of the most obvious things about plants are their overall dimensions. There is an astonishing variety of size found in herbaceous plants. I grow creeping thyme that tops out at a few inches and silphium that towers over my head. Look at the final height of a plant before you consider where in the border it should go. Generally speaking, in a bed that is viewed from several sides, the tallest plants should be placed somewhere in the middle. In a border, plant them toward the rear. The mainstay of flower beds are medium-height plants that take up the central space. In a wide bed, there is room to subdivide the middle portion into mid-front and mid-back. This allows you to see all the plants in your bed. Right at the front are the shortest plants, often tiny treasures. The density of a plant is also important when it comes time to place the plants in the bed. A plant with thick, solid foliage should be planted slightly farther back in the bed than a slender-stemmed, airy plant.

It is also helpful as you plan your garden to know whether the plant achieves its full size in one year. Annuals are fast growers that get to their stated dimensions in a few weeks or months. Perennials are slower to fill in their allotted space. It may take them two or three years to get to the height and width stated in the descriptions. As well as the overall size of a plant, think about its form. The main flowering plant forms are upright, spiky, feathery, mounding, and sprawling. There is also a nearly flat spreading form that is great at the edge of a bed or in a container.

The form of a flowering plant is tied to the shape and texture of its leaves and the way it holds them. Bulbs that flower from spring into early summer often have one flowering stem paired with lower leaves emerging at the base. Later bulbs, like lilies, have an imposing form due to their vertical presence and typically thick, glossy leaves. Plants that grow one central upright stalk look different from herbaceous plants that have multiple stems. Those with strap-like leaves may have fountains of foliage. Combining varied plant forms is a way of making your garden bed dynamic.

The leaves of flowering plants vary tremendously in size, shape, and texture. They range from the slight leaves of many rock-garden plants like sea thrift, through to the enormous leaves of tropical plants like cannas. Most leaves fall somewhere between these two extremes. Leaf shapes are even more varied. They might be linear, round, ovular, or heart shaped. They could be simple leaves with no indentations, or they might be notched, deeply lobed, or highly divided.

Plant texture is a combination of both tactile and visual cues. Think about using a variety of leaves when you are choosing your plants. Some might be smooth, shiny, or glossy, while others may be rough, matte, ridged, or hairy. Taking the time to investigate leaf textures may not seem necessary for a flower bed, but plant leaves affect the way that you see flowers in the garden. Many of our well-loved garden flowers have mid-sized leaves, which can give the bed a samey look. Mix up the textures by adding some large, undivided leaves to bring a striking feel to the bed. Plants like cardoons have an architectural quality that stands out from a distance and provides dramatic contrast. Include plants with more delicate foliage too. Highly dissected, feathery ones, such as bronze fennel or dill, have a fine visual texture that brings a lightness to the overall composition.

Another consideration is the leafiness of a plant. Plants with large, circular, triangular, or oval leaves will add to the general fullness of a bed and provide a great background to flowers. Slender plants with wispy foliage are useful in a flower

In island beds, tall plants like this Joe-Pye weed can be planted in the center and surrounded by lower-growing flowers.

opposite Narrow-stemmed flowers like purple tall verbena and orange sulfur cosmos can be sited at the front and middle of a bed without obstructing the view of plants behind them.

from left Cosmos has wispy foliage that adds airiness wherever they are planted.

The architectural foliage of this cardoon makes a good contrast to flowers with a fine texture.

bed for their see-through, veil-like effect. They don't fill up the bed but instead add variety with their soft appearance. Fine-textured plants can be put anywhere in the border because they don't obscure the view of plants behind them.

Think about foliage color when you make plant selections for your flower garden. The predominant color of leaves and stems is green, a soothing color that is a perfect foil for any flower. The color contrast between leaves and petals makes flowers stand out clearly to you and to pollinators.

Beyond standard green there are many foliage colors to choose from. There is a range of viridescence from deep forest greens to yellowy chartreuse, as well as more unusual colors, including silvery blue-gray and dark burgundy. Plants from tropical regions often have the greatest selection of bright leaves, whereas plants from Mediterranean areas lean toward glaucous coloration.

If you are including brightly colored foliage in your bed, consider how the leaf and flower colors will interact. Some flower cultivars might have vibrantly colored leaves that are difficult to combine with other occupants of the border. If you don't like this look, choose a similar species or cultivar that has calmer-looking leaves. Variegated leaves with contrasting leaf edges, centers, or other patterns can be used where the two-tone leaves will be an asset for flower combinations. Most variegation is either silvery white, easily used in any bed with a white theme, or yellowy gold, which mixes well in bright color schemes. Lean heavily on green leaves if the whole bed looks too busy.

Some flowering plants have leaves that look good for the whole growing season. Others have foliage that withers after flowering. These retreating leaves need to remain in place because they provide the energy for next year's growth. Some of my favorite spring-flowering bulbs and Oriental poppies have this growth habit.

Before you plant these delightful flowers, think whether they are worth the yellowing foliage and the empty spot they leave behind. If they are, there are various solutions to overcome the later blank spot. You can place these plants toward the mid-back of the border, where plants in front and behind will cover the open area as they grow. You can also plant ephemeral beauties in thin, elongated drifts that swish through a bed rather than planting them in a bulky clump that is difficult to disguise. Another trick is to tuck in annuals or tender perennials that use that same space for a second show later in the gardening season. Some people treat spring bulbs as annuals and remove them after flowering, but this can be an expensive proposition!

Flower Color

Gardeners generally agree that there should be a range of contrasting flower shapes and interesting leaf textures in the garden. When the subject turns to flower color, opinions differ about best practices and what is tasteful. Color in gardens has been a divisive issue for generations, with certain hues and combinations going in and out of fashion.

Perceptions of color differ from person to person. You may find this combination of beardtongue 'Hidcote Pink' and bright red Maltese cross delightful, or you may think they clash. A garden allows you to please yourself.

Walk around a garden and look at all the colors. Nature has an incredible range of often subtle colors in bark, twigs, fruit, vegetables, seed heads, and leaves. The predominant color during the growing year is the green of plant foliage, with bursts of other colors according to the seasons. The most vibrant, unique, and beautiful colors are provided by flowers. Repeat your walk at various times of day and see how the colors change with the weather. What you observe will be different when the sky is overcast, if it is noon and intense sunlight is coming from overhead, or in the warm, low-angled light of a sunset. Garden photographers know that strong light washes out flower colors, so many prefer to do garden shoots early in the morning or late in the evening. These golden hours illuminate flowers from one side and bring out their best qualities. Even on rainy days, raindrops on petals act like prisms to create unexpected colors. Enjoy the garden in all its moods.

You may not care about color in the garden at all, or you may feel passionately about it. Our perception of color can also vary. My father-in-law loved red, but he struggled to differentiate between the colors that he saw. He dressed himself in all different types of scarlet, crimson, salmon, and pink and felt that they went well together. To my eye they clashed horribly, but he was happy with his choices. Combining flowers in the garden is rather like this. We each see the colors slightly differently and have our own opinions about what looks good.

The flower colors we perceive are an interaction between sunlight and the pigments within each cell of the flower. The light that reaches a flower travels through it, is absorbed, or is reflected by the petals. Reflected light bounces back

from left The texture and color variations of this tulip 'Apricot Parrot' are fascinating and may inspire creative color schemes.

From a distance, blanket flowers look bright. When you get close, you can see the red and yellow concentric rings and darker venation.

into our eyes and is interpreted by our brains as a particular color. Texture has a great deal to do with color perception. A flower petal is not opaque like the walls of a house, which reflect light evenly. Most flowers have textural variation that alters light reflection. A living petal's surface can look crystalline, opalescent, glossy, or rough, resulting in fascinating variations in flower color. There are petals that are so shiny, such as those of buttercups, that they appear to glow in the garden. Bearded irises and pansies have velvety textures that catch the light in different ways at different times of day.

If you have creative tendencies, you probably think about colors a lot, have strong opinions about them, and have an incredible ability to differentiate between them. There are plenty of people who have never considered colors in an artistic way. If you don't have opinions about flower colors, don't worry. What matters most is that you are choosing flowering plants for all the qualities that they bring to the garden, including flower shape, plant texture, and sensory aspects such as fragrance and touch. Color is one more tool that allows you to show your own style and make your flower bed a personal composition.

When we think about flower color, we usually picture the overall impression from a few feet away as we walk down the garden path. We might describe a flower simply as being pink, blue, or red. When we examine them up close, we can see that they have complex color patterns, fine designs, or subtle textures that are indistinct from a distance. Flowers with wonderful patterns add charm to the garden. When we take the time to observe them in detail, we may find an unexpected dark center or white lines striping down each petal. Look for flowers that have speckles, contrasting edges, or color washes. For harmony you can pick up these secondary colors in other flowers in the same bed. Some of my favorite

Blooms may have surprising details, so check out the back as well as the front of flowers like Japanese anemone 'Robustissima'.

patterned flowers are the tessellated checkered lily, the bright circles of blanket flowers, and the exuberant random brushstrokes on parrot tulips. Other interesting details are petals with different colors on the front and back, like Japanese anemones. Flowers have ultraviolet patterns that are visible to insects but are not seen by us. When bees look at a flower, they see a vibrant display of concentric rings, lines, dots, or other patterns that show them where to go for food.

Contemplate what you want to see when you sit next to your flowers or work in a flower bed. I love pink and purple flowers, and I pack my garden with lots of these colors. I have a friend who refuses to grow yellow flowers but loves every other color. Personal color preferences can help you make flower choices. If you are drawn to a certain color, try to include it liberally in your flower garden. Continue to choose flowers that make you happy, and chances are you will like the way your garden looks. Color choice shouldn't guide all your decisions about what plants to include, but it can help you narrow down your wish list. If you haven't noted bloom colors on your list, now is a good time to do it. You may find that you have inadvertently leaned toward a color or two that please you.

Flower Pigments
and Color Changes

A flower's genetic makeup gives it its basic color and patterns. The pigments in flowers are the same ones that make leaves green, beets burgundy-maroon, and pumpkins orange. Flower appearance and color are affected by where the plant grows and the weather and climate. If the plant is well hydrated, the petals will be lush, plump, and colorful. If it lacks water, the petals wilt and lose their sheen. The ephemeral nature of flowers is shown in color changes that happen over the life of one bloom. This is due in part to the aging process. The petals emerge fresh and hydrated but lose moisture over time, becoming slightly wrinkly in texture without the sparkling iridescence of fresh plant cells. Over the life of the bloom, there is also a reaction between the pigments and the sun. Newly emerged flowers often have strong colors that fade as they are gradually bleached by sunlight. Take daffodils as an example. For the first few days after opening, their blooms are at their most vibrant. If there is a series of hot, cloudless days, yellow daffodils might decline in intensity. The color of the so-called pink daffodils is particularly capricious. Their trumpets are coral pink when they first open, but they quickly change unless they receive protective afternoon shade. There are inventive ways to preserve flowers that fade in strong light. My neighbor used to have a few antique paper parasols that she would bring out and carefully rig up over her tree peonies to shield them from the sun. It was a gardening ritual that she loved, protecting and honoring the once-a-year flowering of her precious peony blossoms.

Pink-cupped daffodils are particularly prone to being bleached by sunlight, so site them in afternoon shade if you want to preserve their color.

Some daffodils like 'Firebrand' have outer petals that open straw-yellow and fade to white.

THE FLOWER RAINBOW

Some of the most dramatic colors in nature are found in a rainbow, which is the result of sunlight being split into its component parts by water droplets in the air. Red is the color that you can see the longest, even as the rainbow is fading. The end of the light spectrum that is visible to humans begins with red then leads to orange and yellow. These are often called warm or hot colors. They are highly visible and appear to advance toward you. Green is the color found right in the middle of the rainbow, and it holds the rest of the colors together. On its other side are blue, indigo, and violet, known as cool colors. Cool colors fade into the background and can be used in large quantities without overwhelming a bed. In addition to the pure, bright colors of the rainbow, there are other vibrant ones that are a mixture of several colors, as well as whites, pale pastels, and somber dark colors.

Red: The Boldest Color

Bright red flowers stand out in the garden and are often the first to catch our attention. Red is a noticeable color used for stoplights and advertising slogans. It is bold and vibrant, but not restful. Red flowers are exceptionally striking when planted in a mass and can be seen clear across the garden. Think of an iconic field of corn poppies and the delight that red brings to the scene.

Channel these thoughts and add a little touch of red to bring a jolt of excitement to a lackluster border.

Red flowers are uncommon in plants from temperate climates but are widely found in warmer areas where they attract pollinating birds. I am lucky enough to have hummingbirds that visit my garden. I have a low-lying rain garden where the vibrant red perennial lobelia known as cardinal flower thrives. There is nothing better than walking out there on a summer morning and hearing the buzz of vibrating hummingbird wings close to my ear as they zip from flower to flower.

Not all red flowers look good planted in close proximity. Scarlet reds have an orangey cast that goes well with other hot colors. Crimson and claret reds have a tinge of blue and are a good choice to enliven an otherwise cool palette of blues and purples. The first true reds of the gardening season are vibrant chalice-shaped tulips. Later on, look for brilliant red salvias and zinnias. All reds are highly contrasting when placed against green foliage but are less obvious against plum or mahogany leaves. Try dahlias like 'Bishop of Llandaff' for a knockout combination of scarlet flowers with dark foliage.

from left For red in the summer garden, try some of the vibrantly colored cultivars of purple coneflower.

Red ladybird poppy, *Papaver commutatum*, is one of the brightest red flowers of late spring and early summer.

LATE WINTER TO MID-SPRING	LATE SPRING AND EARLY SUMMER	HIGH SUMMER	LATE SUMMER INTO AUTUMN
Tulipa 'Red Emperor'	*Antirrhinum majus* 'Rocket Red'	*Canna* 'Cannova Bronze Scarlet'	*Dahlia* 'American Beauty'
	Dianthus barbatus 'Scarlet Fever'	*Lobelia cardinalis*	*Lycoris radiata*
	Papaver commutatum	*Salvia coccinea*	*Salvia elegans*

Orange: Cheerful and Zingy

Orange, like red, is described as a hot or warm color. People have a love-hate relationship with orange: there are gardeners who wouldn't garden with it, and others who can't garden without it. One of my fellow gardeners is addicted to orange and includes it in every garden that he designs to provide sometimes shocking or surprising plant pictures.

Orange is strong and lively, which can make it difficult to find other flower colors that can stand up to its intensity. When a patch of orange butterfly weed is in bloom, it is unmissable even when seen from afar. It needs to be accompanied by other robust warm colors or contrasted with blues or purples. Orange features in some spring bulbs, like crown imperial fritillary, and continues later with the zesty orange of nasturtiums, marigolds, avens, and Mexican sunflower.

from left Orange flowers are easy to find among tender perennials, like this canna 'Orange Punch'.

For more orange in summer beds, combine hardy perennials like orange crocosmia and red hot poker.

LATE WINTER TO MID-SPRING	LATE SPRING AND EARLY SUMMER	HIGH SUMMER	LATE SUMMER INTO AUTUMN
Calendula officinalis	*Asclepias tuberosa*	*Crocosmia masoniorum*	*Chrysanthemum* (various)
Erysimum cheiri	*Eschscholzia californica*	*Hemerocallis* 'Orange Smoothie'	*Kniphofia rooperi*
Fritillaria imperialis 'Rubra Maxima'	*Geum* 'Totally Tangerine'	*Tagetes tenuifolia* 'Tangerine Gem'	

Yellow: Ubiquitous and Sunny

Yellow is one of the most widely available flower colors. It is a cheerful, sunny, highly visible color that invigorates any flower bed. Yellow encompasses a range of colors from hot and dazzling through to pale and cool. The strongest yellows can stop you in your tracks. Pair these rich yellows with oranges or reds to make sizzling, energizing beds. Pale yellows are easy to mix in any color combination and look especially attractive with blue.

Spring brings hot egg-yolk yellow to the garden with the emergence of early trumpet daffodils like 'King Alfred' and cheery basket-of-gold. Yellow continues to be a presence throughout the year. It is found so often in flowers that it is hard to plan a bed that doesn't contain it. Even flowers that have petals of other colors may have yellow-pollen-containing stamens. There is also a plethora of

from left This solid yellow lily makes a strong statement in the summer garden.

This yellow Carolina lupine, *Thermopsis villosa*, provides a cheery touch to the early summer garden.

LATE WINTER TO MID-SPRING	LATE SPRING AND EARLY SUMMER	HIGH SUMMER	LATE SUMMER INTO AUTUMN
Aurinia saxatilis	*Achillea* 'Coronation Gold'	*Alcea rugosa*	*Helianthus salicifolius*
Iris danfordiae	*Coreopsis grandiflora*	*Helianthus* 'Lemon Queen'	*Solidago rugosa* 'Fireworks'
Narcissus (various)	*Thermopsis villosa*	*Lilium* 'Conca d'Or'	*Sternbergia lutea*

daisy-like flowers that contain yellow in their petals, in their centers, or both. Summer and fall are filled with abundant sizes and shapes of yellow blooms such as the classic goldenrod, which when planted with purple asters produces a wonderful autumnal combination. My husband loves yellow in all its forms, so I make a point to include it for his delight.

Green: The Soothing Color

Green brings us to the center of the rainbow. Its position is a natural bridge between the bright hot colors and the cool colors. It is a perfect foil for any of the other colors in your garden, a calming presence that provides a wonderful backdrop and separator for disparate flower colors. There are a few green flowers that add an unusual touch to the flower garden palette. In spring, look for viridiflora tulips that combine pastel colors or cream with brushstrokes of green. Follow this with easy summer flowers like the chartreuse blooms of hare's ear, zinnias like 'Envy', and 'Lime Green' flowering tobacco. Green flowers are elegant partners for any other flower color.

from left Flowering tobacco 'Lime Green' mixes well in both hot and cool color schemes.

This ball-shaped, green-flowered garden zinnia is a subtle addition to a cut flower garden.

LATE WINTER TO MID-SPRING	LATE SPRING AND EARLY SUMMER	HIGH SUMMER	LATE SUMMER INTO AUTUMN
Fritillaria acmopetala	*Ammi visnaga* 'Green Mist'	*Echinacea* 'Green Jewel'	*Chrysanthemum* 'Key Lime'
Narcissus 'Green Eyes'	*Angelica archangelica*	*Gladiolus* 'Green Star'	*Nicotiana langsdorffii*
Tulipa 'Spring Green'	*Aquilegia vulgaris* 'Green Apples'	*Nicotiana* 'Lime Green'	*Zinnia* 'Green Envy'

Blue: Scarce and Desirable

Blue flowers are a peaceful addition to the flower bed. They promote feelings of comfort and tranquility akin to looking at the sea, sky, or distant mountains. Blue is easy to mix into any color scheme in the same way that your favorite denim jeans go with anything in your wardrobe.

Spring bulbs are one of the best blue additions to a flower bed. They can be used liberally as an underplanting to larger plants. Their receding color will unify the bed without overwhelming it. Include grape hyacinths, camas, and squill. Add some rambling forget-me-nots as a mixer and mingler. Blue is carried on by cool-season annuals such as larkspur and love-in-the-mist. Royal blue is one of the rarest flower colors and generally admired, perhaps because it is difficult to find. It is available in some cornflowers and delphiniums. Paler true-blue flowers include bog sage, azure blue sage, and some sea hollies.

Some flowers that are labeled as blue actually lean toward purple or lavender. Blue is so beloved in the garden that plant breeders have been trying to bring blue into flowers of every species. Treat descriptions of blue flowers with a little

from left Classic blue cornflowers are a wonderful choice for the garden or as a cut flower.

Choose true blue delphiniums like this one for the high summer garden.

LATE WINTER TO MID-SPRING	LATE SPRING AND EARLY SUMMER	HIGH SUMMER
Anemone blanda 'Blue Shades'	*Aquilegia caerulea*	*Agapanthus* 'Headbourne Hybrids'
Hyacinthus 'Blue Jacket'	*Camassia leichtlinii*	*Delphinium* (various)
Muscari azureum	*Lupinus* 'The Governor'	*Salvia azurea*

skepticism because it is sometimes wishful thinking. Whether flowers are true blue or slightly blue, they are all cool colors and serve similar functions in color combinations. Blue and bluish flowers combine well with white, yellow, and pastels. Use blue in a garden of red and orange flowers to help tone down the heat.

Indigo, Violet, and Purple: Pollinator Favorites

Indigo, violet, mauve, eggplant, and plum are some of the names of colors found at the purple end of the spectrum. These colors are formed using a combination of red and blue pigments in varying concentrations. Purple flowers are a popular choice for visiting pollinators, so include a few in every season. They are readily available at any time of the year. In spring, choose hyacinths or one of my current favorites, a little glory-of-the-snow called 'Violet Beauty'. For later in the year, choose perennials like blazing star and many irises. Continuing into the fall, the garden year comes to a close with purple autumn asters and dahlias. Subtle

from left The strong purple Japanese water iris 'Royal Robe' blooms at the same time as the softer blue-purple catmint.

Hyacinth 'Miss Saigon' has deep rich purple spring-blooming flowers.

LATE WINTER TO MID-SPRING	LATE SPRING AND EARLY SUMMER	HIGH SUMMER	LATE SUMMER INTO AUTUMN
Crocus tommasinianus	Allium 'Ambassador'	Cleome hassleriana 'Violet Queen'	Dahlia 'Lavender Ruffles'
Iris reticulata 'George'	Iris pallida 'Variegata'	Liatris spicata	Symphyotrichum novae-angliae 'Purple Dome'
Viola odorata 'Queen Charlotte'	Verbascum phoeniceum 'Violetta'	Penstemon smallii	Vernonia noveboracensis 'Southern Cross'

purples do not attract attention to themselves and combine easily with any other colors. Brighter hues of purple draw the eye, especially if the flower is a bold geometric shape like an allium. Pair this color with orange or yellow for an exciting combination. Mixing purples with pinks and whites achieves a quieter look.

BEYOND THE RAINBOW: MIXED COLORS

Not all flower colors are the pure ones described above. There are numerous intermediate mixed flower colors that can be used to great effect in a garden.

Pink Flowers: Soft or Bold

Pink flowers are a common component of the garden that lend softness or vibrancy, depending on their intensity. Vivid pinks can play a role similar to red as a lively, stimulating accent. Paler pinks mix well with various other colors,

from left A pink fall combination of New England aster and border phlox.

This lily has a gradient of soft to darker pink that would be easy to use in a variety of color schemes.

LATE WINTER TO MID-SPRING	LATE SPRING AND EARLY SUMMER	HIGH SUMMER	LATE SUMMER INTO AUTUMN
Armeria maritima	Dianthus 'Bath's Pink'	Cosmos bipinnatus 'Cupcakes Blush'	Anemone 'Robustissima'
Hyacinthus 'Pink Pearl'	Paeonia 'Sarah Bernhardt'	Filipendula rubra	Chrysanthemum 'Pink Crest'
Lobularia maritima 'Rosie O'Day'	Phlox subulata 'Fort Hill'	Phlox paniculata 'Jeana'	Lycoris squamigera

especially if they are of a similar strength. Pinks can lean toward coral on the warm side, or they can have a slight blue undertone that makes them read as cool colors. Whatever pink flower you choose, it will look charming with white to lighten up the bed or with blues for a classic blend. Pink flowers begin in spring with hyacinths, spring starflower 'Tessa', and a wide range of delicious tulip cultivars like 'Angelique', a fluffy double, or the single late 'Menton' in rose-pink. To carry on a pink theme, include a peony or two, followed by some pink lilies, border phlox, and dahlias.

Magenta: Delightful or Malignant

Magenta is a strong garden color that is somewhere between purple and pink. It was described by one of my gardening heroines, the English garden writer Gertrude Jekyll, as malignant, but it is one of my personal favorites. Magenta has been much maligned and reviled in gardens for generations, but I find that it adds punch to a bland border. One of the best magenta flowers is rose campion,

from left Rose campion is my favorite magenta flower.

A magenta celosia.

LATE WINTER TO MID-SPRING	LATE SPRING AND EARLY SUMMER	HIGH SUMMER	LATE SUMMER INTO AUTUMN
Hyacinthus 'Woodstock'	*Dianthus* 'Paint the Town Magenta'	*Gladiolus* 'Plum Tart'	*Celosia* 'Asian Garden'
Matthiola 'Iron Rose'	*Lychnis coronaria*	*Petunia* ×*hybrida* 'Royal Magenta'	*Dahlia* 'Magenta Star'
Tulipa 'Barcelona'	*Paeonia* 'Magenta Splash'	*Phlox paniculata* 'Famous Magenta'	*Zinnia* 'Benary's Giant Wine'

a short-lived perennial that self-seeds for me. It has felty silver foliage and flowers in bright magenta as well as calmer choices of white and white with a blush pink eye. I also love to grow a range of bright magenta zinnias.

Peach, Coral, and Salmon: Mixtures of Pink and Orange

These popular tropical sunset colors blend pink and orange. Flowers in this color range have warmth without the brightness of pure orange, making them easier to bring into successful color schemes. Plant them with soft lilacs, lavenders, or blues, and cool them even further by adding white. Alternately, they can be mixed into a hot-colored garden composition with yellows and oranges. They are seen early in the year in some daffodil cups and tulips like 'Salmon Impression'. Continue the show with 'Coral Charm' peony, and in summer use peach-colored verbena, daylilies, Peruvian lilies, and gladiolus.

from left You could base a late-spring color scheme around peony 'Coral Charm'.

The flowers of this autumn-blooming chrysanthemum open bronzy salmon and mature to a pinky peach.

LATE WINTER TO MID-SPRING	LATE SPRING AND EARLY SUMMER	HIGH SUMMER	LATE SUMMER INTO AUTUMN
		Alstroemeria 'Inca Ice'	
Calendula 'Pink Surprise'	*Antirrhinum majus* 'Chantilly Light Salmon'	*Hemerocallis* 'Lady Georgia'	*Chrysanthemum* 'Sheffield Pink'
Narcissus 'Delnashaugh'	*Dianthus* 'Georgia Peach Pie'	*Verbena* ×*hybrida* 'Peaches and Cream'	*Tropaeolum majus* 'Tip Top Apricot'
Tulipa 'Apricot Beauty'	*Geum* 'Pretticoats Peach'		*Zinnia elegans* 'Zinderella Peach'

White and Cream: Bright or Cooling

White flowers are refreshing in the garden and gleam brightly, especially when combined with crisp greens or darker colors. The gardening year begins with the white of snowdrops and moves on to late-blooming pheasant's eye daffodils, fresh white peonies, delicate columbines, irises, and many more. It is quite possible to have white flowers in your garden throughout the blooming year.

As you look at white flowers, you will see that they are not exactly the same color. Think about when you buy white paint for your home and how many different possibilities there are. The same goes for white flowers. They often have hints of different colors mixed in. A fairly common undertone is green; other blooms are slightly blue, pink, or cream. Not all white flowers look good when they are neighbors. Bright white blooms can make off-white flowers look murky if they are right next to each other.

from left The orange stamens make a feature against the pure white petals of 'Casa Blanca' lily.

For white in spring, combine a daffodil like 'Stainless' with *Allium cowanii*.

LATE WINTER TO MID-SPRING	LATE SPRING AND EARLY SUMMER	HIGH SUMMER	LATE SUMMER INTO AUTUMN
Crocus 'Jeanne d'Arc'	*Ammi majus*	*Echinacea purpurea* 'White Swan'	*Anemone ×hybrida* 'Whirlwind'
Galanthus nivalis	*Digitalis purpurea* f. *albiflora*	*Gaura lindheimeri*	*Colchicum speciosum* 'Album'
Narcissus 'Thalia'	*Papaver orientale* 'Royal Wedding'	*Veronicastrum virginicum* 'Album'	*Symphyotrichum ericoides*

White and cream flowers are the lightest colors in the flower bed. On a hot summer day, white can be glaring in direct sun. In part sun and in the evening, white blooms have a cooling effect on a flower bed. Intermingled with pastels, they come into their own in low-light conditions. The perceived whiteness of a flower also depends on the size and shape of the inflorescence. If it is a frothy weaver and mixer, like white gaura or lady's lace, the whiteness adds a lovely softness to the composition. A large, solid white flower like a fully double dahlia shines back at you clearly. No matter the shape of the flower head, white flowers combine well with all other colors in the garden.

Pastel Colors: Relaxing and Gentle

Pastel flowers are the antithesis of brilliant reds, oranges, and blues, the paler counterparts that bring a peaceful, soft feel to the garden. They blend well

from left The pastel lavender color of iris 'Dawn Waltz' looks pretty next to Canadian columbine, *Aquilegia canadensis*.

Grape hyacinth, *Muscari aucheri* 'Ocean Magic', has flowers in a variety of blues that give a pastel impression from a few feet away.

LATE WINTER TO MID-SPRING	LATE SPRING AND EARLY SUMMER	HIGH SUMMER	LATE SUMMER INTO AUTUMN
Muscari armeniacum 'Valerie Finnis'	*Ageratum houstonianum*	*Campanula lactiflora*	*Chrysanthemum* 'Sweet Peg'
Scilla bifolia 'Rosea'	*Geranium sanguineum* var. *striatum*	*Nicotiana mutabilis*	*Dahlia* 'Mikayla Miranda'
Tulipa 'Honky Tonk'	*Stokesia laevis* 'Color Wheel'	*Salvia yangii*	*Symphyotrichum laeve*

together because they are all of a similar low intensity. Pastel colors are found throughout the gardening year in light straw yellows, lavender purples, watery blues, and pale pinks.

Pastels don't call attention to themselves during the day, so they add flower-iness without clashing with brighter blooms in the bed. Pale yellows and blues are underrated colors in the garden and ones that I appreciate for their ability to go with almost every color. In spring, you are spoiled for choice with an abundance of pastel flowering bulbs. In summer, try wild bergamot, Russian sage, catmint, and giant scabious.

Dark Colors: Intriguing and Unusual

Dark flower colors are unusual choices in the garden. They include the deepest versions of brown, purple, and red. Like blue, black is a highly sought-after flower color. There are very few flowers that are actually black, but they have been bred from the darkest versions of all these colors. White, off-white, and

from left *Scabiosa atro-purpurea* 'Black Knight' has dark burgundy flowers with protruding pale anthers.

Many garden flowers that are normally bright in color have other cultivars available with deep or dark colors, like this annual sunflower.

LATE WINTER TO MID-SPRING	LATE SPRING AND EARLY SUMMER	HIGH SUMMER	LATE SUMMER INTO AUTUMN
Fritillaria persica	*Allium* 'Miami'	*Cosmos atrosanguineus*	*Dahlia* 'Karma Choc'
Tulipa 'Queen of the Night'	*Centaurea* 'Black Gem'	*Digitalis parviflora*	*Hylotelephium* 'Night Embers'
Viola 'Bowles Black'	*Iris* 'Black Gamecock'	*Scabiosa* 'Black Knight'	*Nicotiana* 'Hot Chocolate'

pastels provide a good contrast to the darkest flowers, making them appear even deeper in color. All dark flowers need special placement in the garden, as they can be invisible against dark soil or mulch. Instead, give them a light or green background to show them off. Look for very dark-flowered tulips, pansies, cornflowers, and hollyhocks. There are also a range of deep red and reddish purples that add some depth to color groupings. Try dark celosia and amaranths, several of which have corresponding rich red foliage.

Some of the most unusual color choices in the flower garden are the autumnal shades of brown, russet, amber, tawny, fawn, and chestnut. If you are looking for these colors, include tulips like 'Brown Sugar' and 'La Belle Epoque'. Follow these with a selection of brown-tinged bearded iris, 'Hot Chocolate' flowering tobacco, small-flowered foxglove, and fall chrysanthemums. Pair brown flowers with bronzy oranges and pale yellows.

In this chapter you have learned how to categorize flowers into groups that will eventually help you assemble them into pleasing pictures. Now it is time to learn more about the seasonal changes in the flower garden. The gardening year is cyclical. Each flower has its time in the sun and is followed by ones that bloom later. Understanding the predictable rounds of nature in a flower garden is a key to achieving long-lasting displays. The following chapter takes you through the floral year, highlighting key blooms for each season, looking at some helpful tasks, and showing how to plant for a succession of blooms.

The Flower Gardener's Calendar

A Guide to the Flowery Year

One of the greatest pleasures of gardening in a temperate climate is that your garden is not static. It changes day to day and week to week. Flowers emerge and fade during the gardening year, producing an ever-changing progression of garden pictures. You will never be bored with your garden because it will never be the same, even this time next year. The ephemeral succession of blooms is dependent on seasonal changes in temperature, sunlight, water, and day length. Knowing what flowers bloom in each » season, what growing conditions they require, and what they look like are the art and science of flower gardening. Choosing beautiful plant combinations that bring you joy is an occupation that can fascinate a gardener for a lifetime.

Though spring signals the beginning of the gardening year for most people, your new flower garden can start whenever you are reading this. Flower gardening is a process, and there is always something you can prepare for or do. The first thing you need to learn is which flowers bloom in each season. Flowers bloom in progression, from the earliest blooms of late winter through to flower-packed spring and summer, and then the last precious flowers of the gardening year. Once you know the sequence of bloom times, you can plan an ever-floriferous garden. If you really want a big spring show, choose more for that time of year. If you want to have a year-round display, be sure to pick some flowers for each season. As you explore bloom times, always have your flower wish list on hand to jot down seasonal ideas you come across, especially easy if your wish list is already divided into seasons.

The cyclical nature of flower gardening means that every year you will go through a series of three A's: anticipation, appreciation, and adjustment.

ANTICIPATION The garden is a place of optimism: there is always a sense of things to come. In the same way that part of the fun of a vacation is in its planning, a large part of the pleasure of flower gardening comes from looking forward to what is yet to bloom. You think about what you are going to start from seed, some new perennials to grow, or how you are going to rearrange your flower bed. You dream about the garden that will unfold.

APPRECIATION Once your garden is in bloom, it is time to appreciate it, even if it didn't come out exactly as you planned. Sit among your flowers with a cup of your favorite beverage, or stroll along your garden paths and observe both the big picture and the small details. Be in the moment.

ADJUSTMENT Part of the enjoyment of flower gardening is adjusting your plantings to make them look better to you. Plants are forgiving. They don't mind being moved if you do it carefully at the

previous (clockwise from top left) A trio of pink and purple flowers: purple blazing star, pink and green tulip 'Virichic', and dahlia 'Mary Munns'.

below Imagine the poppies that will unfurl out of these fuzzy buds.

right time of year. My husband sees me out in the garden, shovel in hand, and wonders what I will be rearranging today. It is a bit like being dissatisfied with the arrangement of your living room furniture and tweaking it to suit yourself. (My husband is bemused when I move furniture too!)

Over time, you will move your plants less often as you find flowers that do well in your garden and combinations that please you. However, gardeners are not easily satisfied with their creations and don't like to stand back from the flower bed and say, "There! I am done." We are generally forward-looking optimists who are constantly trying to improve our garden compositions and are always somewhere in this cycle of anticipation, appreciation, and adjustment.

Early to Mid-Spring

Late winter is a season of unpredictable weather where the garden seems to be hovering on the brink of spring for weeks on end. Flowers come in waves; they will wait to open until conditions are just right. The first opportunistic blooms open as the snow melts or there is a break in the cold weather. Little by little, a few more bulbs poke their green noses through the frozen soil, creeping up in height day by day and pausing when the next winter storm rolls in. If you are content to ignore this uncertain gardening season, focus your attention on bulbs that bloom later in spring.

Now is a good time to find out about the minimum temperatures you experience in your area. Each perennial plant can survive down to a set low temperature, below which it is killed. When you buy plants, the labels or descriptions will list their hardiness zones as defined by the United States Department of Agriculture. The zones are easy to access online. If you are gardening in other parts of the world, find your average minimum temperature and check it against the ranges given. Some other countries have their own hardiness ratings.

Crocus flowers like 'Zwanenburg' and 'Zwanenburg Bronze' are small delights that are very cold tolerant.

Each flower that blooms early in the year is precious and admired. These precocious, tiny garden inhabitants bring us joy disproportionate to their size. Differences between flowers that would barely be noticed in the profusion of summer are remarkable now. Blooms may be scented to attract the few pollinators that are out in cool temperatures. Snowdrops, with white dangling bell-like

Grecian windflower 'Blue Shades' and light blue grape hyacinth 'Valerie Finnis' make a cute blue spring combination.

flowers that shed any late-season snow and frost, are the first to bloom, closely followed by chalice-shaped crocus flowers in shades of lavender, purple, white, and gold that pop up and delight early insects. Since there is still a nip in the air, it is nice to walk around the garden rather than sit in it. Plan to create a path where you can walk with dry feet next to your winter bloomers. This need be nothing more than a few stepping-stones where you can stand and admire the first late-winter and early-spring blooms.

The flowering year begins in earnest as the temperatures rise, prompting a rush of spring blooms. The smell of fresh earth and soft breezes greets us as we emerge from the door to rediscover our garden. Our senses, dulled by being inside too much in winter, are sparked back to life along with the emerging flowers. Pick a little bunch of scented flowers and bring it inside, where the warmth of the house will amplify their fragrance. Spring brings hope and anticipation for the flowers we will grow this year.

If you love spring flowers and want more of them in your garden, look at other gardens to see what they have growing at this time of year. I remember one spring years ago, before I really got into bulb gardening, I was frustrated that I had no flowers in my garden when others did. I drove around, stopping at any garden where there were flowers in bloom and tried to identify them. I then ordered a few of each of these early wonders for myself. Of course, it was delayed gratification, because though the bulbs arrived the following fall, I had to wait until the next spring to see them bloom. This cheerful display further fueled my passion for bulbs.

PLANT TYPES

Mid-spring arrives with its own color palette. The winter colors of evergreen foliage, twiggy brown, and barky beige are now accented by splashes of eye-catching yellow, pink, purple, white, and blue flowers. The weather is changeable at this time of year, so the flowers have to be tough. These flowers grow from fall-planted bulbs, cool-season annuals, and early-blooming perennials. As spring progresses, the colors become bolder, with the addition of red and bronzy-orange flowers. Translucent spring-green foliage sets off flowers to perfection. Daffodils have a long season and bloom in tandem with colorful tulips and a plethora of smaller bulbs. Pansies and violas make great instant color splashes, especially in containers.

Classic rock-garden plants burst into bloom in early and mid-spring with greatly varying forms. The flowers of candytuft, purple rock cress, and basket-of-gold sport little clustering clouds of diminutive four-petaled flowers. Creeping phlox covers itself with small, toothed, five-petaled blooms. Pasqueflower has larger-scale fuzzy-backed flowers in purple, claret red, pink, and white punctuated with bright yellow centers.

Spring-flowering bulbs are some of the easiest plants to grow in the garden. You buy the brown- or cream-colored bulbs the autumn before you want them to flower and bury them in the soil. All the plant parts are already present in miniature within the bulb. Once planted, the bulbs start to grow roots. As the days lengthen in spring, the shoot pokes up through the soil and emerges as leaves and a flower. In gardening, the word "bulb" is a shorthand way to describe a range of underground storage structures that we plant to produce flowers. These may include corms, rhizomes, and tubers, as well as true bulbs. Although these structures are different botanically, they all serve the same function of storing energy below the ground when growth is not possible due to the weather.

Bulbs are a fun and useful addition to the flower garden. Planting bulbs in containers or in the ground is one of the easiest ways to have a brilliant show of flowers in spring. They are relatively cheap to buy and produce flowers in an assortment of shapes and colors. Bulbs that are hardy in your area are the best value for money. They should come up year after year and may be so successful that they multiply. Depending on your climate, some bulbs may only flower for one year and should be treated as annuals. For example, in the American South and other warm climates, there is not enough winter cold to chill tulips sufficiently to trigger spring bloom. In this instance, buy prechilled bulbs each year and treat them as a fleeting but enjoyable garden occupant.

Spring-flowering bulbs are perfect to plant right outside your door so that you see them whatever the weather. Mix and match bulbs, thinking about flowering time, height of bloom, shape of flower, and colors. They can be planted directly into the ground or in deep frost-proof containers. In pots or for an annual show in the ground, pack them close together but not touching. Layer the bulbs if you want a spectacular spring display. Put the largest bulbs toward the bottom of a hole, then add the next largest, and the smallest ones on top, separating each with a layer of soil. They will find their way through the other bulbs to bloom. Tiny rock garden iris that flower in shades of blue, purple, or yellow are beautiful paired with little yellow daffodils and cheerful pansies.

Orange and yellow parrot tulips with hyacinth 'Blue Jacket' is a bright and cheery pairing.

Bulbs have different uses in the flower bed, depending on their growth habit and size. Some bulbs like tulips and alliums have a single stem and therefore take up little space in the border. They are perfect to add seasonal drama to the flower bed as they rise up from the froth of lower-growing perennials. Hyacinths have mid-height columns of robustly fragrant bell-shaped flowers that come in both strong and pastel colors to suit any color scheme. Shorter bulbs, planted in groups throughout the bed, are great for lending cohesiveness to the whole scene as they mix and weave between taller plants or as

Cluster spring flowers near your door for daily enjoyment.

a lovely front edging. There is a wide assortment of beautiful smaller-statured spring bulbs that bloom alongside daffodils and tulips and make great companions for them because they cover up the lower stems. These are called minor bulbs, but there is nothing insignificant about their gorgeous flowers. They have petite blooms, so they look best when planted in drifts, either mixed together or singly. Choose from a lovely assortment of squill, grape hyacinth, glory-of-the-snow, striped squill, rock garden iris, spring starflower, and Grecian windflower. They bloom in pastel and mid-tone shades of blues, purples, and pinks, as well as white. The bell-shaped flowers of fritillaries come in dusky brown, pale yellow, plum, mauve, burgundy, and the bright yellow and orange of the crown imperial fritillary. Some are short, while others tower above the tallest daffodils.

STARS OF THE SEASON

Praised by poets for their beauty, daffodils are one of the premier spring flowers. These easy-to-grow bulbs have a wide variety of forms, numbers of flowers to a stem, and differing fragrances. By choosing cultivars that bloom in early, mid, and late spring, you can have flowers in your garden for weeks on end.

The earliest daffodils to bloom are the bright yellow trumpets. These are followed in succession by mid-season daffodils, some with swept-back outer petals, or fluffy double flowers, and others with multiple heads to a stem. The latest daffodils to bloom are sometimes called narcissus, with a pure white flat face and a central disc of red, orange, and green in concentric circles. The smallest daffodils are called miniatures, and they are suited to the front of the bed, a rockery, or a container. Tall daffodils can be planted in the middle or back of flower beds so

from left A simple and effective spring combination of a daffodil like 'Cragford' and lower-growing blue grape hyacinth.

In this group, taller tulip 'Virichic' is planted with the smaller-scale pale yellow 'Honky Tonk' and similarly colored daffodil.

their retreating foliage is hidden by later emerging plants. They can also grow in grass that is not mown until the daffodil foliage has sent energy down to the bulb to fuel next year's growth. Daffodils are not affected by browsing herbivores, as they contain a toxic sap.

I grow plenty of daffodils to enjoy in the garden and use as cut flowers. I have chosen to plant many old-fashioned cultivars that suit the age of my Victorian house. They are not as neat and regular as modern daffodils, but I love their nodding heads and wayward grace. Recent cultivars have been bred for strong stems, bold colors, and unusual shapes. Some daffodils, like jonquil and tazetta types, have the added benefit of delightful fragrance. There are daffodils that will suit any garden.

Tulips are knockout plants in the spring. They are usually chalice shaped, but there are lily-flowered tulips with outturned petal points and doubles with extra petals. There is a wide variety of tulip colors, with almost everything apart from a true blue. Some tulips are fascinating bicolors, and others have subtle shadings from top to bottom. The craziest-looking tulips are the so-called parrot tulips, which have flame-like patterns in multiple colors. If you want to grow tulips as cut flowers, plant as many bulbs as you can fit into a dedicated raised bed, pack

Favorite Flowers for Early to Mid-Spring

Iris reticulata 'Pixie'

Tulipa

Muscari armeniacum

Narcissus 'Croesus'

Fritillaria michailovskyi

Narcissus 'Beryl'

Erysimum

Viola

Hyacinthus 'Splendid Cornelia'

them closer than it says on the bag, and treat them like annuals, removing them after they finish flowering. Tulips are one of the few flowers that continue to grow in the vase, so they add dynamism to your arrangements.

To grow successfully, tulips need to be sited with care. All tulips need good drainage and protection from herbivores. If you are planting in the ground, choose a fenced area or a place that is not browsed by deer. To stop burrowing critters eating the bulbs, plant tulips in sturdy containers that can be left outside or, in cold climates, overwintered in a garage. If you want tulips to perennialize, choose the little species tulips that tend to persist and may even seed in. The taller garden tulips that are most likely to come back for a few years are the Darwins. Tulip season overlaps with the late daffodils to create stunning combinations. Add in early biennials, perennials, and cool-season annuals such as forget-me-nots, wallflowers, pansies, columbines, bleeding hearts, and candytuft.

Orange lily-form tulips underplanted with yellow wallflowers. This display will be changed out in the warm months.

TASKS AND ACTIVITIES

It is such a delight to be outside in spring enjoying the increasing chorus of bird song, the soft light and warmer temperatures, and the gentle color palette as flowers emerge.

Make sure your garden tools are clean, sharpened, and ready to use. Check your supplies of stakes, garden supports, string, and potting soil for containers. It is time to do some clipping back and sorting out of the garden bed, but don't be in a rush to clear away growth if you might get another round of wintry weather. Don't trim back herbs that have shrubby bases, like lavender. Wait until they have started to show a little bit of growth before neatening them up.

If you find bare spots of ground in your spring garden, consider sowing hardy annual seeds straight into the beds. The resulting plants are often tougher and root in more firmly than the ones you grow in pots and then plant out. Nonhardy seeds should be planted inside for the upcoming year. The seedlings will need to be potted into larger pots and eventually hardened off after the last frost date has passed by bringing them outside for a few hours each day over the course of a week or so until they are ready to be planted.

Strive to remove weeds that would rob your chosen plants of sunlight, water, and nutrients before they flower and set seed. Move or divide any large clumps of summer or fall-blooming perennials that have become too big or are in the wrong places. Do this once you can identify them but before they put on much top growth. Spring-blooming perennials should be left in place until the fall.

Late Spring and Early Summer

Spring is the perfect time in the flowery garden, with pleasant temperatures and lengthening days that provide additional light to spur rapid plant growth. Verdant foliage affords a green backdrop for the emerging blooms. The parade of spring bulbs is nearing the end as cool-season annuals, biennials, and early-blooming perennials take center stage. The floral explosion of spring continues with the dramatic blooms of peonies, iris, alliums, lupines, and foxgloves as well as a strong supporting cast of smaller but no less delightful blooms that add to the spring-into-summer floral picture. Spring flowers are varied in shape, fragrance, and color, giving many flowery options to personalize your garden.

PLANT TYPES

In late spring and early summer, the garden is in full swing, and gardeners can experience a rush of joy as a plethora of flowers bloom. Pack your beds full of every type of plant to maximize floriferousness. It is the next peak of the gardening year, with bountiful blooms and lush, ever-expanding greenery.

Hardy or cool-season annuals have a fast and furious life cycle. In one growing season they germinate, grow roots, stems, leaves, and abundant flowers, then set seed and die. They are a quick and easy way to add cheerful early flower power to beds and containers, either purchased as small plants or grown from seed.

Cool-season annuals are tough and can withstand frost. In mild climates, sow their seeds the fall before you want them to flower. The seed may start growing in the autumn and spend the winter as a tiny plant, or it might overwinter and germinate the following spring. In any climate, these seeds can be planted straight into the ground early in spring, and the cool soil temperatures will prompt germination. These annuals will flower as long as the weather is cool, stopping only when true summer heat begins. In moderate climates, cool-season annuals continue to flower throughout the summer. If they finish flowering, pull them out, compost them, and replace them with warm-season annuals to take you through the hot months. Examples of hardy annuals are pansies and Johnny-jump-ups, pot marigolds, sweet alyssum, cornflowers, love-in-a-mist, and honeywort.

A bed of cool-season annuals, including mauve cornflowers, breadseed poppies, and pot marigolds, is backed by a structure supporting sweet peas.

from left Biennials such as this white foxglove and purple dame's rocket are useful because they bloom after spring bulbs and before most perennials and warm-season annuals.

A collection of light blue and dark blue perennial Siberian irises with other yellow irises behind.

Biennial plants grow leaves and good roots in their first year and then flower in the following one, bridging the gap between the end of spring bulbs and the rush of summer perennials.

To establish what appears to be a continuous population of biennials in your garden, you need to sow seed for a couple of years in a row. To get a jump start on the process, buy some second-year plants and let them go to seed in your garden bed or collect seed to sow in trays. Biennials are generous seed producers, so try all methods. Some of the most iconic cottage-garden plants are biennials: the traditional foxgloves, wallflowers, and sweet William, for example.

Perennial plants are the dependable, slow and steady occupants of your flower beds. Unlike the quick, sprinting life cycle of annuals, perennial plants are running a marathon. They take a couple of growing seasons to get completely established, but once they are settled, you can count on them reappearing and getting better each year. Perennial plants are more expensive to buy than annuals, but you get more years of flowering from each one. Some will be in your garden for decades, whereas others may live only a few years.

A perennial plant grows leaves, flowers, and seeds at predetermined times in the growing season. When the frosts arrive in autumn, it seems to perish. However, the plant has already sent extra energy to its roots to fuel next year's growth. As long as the winter is not too cold for that plant, the perennial will sprout again next spring, and the cycle continues. Many will keep growing and expanding, making wider clumps each year, with more flowers. In a few years you can split and divide this type of perennial to make additional plants for your garden. Perennials that bloom at this time of year include hardy geraniums, catmint, veronica, perennial salvia, bluestar, and avens.

STARS OF THE SEASON

Peonies are some of the largest and most beloved flowers of the late spring and early summer. Their sheer opulence makes them a favorite both in the garden and as a cut flower. Herbaceous peonies range in shape from delicate singles to blowsy, full-petaled doubles in colors of white, light pink, magenta, crimson, and coral. Some are deliciously scented. They are also quite long-lived and can survive in your garden for decades.

Bearded iris and allium are two stars of the late-spring season.

I have peonies that came from my husband's great-grandmother's garden. Site them carefully, as they take a few years to settle down in their new soil and don't like to be moved. If you need to change their location, the best time is in the autumn.

Alliums, with their globe-shaped flowers, are one of the last bulb groups to bloom. They are often purple, though some are white, blue, burgundy, yellow, or pink. The dramatic spherical shape of the tall alliums makes a strong statement in the flower bed. Short alliums have a softer look and are perfect at the front of the bed or in a rockery. Tall irises are another star of the late-spring flower palette, with their characteristic tri-cornered blooms. There is an iris for each part of the garden, with Siberian and Louisiana iris in the damp areas, and bearded iris in dry soil where their rhizomes can bake in the sun. Perennial and annual poppies are a great addition to the late-spring garden. With their translucent petals, bold centers, and myriad colors, poppies are always a standout. The earliest one to bloom is the Iceland poppy, followed by the Shirley poppy, breadseed poppy, Oriental poppy, and California poppy.

Favorite Flowers for Late Spring and Early Summer

Digitalis purpurea

Geum 'Mai Tai'

Lupinus 'Persian Slipper'

Papaver rhoeas

Iris

Paeonia 'Do Tell'

Achillea millefolium

Allium 'Pink Jewel'

Aquilegia vulgaris

TASKS AND ACTIVITIES

Late spring into early summer is one of the busiest seasons in the flower garden. It is a good time to buy perennials and annuals to add to the garden. Wait until after your last frost to put out and plant half-hardy annuals. They may be available for sale before your last frost date. Feel free to buy them, but bring them inside if you are meant to have a cold night. As you plant in your flower beds, do not remove or tie up old bulb foliage. Instead, gently direct it through the bed where surrounding plants will cover it but not smother it.

After the last frost, any nonhardy seedlings you have been growing inside should be hardened off before planting outside. Transplant them on a cool, cloudy day, and water them well. Also bring out any tender perennials, corms, and tubers. They can be planted in well-prepared soil with plenty of compost. If you are growing dahlias, the tubers need to be laid horizontally in a hole about six inches deep. When you set out your tubers, put in a suitably sized stake at the same time, as adding it later could risk piercing the tuber. Cover the tubers with about an inch of soil and then backfill the hole as it grows. Plant some gladiolus corms now and then later in succession every two weeks to prolong the show. Stake any other plants like peonies that may flop. Do it judiciously so as to hide the stakes from view. The point is to hold up the flowers but not to make an eyesore in the bed. Alternately, choose stakes that you don't mind seeing among your flowers.

Hardy annuals like this cornflower 'Lady Mauve' can be sown in place or grown inside and then set out later.

One way to reduce the need to stake tall perennials later in the year is to cut them back at the end of spring. Doing this makes them flower at a shorter height, slightly later than they normally would, and often with more numerous, though smaller, flowers. The closer to their regular flowering time you cut them back, the greater the delay will be in flowering. Cut them back by a third to a half of their height. This is sometimes called the "Chelsea chop," as the timing coincides with the prestigious Chelsea Flower Show held in London, England, at the end of May. Plants that respond well to this treatment include many late-summer and fall-blooming perennials such as sedum, border phlox, New England asters, and common sneezeweed. Pinch back hardy chrysanthemums several times before midsummer to reduce their eventual height and encourage more flowers.

As flowers fade, cut off the spent blooms from perennial flowers like peonies or irises. This deadheading improves the overall look of the flower bed and redirects energy into growing stronger roots and better flowers for next year, instead of producing seed. Some perennials, like hardy salvias, may even rebloom. If you feel that something you just planted is in the wrong place and it is still early summer, you may be able to move the plant right now. Just shelter it from the strong sun and water it every day.

Self-Sowing or Volunteer Plants

If you enjoy a loose or spontaneous planting style, develop a set of plants that will self-sow. Self-seeders may be hardy annuals, biennials, or short-lived perennials and can be some of the most exciting additions to the garden because they add spontaneity to your design. They add bargain fullness and visual continuity to a flower bed. They may produce unanticipated combinations or pop up in unexpected places where you wouldn't have been able to grow anything else—like in the cracks of paving or between other plants. Keep them or remove them, depending on your preference. Self-sowing plants are characterized by their ability to set copious amounts of viable seed. To some gardeners, this massive seed output is a negative feature, as they end up with too many plants. To the proponents of a free-wheeling garden style, these self-sowers are an incredible gift. They love the free plants that show up with no effort on their part and add a randomness to their planting schemes. Self-sowers are an important component of cottage gardens and contribute greatly to naturalistic ones.

Add extra flower power to your garden with self-sowing plants like these orange Atlas poppies, *Papaver atlanticum*; garden catchfly, *Silene armeria*; columbine, *Aquilegia*; and common foxglove, *Digitalis purpurea*.

High Summer

High summer arrives with long days and the warmest temperatures of the year. I love to be out in the garden as early as I can—at dawn if I wake up in time. The hustle and bustle of the human world has not yet begun, but it is prime time for other occupants of your garden. Birds are in full voice, reminding me of my grandfather whistling along with their tunes. A lonely bumblebee is fast asleep in the soft center of a dahlia flower, waiting for the sun to reach that part of the garden and warm up its body. Some flowers open only when the sun hits them. Night-blooming flowers are starting to close but may have the vestiges of last night's fragrance clinging to their petals. It is a peaceful time to breathe in the soft morning air and watch the garden unfold around me.

The buzzing of bumblebees on a sunflower is one of the joys of summer.

One of my goals in summer is to eat as many meals outside as I can, so I have added places to sit and enjoy a cup of tea or lunch where I can watch the goings on in the garden. So much changes from day to day in summer that I make sure to explore regularly because I don't want to miss a favorite flower opening up for the first time, and I need to check particular plant combinations to see if they work well. My camera is my constant companion as I walk around. I use it to record special flowers for later review. Being able to zoom in on a flower is a way to focus my attention on just that one bloom and not get overwhelmed by the whole scene. It is also my window into the tiny world of creatures that inhabit the garden. I might pick a bunch of flowers to bring inside so that I can closely examine their forms and colors together. Flowers that look nice in a vase usually also coordinate well in the garden.

The long days of summer mean that there is enough time to take extended garden trips. Revisit your favorite local public gardens and add new gardens to vacation itineraries because it is fun to see what other people are doing. Visiting each one enhances your understanding of how to garden and what possibilities exist for your space.

PLANT TYPES

As spring flowers fade away and are cut back or pulled out, you gain space for the next inhabitants of your bed. There is a wide range of plant types that contribute to the flowery picture in summer. Hardy perennials form the backbone of plantings, with half-hardy annuals and tender plants added to customize your garden with the colors, shapes, and forms that you prefer. Summer is the height of flowery glory in gardens with lots of annual plants. Almost all plants grow fast at this time of year, harnessing energy from the sun to generate abundant, lush, leafy growth, and power prolific flower production.

Warm-season annuals originate in hot climates around the world and enrich the summer flower palette. They need a long growing season, warm soil, and balmy air temperatures to grow well and flower. Grow half-hardy annuals for a broad range of colors and shapes that bring pizzazz to the garden. These plants can be grown in a flower bed composed solely of annuals arranged decoratively for visual effect or in rows or blocks for cutting. They are perfect in containers where you want an exciting summer floral display. In a mixed bed, annuals can be added to fill in any bare spaces among perennials or used in drifts to unify a bed. Plant them next to daffodils and other spring bulbs to cover the waning foliage or next to plants that go summer dormant like Oriental poppies. These annuals are easy to start inside in spring or to buy as small starter plants. If you care for them with plenty of water, they will bloom reliably for the whole summer.

Tender perennials produce sizzling flowers that bring exotic glamour and hot colors into your garden for weeks on end. They are long blooming and heat tolerant, pumping out bright red, lipstick pink, dazzling orange, blazing yellow, and other colored flowers. These plants have the potential to be long-lived in warm climates but will be killed by frost, so they are treated as annuals in temperate areas. Buy them anew each year or overwinter them by protecting them from cold. This can be done by leaving borderline tender perennials in the ground with a thick layer of protective mulch, or by digging them up and storing them inside. It may be easiest to grow these plants in a container so that they are simple to move in and out of the house. For example, flowers like canna can be grown in large pots that are taken indoors, or lifted out of the ground and stored in a frost-free area. Once the weather has warmed the following spring, they can be replanted, or the pots can be moved outside.

STARS OF THE SEASON

opposite Keep the flowery show going in your garden by including a collection of warm-season annuals like celosia and zinnia.

Lilies are treasured summer plants, grown for their theatrical open-faced trumpet shapes, or for their swept-back petals that curl and touch their stems, depending on the variety. Some lilies tower over every other garden occupant, while others are perfect for mid-border. Lily species and cultivars vary widely

from left Bright, large-flowered lilies like this one shine out in the summer garden.

Vertical purple blazing stars break up a mass of lavender daisy-shaped Stokes' asters.

in bloom time, so to keep the show going throughout the summer, try early-summer-blooming Asiatic and martagon lilies, followed by trumpet lilies and Oriental hybrids. Lilies have to be protected from browsing herbivores, as they are particularly attractive to them. Their shapes contrast well with other blooms, including daisy-shaped flowers like cosmos and the spires of blazing star.

Daylilies are another popular summer garden flower. Unrelated to true lilies but with a similar trumpet-like flower, daylilies live up to their name because each flower is only open for about a day. The plant produces blooms over a long period of time, so look for types that have a high flower count. Their green, strap-like leaves provide a backdrop for other flowering plants. There are some cultivars with flowers that soar up on long stems, and others that are suitable for the front of the border.

There is a plethora of daisy-like flowers that bloom in high summer to enhance the garden picture and entice pollinators, including zinnias, marigolds, rudbeckias, and coneflowers. Pair these blooms with the upright spires of delphiniums where summers are cool, or larkspurs where it is hot and humid. Add perennial lobelias, mulleins, and turtleheads for verticality.

Favorite Annuals, Tender Perennials, and Bulbs for High Summer

Gladiolus

Nicotiana alata

Celosia argentea

Helianthus annuus

Tagetes erecta

Petunia

Cosmos 'Double Click Mix'

Zinnia 'Queen Lime Red'

Cleome hassleriana

Favorite Hardy Perennials for High Summer

Coreopsis verticillata 'Zagreb'

Phlox paniculata 'Lavelle'

Lilium

Echinacea 'Double Scoop Bubble Gum'

Kniphofia 'Little Maid'

Monarda 'Balmy Pink'

Rudbeckia subtomentosa 'Henry Eilers'

Gaillardia ×grandiflora 'Arizona Apricot'

Leucanthemum ×superbum 'Becky'

TASKS AND ACTIVITIES

Summer is the time for enjoyment and assessment. As your floral combinations take shape, consider whether you like them as they are or if you want to change anything, and make notes about what to move in fall. Keep up with watering annuals and tender perennials, especially plants growing in containers. Potted plants dry out very quickly in the summer, so you need to check them every day. Add water until it flows out of the bottom of the pot, but do not keep containers sitting in water unless they hold a wet-tolerant plant. Fertilize pots with a low dose of organic fertilizer every few weeks. Choose one that is low in nitrogen and high in phosphorus and potassium to promote root growth and flower development. Flowering plants growing in the ground should need minimal fertilizing if you have prepared the soil well and added lots of compost.

Zinnias and other annuals need regular deadheading to keep the plants producing more flowers.

Deadhead regularly to remove spent blooms and encourage repeat flowering. Buds continue to open on annual plants as long as the weather and day length suit their requirements. Flowering stems of early-blooming perennials like hardy salvias, yarrows, and catmint can be cut to the ground after they finish blooming to encourage a second flush of flowers at the end of summer. Trim back leggy growth on plants if they are crowding their neighbors. Stake and tie up plants that have grown tall and look like they might flop over.

If you love sowing seeds, summer is the time to sow biennials for flowering next year. Try sprinkling them sparsely onto a gravel-covered bed or plant them into pots that can be kept outside in a sheltered place. It is also the time to plant early-autumn flowering bulbs like colchicum. Take time to really enjoy your garden and watch the flowers and pollinators interact. Cut plenty of flowers, particularly annuals, for your house and to give away. The summer garden is abuzz with life, and it is great to be part of it.

Late Summer into Autumn

As the end of summer rolls around, every warm day is particularly sweet because you can feel the season changing. The quality of light is softer, with misty mornings and golden evenings. The end of summer into autumn is dominated by late-blooming hardy perennials, tender perennials, and annuals that continue to flower until the first frost. The flower colors of autumn are rich with saturated

Enjoy fall flowers like
Japanese anemone
and rudbeckias.

goldenrod yellows, aster purples and pinks, amaranth burgundy, and Mexican sunflower orange that echo the changing colors of deciduous tree leaves. Late summer is one of the most productive for the harvest of cut flowers. There are armloads of dahlias, celosias, globe amaranths, and zinnias. Make the most of this and pick lavish bunches for your friends and yourself.

As autumn brings cooler temperatures, summer plants produce fewer flowers, but each one lasts longer. They are brighter and more vibrant in color because they are not bleached by the hot summer sun. Even when you think the flowery year is winding down, new plants come into bloom. Autumn is sometimes forgotten when people make their flower wish lists, but it is fun to include a few late-bloomers to delight you. It is a lovely time to be out in the garden as the rush of the gardening season winds down. I relish the last warm, peaceful evenings by sitting outside on the porch long after dark and looking back on the gardening year. The first frost brings the end of the flowering annuals and tender perennials. It is a bittersweet day in the garden, with the frost outlining frozen flowers.

STARS OF THE SEASON

Some of the annuals and tender perennials that have been flowering all summer continue to bloom well into autumn as long as they were regularly deadheaded, grown in good soil, and given sufficient water. Zinnias keep up their show with brilliantly colored flowers that attract both butterflies and bees. Flowering tobacco is still blooming and filling the night air with fragrance. The fabulous bright orange Mexican sunflower is at its prime now, tempting passing butterflies with its bold orange daisy-like flowers held high on long stems. Marigolds and pot marigolds are blooming in orange, yellow, and creams. Nasturtiums get a second burst of growth in the cooler temperatures with their round, disc-like leaves and trumpet-shaped flowers in red, orange, cream, coral, yellow, and salmon.

A soft orange dahlia is the star of this autumn border with tall verbena, crocosmia, and nasturtium.

Dahlias are one of the stars of the late-summer and fall garden. They are flowering machines once they have put on strong vegetative growth. Their leaves are usually green, though a few well-loved cultivars, such as 'Bishop of Llandaff', have dark mahogany-brown foliage. Dahlia flowers come in a spectacular range of colors, including pinks, purples, magentas, yellows, oranges, whites, and reds—every color except blue. Bloom sizes range from minute flowers an inch across to ones the size of dinner plates. The flower shapes are classified using wonderful names such as pompon, waterlily, anemone, cactus, balls, and informal decorative.

There is a dahlia for everyone, both in the garden and as cut flowers. You can visit dahlia displays to get an idea of what is available and write down the kinds you want to grow. Plant height varies, with short dahlias for the front of the bed or in containers, and six- to eight-foot-tall plants for the back of the bed

from left Many of the annual and tender-perennial salvias are at their best in late summer and fall, such as the fuzzy purple Mexican bush sage, *Salvia leucantha*.

Melon-colored golden surprise lily, *Lycoris chinensis*, adds flair to a late-summer garden.

or a cutting garden. Tall dahlias have to be staked and regularly tied in with figure-eight loops around the stem and the supporting structure. To continue flower production until frost, water and fertilize the plants and pick flowers regularly to prevent them from setting seed.

Some of the tender salvias that come from subtropical areas start to bloom as summer comes to an end. Salvias have upright or gracefully horizontal spiked flower heads that contrast well with the daisy-shaped flowers predominating at this time of year. Blue anise sage blooms for a long season that continues into fall, with coveted royal blue or emperor purple flowers that are a useful complement to warm-colored blooms. The pineapple sage has a fruity fragrance to its foliage and red flowers that don't start blooming until the tail end of summer. Mexican bush sage has soft flowers that are white with purple bracts, or all purple. In places with an early frost, plants native to hot climates may not have enough time to bloom, so grow some of the tender perennial salvias that bloom all summer until frost, like mealycup sage and scarlet sage. In warm climates, salvias are a standout and a food station for the last migrating hummingbirds, if you are lucky enough to have them visit your garden.

Several bulbs bloom toward the end of the flowery year that are summer dormant instead of winter dormant like spring-flowering bulbs. Late-summer and autumn-flowering bulbs grow their leaves in the spring to send energy to the bulb. The foliage withers during summer, and as the end of the season arrives, they send up flowers that appear to pop out of nowhere, surprising you. During their summer dormancy they have to be dry, so they can't be planted in a regularly irrigated flower bed.

Surprise lilies have clusters of trumpet-shaped or spidery flowers held up on sturdy stalks. There are several species available, with flowers of red, pink blushed with blue, or peachy yellow. Some cannot take cold winters, so check their hardiness before you buy them. Another autumn surprise are colchicums, which look like a large lavender, purple, or white crocus. Some are goblet shaped, while others have strappy petals that splay out from the center. The flowers are a welcome early-autumn treat, but be aware that all colchicum are toxic if ingested. There are also true crocus that bloom in the fall, including the species from which the spice saffron is harvested, *Crocus sativus*, and an autumn daffodil, *Sternbergia lutea*.

A classic autumnal pairing of yellow goldenrod and dark purple New England asters.

The classic perennial flowers of the autumn are asters, goldenrods, sedums, and chrysanthemums. They have spent the summer growing tall and leafy, so they are at the peak of their growth with plenty of energy to put into making flowers now. These plants bloom as the days get shorter and the nights lengthen. On sunny days, they are covered in pollinating insects trying to get their last stores of pollen and nectar before winter sets in. Asters, with their gorgeous and profuse purple, pink, and white daisy-shaped flowers, are iconic fall plants. Different species and cultivars vary in plant size, shape, leaves, and flowers. Asters pair well with goldenrods, which bloom at the same time with fuzzy golden-yellow flowers. The shapes and colors complement each other, especially if the plants intermingle. The flat tops of sedums are a good strong shape to add to the mix. Some cultivars have reddish or dark foliage.

Short sedums are perfect at the front of the bed as an edging, and taller cultivars are a wonderful presence in mid-border. Japanese anemones are some of the most graceful autumn-blooming hardy perennials. Their long, airy stems rise above the flower bed, holding cup-shaped blooms high for passing pollinators. The petal colors come in white, pink, and lilac surrounding the central yellow stamens. Pair Japanese anemones with the spikes of obedient plant for a combination of contrasting shapes.

Hardy chrysanthemums, sometimes called mums, are the last perennials to come into bloom in the garden. Some varieties are so late that you feel they

Favorite Flowers for Late Summer into Fall

Salvia elegans 'Golden Delicious'

Anemone ×hybrida 'Honorine Jobert'

Crocosmia 'Anna-Marie'

Hylotelephium 'Matrona'

Solidago 'Crown of Rays'

Chrysanthemum

Gladiolus murielae

Symphyotrichum oblongifolium 'October Skies'

Colchicum speciosum

cannot possibly open before winter arrives. When they do bloom, their rich colors and spidery, daisy, or button shapes are worth waiting for. Fully double ones, with their extra rows of petals, are a bold presence in the garden. Choose single-flowered cultivars with obvious yellow stamens for the last pollinators. Chrysanthemums are available in bronze, orange, red, peach, pink, lavender, white, yellow, and more. The compact domed chrysanthemums that you can buy in the fall at plant nurseries are fabulous additions for containers, but they may not be hardy enough to survive the winter.

TASKS AND ACTIVITIES

Enjoy the late-blooming perennials that are the last flowery delight of the gardening season. As their flowering wanes, it is a great time to do an assessment of your flower beds and see where you have empty spots. Move and divide perennials that have finished blooming. Pick an overcast day to do your digging, and water the plants well once you have moved them. Decide how much you will trim back old stems and foliage in the fall and how much you will leave on the bed over winter. Keep plants with great winter forms to add interest in the coming months and provide habitat for insects and seeds for birds.

Annuals still need care and attention at this time of year. Some annuals, like nasturtiums and marigolds, get another flush of flowers as the temperatures moderate. If you want to keep your garden looking good, deadhead old blooms, tie up tall stems to prevent flopping, and water plants, especially if you have a dry spell. If you want to save seeds for next year, let them ripen on the plant and harvest them once the seed head has fully dried. After the first hard frost, the soft green stems of annuals usually turn to mush, so pull them out and compost them. This gives you spaces in the bed to plant spring-flowering bulbs. Planning and planting your flowery bulb display for next spring is one of the most exciting activities of the fall season. Hardy annual seeds can also be planted in these just-cleared spots.

Enjoy your tender plants in the garden for as long as you can, though they will start to decline as temperatures cool. Be prepared to dig up any plants you want to save for next year before the nighttime temperatures get too cold. If they are not hardy in your area, dig up tender tubers and corms, such as dahlias, cannas, and tender gladiolus, a week after the tops get blackened by the first icy weather. Store them in a frost-free area for winter.

Work out a management strategy for dealing with fallen deciduous tree leaves. Keep as many as you can to use as a soil improver. Shredding the leaves first helps them decompose quickly. There are two main strategies you can take: spread the shredded leaves onto your beds as a mulch, or put them in a compost bin or pile to use in the coming years. I do a combination, taking some away and putting the rest back on the beds.

Take a look at summer containers and see what plants still look good. Remove or trim back any plants that are past their prime and pop in a couple of new ones to add to the overall look for fall, or overhaul the entire container. You can prepare for spring by potting up spring bulbs. If you live in an area with harsh winters, they need to be kept inside in a cool, frost-free area and barely watered. In mild climates, you can keep your pots outside and overwinter hardy plants such as pansies in the same containers as the bulbs.

opposite Some plants retain their structure in winter, such as this Jerusalem sage with its whorled seed heads, so leave them standing in autumn.

Winter

Winter in the temperate flower garden is the time for small, quiet floral joys. If your garden is not under a blanket of snow, you may have a few flowers to carry you through the darkest days of the year. Relish each tiny, often scented bloom, and look for the grateful pollinators that emerge on days warm enough to fly. We have several honeybee hives and a variety of other native solitary bees. When the temperatures rise, they come out to get water and look for pollen and nectar. I have added cold-season flowers to my garden for my pleasure and to supply the bees and other pollinators with a little food.

Bees appreciate any flowers that bloom in winter, such as this snowdrop.

Whatever your weather, there is a lull in activity during winter that gives you time to think and plan. Draw on memories of the floral delights of this year, and anticipate the ones to come. Use the long evenings to reflect on past successes and imagine what you would like to change. Pull out all your notes, photos, seed packets, plant tags, and anything else that helps you remember. Look through your pictures and note what you thought were the best combinations of flowers. Think of things you want to improve. One of the most uplifting activities is dreaming about the flowering plants you might buy and new seeds you want to grow. Check possible purchases against your flower garden wish list. My desired list always initially exceeds my space and budget, but the process of narrowing it down helps solidify my vision. The entire wish list construction and reduction gives me lots of pleasure as I daydream about the future of my flower garden.

TASKS AND ACTIVITIES

In winter there are some gardening activities that can be done outside, but they are very weather dependent. The majority of your flower gardening activity takes place indoors as you plan for the coming year.

Winter is the time to take an inventory of any saved or purchased seeds you have and plan what you need to sow for next year's garden. Gardening groups might organize seed exchanges or swaps at this time of year. They are a great way to share the treasures from your garden and get some different ones to try. To decide when each seed should be planted, check the back of the seed packet. It will state whether the seeds are better started indoors or directly out in the garden soil. Some of the flowering plants you may want to grow, particularly half-hardy annuals, will not tolerate frost, so they need to be started inside in seed trays and planted out once the soil has warmed up. Divide the seeds into groups according to the number of weeks prefrost they should be planted and make a seed-sowing calendar to keep you on track.

Leave seed heads like those of lilies of the Nile to provide winter garden accents in the snow.

The weather you experience in the cold months of winter will determine how much you can do. Consistent snow cover is a natural protective blanket for the flower bed. Snow is a great insulator of soil, which protects perennials from frost heaving and drying winds. In winters without snow or with erratic snowfall, you have to protect your plants in another way. A covering of loose mulch or cut evergreen branches laid on the soil are some of the ways to maintain a steadier soil temperature. One of the worst enemies of herbaceous perennials in this type of climate is the cycle of the soil freezing and thawing. Just like water repeatedly freezing and melting forms potholes in roads, water in the soil expands and contracts with the weather and creates an unstable environment for your perennials. If a plant is not firmly rooted in, freezing temperatures can pop the whole root ball out of the soil, where it may desiccate and die. If your garden experiences cycles of freezing and thawing during winter, be sure the perennials you add to your garden during the growing season have enough time to become well rooted before cold weather sets in.

In mild climates, you have plenty of opportunities to get out into the winter garden. There are a range of winter-blooming plants you can enjoy that are not hardy elsewhere. In colder climates, you can experiment with some of the winter bloomers that are borderline hardy for your zone. I have had luck growing some plants that should not survive winters in my area by finding warmer mini microclimates in the garden. These are often places where the snow melts first or areas that trap the sun and are sheltered from prevailing winter winds, maybe between a porch and a house wall. There are some plants that flower in winter, even in cold areas. These are either tiny bulbous plants that come from frozen mountaintops or cold-hardy shrubs that provide some winter flowers, as they are able to resist snow and frost. If they have areas highlighting winter flowers, visit local public gardens to get inspiration and information on what you could grow.

I like to get outside at some point every day. There is the old adage that there is no bad weather, just bad clothing, so I do try to emerge from my writing nook, dress up in layers, and take a walk around the garden. If the flower beds are not covered by snow, there is a chance to pull opportunistic winter weeds that seem to germinate no matter how cold it is. I have developed an area of my garden to highlight winter flowers where I have clustered many cold-weather bloomers. It is near the back door and has a nice path for easy access regardless of the weather. The beds face the midday sun so the plants get any rays that they can. The path is lined with witch hazels (*Hamamelis*), sweetbox (*Sarcococca*), and snowdrops for blooms when little else is out. The very earliest daffodils, like 'Rijnveld's Early Sensation', are here too. Occasionally, some days are so cold that I just stay inside, drink hot tea, and do some garden reading. My neighbor is content to stay indoors all winter, preferring to hang up her cleaned garden tools at the end of fall.

Gardeners are eternal optimists. We look forward to seeing each of our favorite seasonal flowers emerge from the ground. We love the process and the cyclical nature of flower gardening because there is always something to look forward to and hope for. It is a rolling sequence of floral anticipation, appreciation, and adjustment. As you water your little seedlings or gaze through the windows at the wintry garden, remember the joys of past gardening seasons and look forward to your most floriferous garden ever.

The following chapter makes for good winter reading. Carefully go through the flowering plants and see which ones you might enjoy growing. Find ones that spark your interest, and if they are perennials make sure that they suit your climate and conditions. If you are in the early stages of your flower gardening adventures, look closely at annuals, as they are a cheap and cheerful way to add flower power to your beds and containers.

Seeing the tiny green noses of snowdrops coming up gives you a sense of hope for the gardening year to come.

The Flower Gardener's Palette

Choosing Plants for Your Garden

Once you have a flower wish list but before you acquire plants, make sure that your choices will succeed in your garden conditions. In this chapter I have compiled a list of my favorite flower garden genera and the best species and cultivars for home gardens. Use it as a jumping-off point and a reference as you continue to explore flower growing. This list of flowering plants is sorted alphabetically by genus and includes their common names. All the plants in this book are for a sunny garden where they will receive six or more » hours of sun per day during the growing season unless otherwise specified. Most of the plants need moist, well-drained soil, but I have indicated if this is not the case. In the descriptions, I also note if the plant might be considered invasive, so check your local municipality to find out whether it should be avoided in your area.

To help you understand which flowering plants will fit your design preferences, each entry lists flower shape and role, season of bloom, position in the bed, if it is suitable for containers, height and width, hardiness, and plant life cycle. Further description follows, including key flowers and colors within the genus, deer and rabbit resistance, and anything else noticeable about the plant's presence.

Height and width are the range for the genus and are listed in inches. For perennials, this is their size after about three years' growth. Annuals tend to attain their dimensions in one growing season. The size of tender perennials also represents their growth during one summer. Where they are hardy, they may attain a larger size. Hardy bulbs usually get to their full size in the first year. All plants' sizes are linked to growing conditions and may vary according to how they are grown. Hardiness zones are those listed on the United States Department of Agriculture website, with the lowest number referencing the coldest zone in which it is likely to survive the winter. I have listed general hardiness ratings for plants in each genus. The species and cultivars may vary, so check before you buy.

previous (clockwise from top left) Three bright red flowers: a single dahlia, a spike of annual salvia, and a glossy cup-shaped poppy.

Achillea 'Firefly Amethyst'

Achillea 'Pretty Belinda'

Achillea 'Moonshine'

Achillea / YARROW

SHAPE horizontal
ROLE mid-border delight
midsummer to autumn // mid-front to mid-back //
12–36 in. × 12–24 in. // zones 3–9, perennial

Yarrows all make extremely reliable, drought-tolerant perennials that thrive in sunny areas with soils that drain well. They are classic plants that add flat-topped, plate-shaped flowers to the late spring through summer garden. The strong horizontal lines of their blooms contrast well with the upright spikes of perennial salvias, red hot pokers, and the spiky domes of sea hollies. Yarrows can make significant patches once established that can then be divided after a few years. Their aromatic foliage deters herbivore browsing. All types make great long-lasting cut flowers, which can be dried. Deadhead the spent flowers to promote rebloom.

There are several different species to look out for and lots of cultivars. *Achillea millefolium* is the common yarrow that grows in the wild with off-white blooms. It has undergone some interesting plant breeding to produce a large choice of flower colors, including yellow, pink, magenta, purple, orange, and colors in between. *Achillea filipendulina*, fern-leaf yarrow, needs good drainage. It has tall stems that hold golden-yellow flowers in the height of summer. Look for the lofty cultivar 'Gold Plate'. Other good yarrow cultivars for the garden include 'Coronation Gold', a well-loved cultivar with gray-green foliage and very flat yellow flowers, 'Moonshine' with soft yellow flowers and silvery foliage, 'Terra Cotta' with bronzy yellow and orange flowers, and 'Pink Grapefruit', which flowers in shades of pink. *Achillea ptarmica* and its cultivars have small white flowers rather like baby's breath that mingle well in perennial beds.

Agapanthus

Agastache 'Black Adder' in a bed with other flowers.

Agapanthus / LILY OF THE NILE

SHAPE loose ball
ROLE bold beauty or mid-border delight
late summer to autumn // mid-front; containers // 12–48 in. × 12–24 in. // zones 7–11, tender perennial

Lilies of the Nile are summer through fall bloomers that have loose, rounded clusters of usually blue flowers. *Agapanthus* is a fairly tender perennial that will survive outside in warm climates. Some cultivars have been bred to be hardy, like *A.* 'Headbourne Hybrids', which may survive outside in well-drained soil with a heavy winter mulch in zone 7. In cold-winter areas, grow lilies of the Nile in pots that are brought inside for the winter. You can plant them in decorative containers and use them to flank paths, or you can place their pots into the bed to cover holes left by the retreating foliage of daffodils or Oriental poppies. Lilies of the Nile are bold late-summer companions for crocosmia.

Agastache / HUMMINGBIRD MINT OR GIANT HYSSOP

SHAPE spike
ROLE mid-border delight
high summer to autumn // mid-front; containers // 12–48 in. × 12–36 in. // zones 5–9, perennial

Agastaches have numerous small, tubular, lipped flowers clustered along upright or flexible stems. Their anise or minty-scented foliage is delightful in the summer garden and has the added benefit of making the plants deer and rabbit resistant. They have a long season of bloom. There are two main categories of garden *Agastache*. The easiest to grow plants are *A. foeniculum*, anise hyssop, that flower for weeks in the summer garden. Look for some of the hybrids and cultivars that have a similar habit. I have really enjoyed growing 'Black Adder', which copes well with hot summers and high humidity. I also like 'Blue Fortune'.

Agastaches of this type are called hummingbird mints.

Ageratum houstonianum

The second group are the hummingbird mints such as *Agastache cana*, or the cultivars like 'Rosie Posie' that can take heat and dry conditions. They may be short-lived if they are not given adequate drainage. As the name suggests, they attract hummingbirds, but they are also loved by butterflies. Their flowers come in a range of sunset hues from yellow and coral to orange, pink, and more. They are wonderful for mixing with bold plants in the flower bed like coneflower or with other summer bloomers like white gaura.

Ageratum / FLOSSFLOWER

SHAPE button
ROLE tiny treasure or mid-border delight
late spring to autumn // front to mid-front; containers // 12–30 in. × 6–18 in. // half-hardy annual

Ageratum houstonianum is grown as an annual in most climates. In shades of blue, purple, or white, flossflowers' powder-puff shaped flowers are clustered above slightly fuzzy green leaves that fit easily into the garden. Short cultivars are perfect in containers or at the front of the border. Tall cultivars integrate well in the mid-front with yarrows, columbines, and salvias. They are good in cut flower arrangements. Flossflowers all grow well in soil amended with extra compost to keep the roots moist but not wet. Trim back the plants if their stems get too long and you will get a rebloom later in the summer. Flossflowers can be purchased as seed for starting indoors in spring or as small bedding plants.

Alcea rosea in a flower bed.

Alchemilla mollis

Alcea / HOLLYHOCK

SHAPE spike
ROLE background or bold beauty
late spring to autumn // mid-back to back //
42–96 in. × 12–24 in. // zones 2–9, perennial or biennial

Hollyhocks are charming old-fashioned cottage-garden favorites that are easy to grow and adaptable to a wide range of conditions. These tall biennials or short-lived perennials are great for the back of the border, where their upright stems hold a series of outward-facing flowers. *Alcea rosea*, common hollyhock, has single blooms that are cone-shaped with a central boss and doubles that look ruffled and full. Both forms come in rosy pink, red, yellow, white, and nearly black. Give them a sunny, well-drained spot. They do well in lean soil. Grow your own hollyhocks from seed and they should flower next year. They are prone to a disease called rust, which looks like little brown dots on its leaves. If the fungus affects your plants, remove the infected leaves and throw them away. The species *A. rugosa*, yellow-flowered Russian hollyhock, and *A. ficifolia*, fig-leaf hollyhock, available in multiple colors, seem to be less prone to rust.

Alchemilla / LADY'S MANTLE

SHAPE cloud
ROLE mixer
late spring and early summer // front of the border //
12–18 in. × 18–30 in. // zones 4–8, perennial

Alchemilla mollis, lady's mantle, is a perfect plant for the front of a flower bed where you can admire the airy sprays of yellow-green flowers. Use lady's mantle in a cottage-garden-style bed or to soften a path edge. The wavy-edged, rounded leaves are known for their ability to catch water droplets and make them look like little circular mirrors. *Alchemilla* thrives where summers are cool and can seed into beds aggressively. In areas with hot and humid summers, it can be hard to establish. Site the plants in afternoon shade and give them plenty of water in their first year. Use them as an edging or an underplanting for taller perennials.

Allium 'Gladiator'

Allium cowanii blooms in late spring and is great mid-border.

Allium sphaerocephalon

Allium / ALLIUM

SHAPE ball or dome
ROLE bold beauty, mid-border delight, or tiny treasure
late spring to autumn // front to mid-back; containers //
12–60 in. × 6–12 in. // zones 4–9, hardy bulb

The genus *Allium* contains a plethora of wonderful globe or dome-shaped flowers. Each flower head is made up of a collection of little star-like flowers that attract bees. Most alliums are planted in the fall as bulbs. They need well-drained moist but not dry soil. Choose your allium by color, plant height, and season of bloom. They are often purple, but may be creamy white, pink, or other colors. Allium are an ornamental onion so they are not eaten by deer or rabbits.

Allium giganteum, giant allium, is the dramatic punctuation that the late-spring and early-summer garden needs. Its height and bold spherical shape make it stand out in a sea of lower-growing perennials such as catmint and lesser calamint. I like to grow it with other tall alliums that bloom at the same time such as A. 'Ambassador', A. 'Globemaster' and A. hollandicum 'Purple Sensation'. I also enjoy the shorter A. schubertii and A. christophii with their large loose blooms that resemble fireworks. Blooming at

the same time is A. siculum, formerly called *Nectaroscordum*, which has nodding bells of dusty red, green, and cream held on tall stems. In my garden I grow A. schoenoprasum, chives, which flowers in spring. This edible onion produces roundish puffs of small-scale flowers for a neat edging to an herb bed. You can pick petals or leaves for cooking.

Allium sphaerocephalon, drumstick allium, has tightly ovular flowers with a burgundy top and green base. It looks good in mixed borders or dry gardens and flowers in the first part of summer. It can seed aggressively. The tallest allium is A. 'Summer Drummer', which blooms on long stems in midsummer. Both its buds and its flowers grab your eye, first with pointed buds and then round purple flowers on tall stems. There are some excellent summer-blooming alliums that are clump formers for the front of the bed. They have rounded flower heads in the pinky purple range with strong green foliage. Look for cultivars such as 'Millenium' or 'Windy City', which of course is a Midwest favorite. The final allium of the year in my garden is A. thunbergii, Japanese onion, which blooms in fall on a short to medium plant suitable for the front of a well-draining bed or rock garden. Its flowers are drooping balls in purples, pinks, and white.

Allium, continued

Allium 'Mount Everest'

Allium siculum with *Allium* 'Purple Sensation' behind it.

Allium 'Millenium'

Alstroemeria 'Koice',
Inca Ice alstroemeria

Amaranthus
caudatus

Alstroemeria / PERUVIAN LILY

SHAPE loose trumpet
ROLE mid-border delight
late spring to autumn // mid-front to mid-back //
24–36 in. × 24–36 in. // zones 6–10, perennial

Peruvian lilies have open, vaguely trumpet-shaped
flowers in orange, purple, white, pink, coral, and
mauve with dashed interior markings. They bloom
from summer to fall, depending on the cultivar, and
are a hummingbird favorite. They may or may not be
hardy, so pay attention when making your selection.
They perform well in sunny spots with afternoon
shade in hot areas. Site them in a place that is sheltered from wind and has fertile soil. They may require
support during growth and need regular watering.
They make a very long-lasting cut flower. *Alstroemeria* ligtu hybrids are some of the most vigorous
where they are hardy.

Amaranthus / AMARANTH

SHAPE plume or tassel
ROLE background or mid-border delight
high summer to autumn // mid-back to back //
36–72 in. × 12–30 in. // half-hardy annual

Amaranths are tall annuals that bear long, dangling
tassel-like or feathery flowers. Their flowers and leaves
are often vibrantly colored. Amaranths make great cut
flowers, and their unusually shaped blooms contrast
well with others in summer bouquets. They are easy to
grow from seed and will self-sow for next year. *Amaranthus caudatus*, love-lies-bleeding, has dramatic,
dripping inflorescences of tiny reddish pink flowers.
Amaranthus cruentus, red amaranth, is a statuesque
plant that is great for the back of the border. In some
parts of the world, they are grown as a food crop, but
they are equally useful as a decorative plant. If you
are growing it as a cut flower, be sure to pinch out the
growing tip early in the season to produce multiple
smaller-scale flowers. I like the cultivar 'Hopi Red Dye',
with its maroon-red foliage and flowers. It looks great
in late summer and fall with Mexican sunflower.

Ammi majus

Amsonia tabernaemontana

Ammi / LADY'S LACE

SHAPE horizontal
ROLE mixer
late spring, early summer to high summer // mid-front to mid-back // 36–48 in. × 12–24 in. // half-hardy annual

Ammi majus, lady's lace, is a tall half-hardy annual with white, domed to flat-topped blooms good for cut flowers that adds a lovely filigree touch to a flower bed. *Ammi* flowers look similar to the roadside wildflower Queen Anne's lace, but are not as aggressive. Try them with delphiniums and milky bellflowers or with other cutting flowers. They may benefit from some support as they grow. *Ammi visnaga* is grown for the similar-looking flowers and delicate foliage. Try the unusual cultivar 'Green Mist'. Wear gloves when cutting them, as the sap can cause skin problems.

Amsonia / BLUESTAR

SHAPE star-like
ROLE mid-border delight
late spring and early summer // mid-front to mid-back // 24–36 in. × 24–36 in. // zones 5–9, perennial

Bluestars are mostly native to North America. They have a milky sap, so they are unbothered by browsing herbivores. *Amsonia hubrichtii*, narrowleaf bluestar, has clouds of slender wavy foliage and sprays of star-shaped blue spring flowers. The leaves turn bright yellow in the fall. It is a good weaver and mixer in a flower bed and its fine foliage texture contrasts well with the coarse leaves of coneflowers and rudbeckia. It is easy to grow in beds or informal gardens and may self-seed in the right conditions. *Amsonia tabernae-montana*, willow bluestar, has similar flower color and structure with larger leaves and a slightly shorter habit. These two species both prefer moist soils but can take some drought.

Anemone blanda 'Blue Shades'

Anemone hupehensis 'Hadspen Abundance'

A planting of Japanese anemones.

Anemone / ANEMONE

SHAPE bowl or daisy

ROLE tiny treasure or background

early to mid-spring; late summer into autumn // front or back // 6–48 in. × 6–36 in. // zones 4–8, hardy bulb or perennial

Anemone is a large genus that contains several garden-worthy flowers, starting in spring with the petite blooms of *A. blanda*, Grecian windflower, through to the late-summer tall Japanese anemones. Grecian windflowers have many-petaled flowers only a few inches above the ground, making them a great gem for the front of the border. In fall, tuck their tiny black tubers between daffodil bulbs, and in spring they will carpet the soil with their adorable blooms. The flowers may be blue, white, or occasionally pink with a light yellow center.

Japanese anemones *Anemone* ×*hybrida* and *A. hupehensis* are welcome additions to the late-summer garden. Their long stems hold bowl-like blooms above lower-growing good-quality foliage. The form of the plant and the flower make a lovely fresh contrast to other plants of the season. They have a see-through quality, which means they could be placed in the middle of the border. My favorites are any white flowering ones, particularly the old-fashioned 'Honorine Jobert'. They charm me with their green center and yellow stamens encircled by pristine white petals. Other cultivars are pinky mauve and may have contrasting colors on the outside of their petals. They are best planted in spring to help with establishment, but once they get going, they can take over large areas. Try tucking a few colchicums at the base, as they bloom at a similar time.

Anethum graveolens

Angelica archangelica

Anethum / DILL

SHAPE horizontal
ROLE mixer

early to mid-spring; high summer // mid-back to back; containers // 36–60 in. × 24–36 in. // hardy annual

These airy plants are a lovely counterpoint to flowers that have large leaves, with their yellow lacy umbels and thread-like green fragrant foliage. They are annual plants that are easily grown from seed. Dill is a traditional occupant of an herb garden, where it is often grown with other herbal plants like tansy and feverfew in rich, light soils in sunny positions. It is used fresh and dried in cooking. It is a butterfly host plant and a pollinator favorite.

Angelica / ANGELICA

SHAPE ball or dome
ROLE bold beauty

high summer to autumn // back of the border // 36–72 in. × 24–48 in. // zones 5–7, perennial or biennial

Angelica gigas, giant angelica, has dark purply rounded umbels borne on statuesque biennial or short-lived plants. Its dark stems and large green foliage have an impressive presence in the back of the flower bed in late summer. It thrives in consistently moist soil that is rich in organic matter. In hot areas it will need some afternoon shade. *Angelica archangelica*, garden angelica, is a similarly large plant grown for its bold, multiple clustered balls of green flowers

Angelica gigas

Angelonia
angustifolia

and huge leaves. Plant it where you want to make a statement. It is suitable for an herb garden, as it has a few culinary uses. Both these angelica plants can set plenty of seeds, so deadhead them if you don't want lots of seedlings. Sprinkle some seeds around the original plants if you would like replacements two years later. Angelicas are pollinator magnets.

Angelonia / SUMMER SNAPDRAGON

SHAPE spike
ROLE container or front-border treat
late spring to autumn // front; containers //
12–18 in. × 12–18 in. // half-hardy annual

With upright stems that hold a spike of miniature bilaterally symmetrical flowers, *Angelonia angustifolia*, summer snapdragon, vaguely resembles a true snapdragon, though on a smaller scale. It is a tender perennial that is grown as an annual. Colors are dusty pink, blues, purple, white, and bicolors. Plants in the genus are heat tolerant and do well when planted in containers. Combine them with other summer annuals and tender perennials like Egyptian starcluster or canna.

A coral-red cultivar of *Antirrhinum majus*.

Upright cultivars of *Antirrhinum majus* make great cut flowers.

Antirrhinum / SNAPDRAGON

SHAPE spike
ROLE tiny treasure or mid-border delight
early spring to autumn // front to mid-front //
12–36 in. × 6–12 in. // half-hardy annual

Antirrhinum majus, common snapdragon, is the most widely grown plant in this genus and comes in a large selection of possible cultivars. They are tender perennials usually grown as half-hardy annuals and are available in a wide range of single colors and bicolors such as yellow, white, pink, peach, lilac, and crimson red. They typically have a characteristic mouth-like flower that is beloved by children, who squeeze its sides to get the "mouth" to open and close. Snapdragons, or "snaps," are normally purchased as small plants but can be grown from seed sown inside and then planted out as seedlings after the last frost. They do well in good garden soil. My favorite tall snaps are the Rocket Series and Potomac Series, which are wonderful for cutting. For the front of the bed, I use 'Magic Carpet Mix'. Snapdragons do best in cool weather but will bloom all summer where temperatures are moderate. They can also be used as a winter annual in warm climates.

Aquilegia / COLUMBINE

SHAPE bell
ROLE mid-border delight
late spring and early summer // front to mid-front //
12–30 in. × 12–24 in. // zones 3–8, perennial

Columbines are delightful flowers of late spring and early summer. They are slender in form and easily slip between some of the larger occupants of the border. They are available in a broad range of colors from white to pinks of varying intensities, purples, blues, reds, yellows, and some fabulous near-black ones. They are perennials that are easy from seed scattered

A daintily colored *Aquilegia vulgaris* in the Songbird Series.

in place, started in pots, or purchased as plants. If you have several different colors or shapes in your garden, the pollinators will get to work and cross them with each other. They have a tap root but will move easily when young. Any average well-drained garden soil will suit their needs. Some of my favorites are the red and yellow *Aquilegia canadensis*, Canadian columbine, which is beloved by hummingbirds, and *A. vulgaris* 'Nora Barlow', which has layers of spiky petals in pink and white with touches of green. For an arid climate, try *A. caerulea* with its large, delicately colored light blue and white flowers. They are native to the Rocky Mountains of North America but grow well in other areas of the world given good drainage and a sunny position. All columbines make endearing companions for alliums, hardy salvias, bearded iris, and late tulips and don't mind being lightly shaded by surrounding plants.

Aquilegia vulgaris

Armeria maritima growing in a terracotta pot.

Asclepias syriaca

Armeria / THRIFT

SHAPE ball
ROLE tiny treasure
late spring and early summer // front of the border //
6–12 in. × 6–12 in. // zones 4–8, perennial

Armeria maritima, sea thrift, has short, grassy foliage held in a tight clump. The rounded button-like flowers shoot up from the base in late spring and early summer. The usual bloom color is pink, but there are also pinky red or white versions. Sea thrifts grow naturally on cliffs near the sea, so give them a sunny, dry spot that is not smothered by surrounding plants. Increase drainage by planting between rocks and adding a gravel mulch. They are little plants, so place them at the front of a bed, a raised rockery, or container. You could also try them in a rock wall with creeping thyme and purple rock cress.

Asclepias / MILKWEED

SHAPE ball or dome
ROLE mid-border delight or background
late spring to autumn // mid-front to back //
12–48 in. × 12–24 in. // zones 3–9, perennial

Asclepias, milkweed, has shooting-star-shaped individual flowers arranged in flat to dome-topped inflorescences that are the darling of pollinators. The plants are host to the larval stage of the monarch butterfly, so they are must-have plants in North American gardens. They typically grow from tap roots and make a milky sap that prevents them from being browsed. Their seed heads are decorative, with silken strands on the seeds that help them blow away and spread in your garden. *Asclepias tuberosa*, butterfly weed, has bright orange cushion-shaped clusters of flowers that are standouts in summer gardens.

Asclepias
tuberosa

Asphodeline
lutea

I grow mine in a gravel garden with California poppies, but they are also comfortable residents of the mid-front of a flower border. *Asclepias incarnata*, swamp milkweed, is a good choice for a wet spot in the garden. In the height of summer, it carries scented pink or white flowers for the mid-back of the border. Grow it with Joe-Pye weed and queen-of-the-prairie. *Asclepias syriaca*, common milkweed, flowers at a similar time, with drooping ball-shaped collections of dusty pink and white flowers that smell a little like lilac. Plants have large leaves held on tall stems and can grow in average to dry soils. Because they may spread aggressively, they are a good choice for a wild planting.

Asphodeline / KING'S SPEAR

SHAPE spike
ROLE mid-border delight
late spring and early summer // mid-front to mid-back // 36–48 in. × 12–24 in. // zones 6–9, perennial

Asphodeline, king's spear, has spikes of fragrant yellow flowers that emerge late spring into summer from tufts of narrow blue-green foliage. This tall, elegant flower makes a good vertical accent in a gravel garden or seaside bed. Grow it with other flowers that need great drainage like sea hollies, red valerian, and rose campion. The nectar-rich flowers attract a variety of insects and when pollinated form attractive spherical seed pods.

Aster ×frikartii 'Mönch'

Aster tataricus

Astrantia major

Aster / ASTER

SHAPE daisy
ROLE background, mid-border delight,
or front-border treat
high summer to autumn // front to back; containers //
12–72 in. × 12–36 in. // zones 4–8, perennial

Asters, sometimes called Michaelmas daisies, are
known for their late-season show of multiple flowers
on branching stems. They have a yellow central disc
surrounded by florets primarily in purple and blue.
Tatarian asters, *Aster tataricus*, are unassuming perennials for the back of the border until they burst into
bloom in early autumn. They have open groupings of
lilac-purple flowers that attract monarch butterflies.
You can also try the more compact cultivar 'Jindai'.
Aster ×frikartii 'Mönch' is a bushy, mounding aster for
the mid-front of a border with lovely lavender-blue,
yellow-centered flowers that starts blooming in the
height of summer. Try it with red hot pokers, tall vervain,
and border dahlias. This genus used to contain some
of the garden plants that are now in *Symphyotrichum*.

Astrantia / MASTERWORT

SHAPE dome
ROLE mid-border delight
late spring, early summer to high summer // front to
mid-front // 12–30 in. × 12–24 in. // zones 5–7, perennial

Astrantia is a great genus of underused summer-
flowering perennials that perform well in a slightly
damp spot in full sun or part shade. Their dome-
shaped flowers are surrounded by slightly bristly
papery bracts. The flowers are in shades of plum-red,
wine-dark, white, and pink. Grow masterworts with
common foxgloves, short meadow rues, hardy geraniums, and alliums. They can be grown as cut flowers.
Place them at the mid-front of a bed. I have had best
success in my hot summer climate by planting them
at the bottom of a downspout so that the soil doesn't
completely dry out. I like the cultivar 'Roma' with its
shades of pale pink.

Aubrieta deltoidea

Aurinia saxatilis

Aubrieta / PURPLE ROCK CRESS

SHAPE four-petaled
ROLE tiny treasure
early spring to early summer // front of the border //
6–12 in. × 12–24 in. // zones 4–7, perennial

Aubrieta deltoidea, purple rock cress, is a lovely
spring bloomer for the front of a sunny rock wall or
well-drained raised bed. Plant it with extra grit or sand
in the soil and in a place where you can admire its little purple, white, or pink blooms. Cut the stems back
after flowering to keep the plant compact, or allow it
to set seed and sprinkle them around to maintain this
short-lived perennial. Try it with miniature daffodils,
creeping thyme, or low-growing pinks.

Aurinia / BASKET-OF-GOLD

SHAPE clusters
ROLE mixer or front-border treat
early spring to early summer // front of the border //
6–12 in. × 12–18 in. // zones 3–7, perennial

Aurinia saxatilis, basket-of-gold, provides a welcome
splash of bright egg-yolk yellow in the spring garden.
Plants bear a plethora of tiny four-petaled flowers
on a low-growing airy plant with silvery leaves. They
require perfect drainage to do well in the garden and
dislike being smothered later in the season. Plant
them on a raised bank, rock garden, or graveled area
for best performance. Try them among spring bulbs,
wallflowers, and purple rock cress for a bright display.

Baptisia sphaerocarpa 'Screamin' Yellow' with B. australis behind it.

Baptisia / FALSE INDIGO

SHAPE spike
ROLE mid-border delight or background
late spring and early summer // mid-back to back //
36–48 in. × 36–48 in. // zones 3–9, perennial

Baptisia australis, blue false indigo, is a large, tough plant that can almost act like a medium-sized shrub in your flower bed. It has excellent form and divided leaves that maintain their good looks until fall. The flowers emerge in early summer and are held in showy spikes on upright stems. Their inflorescences resemble those of lupines, with many pea-like individual flowers clothing the stalk. The old *B. australis* flowers were almost entirely blue, but a flurry of breeding has produced garden-worthy plants in an array of colors and heights. Try the unusual brown flowers of 'Dutch Chocolate', the white flowers of 'Ivory Towers', and the yellow and rust bicolored 'Cherries Jubilee'.

I also like the sunny yellow 'Lemon Meringue' with its dusky buds. If you have a smaller garden, try 'Blueberry Sundae'. The related yellow-flowered *B. sphaerocarpa* 'Screamin' Yellow' lives up to its name.

All *Baptisia* take a couple of years to come into their full glory, but they are worth waiting for and can live a long time. They grow to be substantive plants that look great at the back of a flower border, as a specimen, or in a meadow planting. Try it in combination with narrowleaf bluestar. They have a long taproot, so they are perfect for a dry or gravel garden and will tolerate poor soils. Think where you want your false indigo to be, as they are not easy to move once established. I received my first one as a pass-along plant from a friend, but the deal was that I had to dig it myself. It was a lot of work! I love their seedpods and leaves in flower arrangements. False indigos are left alone by deer and rabbits but are good pollinator plants.

Borago officinalis

Bupleurum rotundifolium

Borago / BORAGE

SHAPE five-petaled
ROLE mid-border delight
late spring, early summer to high summer // mid-front //
18–30 in. × 12–24 in. // hardy annual

Borago officinalis, borage, is an herbal annual that has
distinctive star-shaped light blue or white flowers.
The blooms are edible and can be tossed into salads
or drinks, where their slightly cucumbery taste is
refreshing. They are also pretty when frozen into ice
cubes. The plant has bristly stems and green leaves.
Its habit may be upright, but it has a tendency to
slump in rich soils. Borage is easy to grow from seed
and looks great with pot marigolds for a spring show.
It is a fabulous nectar source for early flying insects.
Borage grows best in cool weather, so grow it in the
springtime if you're in a hot climate.

Bupleurum / HARE'S EARS

SHAPE flat top
ROLE mixer
late spring, early summer to high summer // mid-front
to mid-back // 30–36 in. × 6–12 in. // hardy annual

Bupleurum rotundifolium, hare's ears, is an annual
with chartreuse-yellow flower clusters surrounded by
bright green bracts above blue-green foliage. They
have medium-tall branching stems that act as a good
mingling plant, and they make an excellent summer
cut flower for fresh or dried arrangements. Grow them
in medium to moist soil that is well drained. They add
a fresh look to hot-color beds and enliven a cool color
scheme. They look exciting in an annual planting with
poppies and cornflowers.

Calamintha 'White Cloud'

Calendula officinalis

Calamintha / CALAMINT

SHAPE cloud
ROLE mixer
high summer to autumn // front to mid-front //
12–24 in. × 12–24 in. // zones 5–7, perennial

Calamints are soft and airy perennials for late-summer bloom. Their petite white or light blue flowers line the stems and are much sought after by bees. The plants and flowers are not eaten by herbivores, as they have minty-scented foliage. Grow multiples throughout a medium to dry bed where their delicate upright stems mix and mingle well. Calamint makes a good companion in a flower bed for hardy salvias, sedum, low-growing asters, lamb's ears, and blazing star. Some of the cultivars have slightly more showy flowers. Look for a variety called *C. nepeta* subsp. *nepeta* and the cultivars 'Blue Cloud' or 'Montrose White'. In areas with cold winters, plants should be cut back to where you see fresh growth in the spring.

Calendula / POT MARIGOLD

SHAPE daisy
ROLE container or front-border treat
early spring to autumn // front to mid-front; containers
// 12–24 in. × 12–24 in. // hardy annual

Calendula officinalis, pot marigold, has cheery single or double daisy-like flowers that can be bright orange, yellow, apricot, or cream, and may have contrasting centers. These hardy annuals are easy to grow in early spring from directly sown seed in most climates, or as a fall flower that will overwinter where conditions are mild. Pot marigolds grow well in cool weather but stop blooming when the summer gets hot. They are fun flowers that are great for the front of a border or in a container. They are not fussy plants and will grow in regular garden soil. *Calendula* was in my first garden after I was married, and I wouldn't be without it in my herb garden now, where I combine it with chives and borage. The flowers are edible, so try a few petals as a garnish on salads for a splash of color. Pot marigolds also make good cut flowers. I try a new cultivar almost every year and have never been disappointed.

Calibrachoa 'Uno Pink Star'

Camassia leichtlinii

Calibrachoa / MILLION BELLS

SHAPE trumpet
ROLE container or front-border treat
late spring to autumn // front; containers // 6–12 in. ×
12–24 in. // half-hardy annual

Calibrachoa is similar in shape to a trailing petunia but with smaller-scale flowers. There is an incredible choice of hues to suit almost any garden color scheme. Look for terracotta, orange, violet, magenta, yellow, bronze, pink, white, and various bicolors, mostly with yellow or otherwise contrasting throats. This is a tender perennial normally grown as an annual. Million bells are useful in containers, window boxes, and hanging baskets, or at the front of a bed where they flower nonstop all summer when conditions are favorable. Provide them with rich, well-drained soils. Some cultivars are self-cleaning and so do not require deadheading. Buy them as small plants in spring. You may find these plants sold as petunias.

Camassia / CAMAS

SHAPE spike
ROLE front-border treat or mid-border delight
late spring and early summer // front to mid-front //
12–36 in. × 6–12 in. // zones 4–8, hardy bulb

The beautiful spikes of blue or white star-like flowers of *Camassia*, camas, are an excellent addition to a late-spring garden. Easy to grow from a fall-planted bulb, this is one of the bulbous plants that will take moist soil. It is perfectly at home in a flower bed with columbine, tulips, and allium or in grass for a meadow-like planting with pheasant's eye daffodil. There are a few species that range in size from the slender, dark blue-purple *C. quamash* and the paler *C. cusickii,* to the taller *C. leichtlinii,* which has a number of lovely cultivars with flowers of white, blue, and pink. *Camassia* are mostly native to western North America.

Campanula
glomerata

Campanula takesimana, Korean bellflower, is a great choice for summer blooms in a part sun section of your flower border.

Campanula 'Birch Hybrid'

Campanula / BELLFLOWER

SHAPE bell
ROLE front-border treat, mid-border delight, or background

late spring, early summer to high summer // front to back // 6–48 in. × 12–36 in. // zones 3–8, perennial

Campanula is a large group of plants and a mainstay of traditional flower gardens. There are several different plant forms, from low spreaders to tall ones for the back of a bed. They have variations on bell-shaped flowers in colors of bluish purple, dark purple, pink, or white. Campanula are rarely browsed by deer.

Campanula portenschlagiana and *C. poscharskyana* are low-growing plants that can spread where conditions suit them. They require really good drainage and no smothering neighboring plants, so place them in a rocky area, gravel garden, dry-laid wall, or at the front of the border. Both have purply-blue flowers that cover the plants in late spring and early summer. *Campanula glomerata*, clustered bellflower, is a very hardy plant that bears globular heads of flowers on upright stems. Flower colors are rich purple or pure white, and they bloom in early and midsummer. Their vaguely rounded shape adds a different look to the mid-front of a bed. *Campanula medium*, Canterbury bells, is a biennial plant that is infrequently used. Its spikes of prominent early summer flowers come in purple, pink, blue, and white and can be cut for arranging.

The tallest perennial bellflower for the garden is *Campanula lactiflora*, milky bellflower, which can be placed in the mid to back of a bed. Blooming in mid and late summer, it produces branching stems with a multitude of purple, pale lavender, pink, or white flowers that pair beautifully with hollyhocks and lilies. Provide it with medium to moist soil that is well drained. Try the cultivars 'Loddon Anna' or 'Prichard's Variety'.

Canna 'Cleopatra'

Canna 'Pretoria'

Canna / CANNA

SHAPE loose trumpet
ROLE bold beauty

late spring to autumn // mid-front to back; containers // 24–72 in. × 12–36 in. // zones 7–10, tender perennial

While gardeners often grow cannas for their leaves, there are some hybrids that also have valuable flowers. They are held at the top of tall stems in luscious hot colors. Cannas vary by height, so choose an appropriate one for your situation and look for color combinations that suit you. Their large leaves vary from solid green to bronze and may have stripes of purple, yellow, orange, or other variegations. Flower colors can be scarlet, dark red, yellow, or orange, but may also be cream or pink. Plant them at the back of a border to make a bold backdrop. Shorter ones make nice focal points throughout a bed. The smallest cultivars are suitable for a large container, but make sure that it has enough soil volume. Amend the soil with plenty of compost and add lots of water and some fertilizer. Your plants may be slow to grow while the weather is cool, but they start to shine when the heat of summer kicks in. In places with warm winters, some cannas may survive in the soil outside. In colder zones, dig them to bring indoors until spring. The cultivar 'Tropicanna' is one of the most well known, with orange flowers, striped leaves, and a red midrib. I grow 'Cleopatra' in a large pot and enjoy its multi-colored yellow and red flowers and irregularly patterned purple and green leaves.

Celosia argentea
'Dracula'

Celosia argentea
'Flamingo Feather'

Celosia / CELOSIA

SHAPE spike, plume, or crest
ROLE mid-border delight or containers
late spring to autumn // front to mid-back; containers //
12–48 in. × 12–24 in. // half-hardy annual

Celosias are grown in gardens as half-hardy annuals. Choose your celosia by plant height, leaf and flower color, and bloom shape. Foliage can be green, bronze, or maroon-red. Bloom colors range from silvery pink through cerise, magenta, bright orange, and red. Celosia are often grown as a cutting flower and make an interesting addition to the middle of a border or a container planting. There are three main types of *C. argentea*, sometimes referred to as cockscombs. The weirdest-looking flowers are those of the Cristata Group, with their congested, brilliantly colored flowers that look rather like a velvety brain or sea coral. The second type is the Plumosa Group, which have plume-shaped flowers, and the third, Spicata Group, sometimes called wheat celosia, have slender upright flower spikes.

Celosia can be grown from seed sown in place outside after frost or started inside in early spring. Plants will self-sow for next year in well-drained soil. Dwarf ones are used as carpet bedding and in containers. Tall cultivars can be used as cut flowers, either fresh or dried. Pinch out the growing tips of young plants to encourage branching. I find that the single-colored spiky and plume-like blooms are the easiest to incorporate into a mixed bed. One special favorite is the upright 'Flamingo Feather', with silvery pink inflorescences. Combine celosias in the garden with zinnias and globe amaranth for summer-long color in a variety of flower shapes.

Annual
Centaurea
cyanus

Perennial *Centaurea*
montana 'Alba'

Centaurea / KNAPWEED OR CORNFLOWER

SHAPE button or daisy
ROLE mid-border delight or front-border treat
late spring, early summer to high summer // front to mid-back; containers // 12–48 in. × 12–30 in. // zones 3–8, perennial or hardy annual

The genus *Centaurea* has both perennial and annual plants that are worth including in garden borders and as cut flowers. The annual *C. cyanus*, cornflower, is charming, with some of the bluest flowers of mid-spring and early summer. Traditionally, it was used as a flower for buttonholes, hence one of its common names, bachelor's button. Plants are grown from seed sown in place. Extend the flowering season by successive sowing. They need good drainage and a sunny spot and will self-sow. The flowers are gently fragrant and are delightful in a bouquet. If you are growing for cutting purposes, choose tall cultivars with long stems and keep picking them regularly. Dwarf cultivars can be tucked at the front of a bed or in containers. Beyond blue, there are also dark maroon, pink, white, and light purple cultivars available. Some flowers are single, and others are double. I favor the cultivars 'Blue Boy' and the purple mixture 'Classic Magic'.

Perennial cornflowers vary in flower color, shape, and height. The most widely grown is *Centaurea montana*, which has delicate, star-like flowers that are usually blue but may be white or purple. *Centaurea macrocephala*, giant knapweed, is an underused large plant with a real wow factor when in bloom. It has a bright yellow thistle-like tuft that emerges out of a brown basket-like bud. Both of these perennial species can grow in unfavorable, dry conditions but can also grow in regular garden soil. In the right conditions, they can be aggressive spreaders.

Centranthus
ruber

Cephalaria
gigantea

Centranthus / RED VALERIAN

SHAPE cluster
ROLE mixer

late spring, early summer to high summer // mid-front to mid-back // 24–30 in. × 12–18 in. // zones 5–8, perennial

Centranthus ruber, red valerian, is an easy plant to grow where soils are extremely fast draining and sun-baked. It loves to seed itself into limestone walls, so if you are on a neutral soil, give it a little lime and add plenty of grit or try sowing it into a gravel garden. Its delicate clusters of reddish pink or white flowers are held high above slender blue-green foliage in summer. Where it has the right conditions, red valerian may seed in enthusiastically. Grow it with triplet lily, Jerusalem sage, and lavender.

Cephalaria / CEPHALARIA

SHAPE mixer
ROLE button

late spring, early summer to high summer // mid-back to back // 48–60 in. × 24–36 in. // zones 3–7, perennial

Cephalaria gigantea, giant scabious, has summer-blooming, palest yellow pincushion flowers atop very tall wiry stems above dark green, divided basal leaves. It attracts many butterflies and bees and looks appropriate at the back of a cottage garden, in a large-scale gravel garden, or anywhere you would like a bobbing, see-through plant. Plant giant scabious in well-drained soils and in a sheltered location if you garden in a windy area. It makes a sweet cut flower. Remove the stems to the ground after flowering or allow it to set seed. It looks great with tall sea hollies and mulleins.

Cerastium
tomentosum

Ceratotheca
triloba

Cerastium / SNOW-IN-SUMMER

SHAPE five-petaled
ROLE front border treat

late spring and early summer // front of the border //
6–12 in. × 12–36 in. // zones 3–7, perennial

Cerastium tomentosum, snow-in-summer, is a
fabulous easy-care plant for a rocky area in full sun.
It needs perfect drainage, so add extra grit to the
planting hole. Light silvery gray foliage is topped in
late spring and early summer by small, flat-faced,
five-petaled white flowers. Plants have a carpeting
or cascading habit, depending on where they are
planted. Where it is happy, it can spread to form
large mats. In some climates it can be short-lived,
whereas in others it is considered invasive. Grow it
with mat-forming pinks, rock garden iris, and creeping
phlox for a low-maintenance combination. I remember this flower hanging down the sides of a raised
bed where, as a child, I could easily reach it and pick
the little flowers to add to mud pies. These plants are
left alone by deer.

Ceratotheca / SOUTH AFRICAN FOXGLOVE

SHAPE spike
ROLE mid-border delight

high summer to autumn // mid-back // 36–48 in. ×
12–24 in. // zones 9–10, tender perennial

Ceratotheca triloba, South African foxglove, is a tall
tender perennial that is usually grown as a summer-
flowering annual. Its slightly arching spike of tubular,
subtly veined, white or lavender fuzzy flowers resembles its namesake foxglove. The soft gray-green foliage has an unusual peanut-butter scent once rubbed,
which repels herbivores. Start this plant from seed
sown inside or sown directly outside in very mild climates. Grow this plant in any reasonable well-drained
garden soil. Combine it with border phlox, flowering
tobacco, and salvias.

Cerinthe major

Chelone lyonii

Cerinthe / HONEYWORT

SHAPE bell
ROLE front-border treat or container
early spring to early summer // front to mid-front;
containers // 12–24 in. × 12–24 in. // hardy annual

Honeyworts, *Cerinthe major*, are cool-season annuals with dangling tubular flowers in a fascinating dusty-purple that shades to blue. They smell like honey and are a favorite of bees. They are easy to grow from seed started indoors and then planted out in spring. Leaves are a pretty blue-green. They look fabulous in a container with other annuals like pot marigold and sweet alyssum. They also make an unusual cut flower. They bloom well until the summer gets hot, and then they need replacing with a heat-tolerant alternative. They perform best in fertile and well-drained soils that are regularly watered.

Chelone / TURTLEHEAD

SHAPE spike
ROLE mid-border delight
high summer to autumn // mid-front to mid-back //
24–36 in. × 12–30 in. // zones 3–8, perennial

Turtleheads are lovely perennial plants for moist soil. These upright plants have spikes of white, lilac pink, or bright pink flowers. Their summer blooms have an interesting hooded shape that resembles the head of a turtle. Any of the turtleheads are good for rain gardens or any humus-rich, medium to wet, well-drained soil. They can be grown in a flower bed as long as they are not allowed to dry out. Top-dress them with well-composted leaf mulch. *Chelone lyonii*, pink turtlehead, has stiff stems that hold up pinkish-purple flowers. The cultivar 'Hot Lips' is widely available. For small spots, try the short, dark-leaved cultivar

Chelone glabra

Chionodoxa 'Violet Beauty'

'Tiny Tortuga'. *Chelone obliqua*, red turtlehead, has slightly darker flowers than its cousin and blooms in the height of summer. *Chelone glabra*, white turtlehead, has white or palest pink blooms in late summer into fall and is a slightly taller plant. All turtleheads are deer resistant and are favorites of butterflies and hummingbirds.

Chionodoxa / GLORY-OF-THE-SNOW

SHAPE star-like
ROLE tiny treasure
early to mid-spring // front; containers // 4–10 in. × 2–4 in. // zones 3–8, hardy bulb

Chionodoxa, glory-of-the-snow, is a short-statured spring-flowering bulb with star-like flowers in light blue, white, or lavender purple with a white eye. There are several species that look very similar, so buy them according to the color that you like. Whichever glory-of-the-snow you choose, they make good companions to taller bulbs. One of my favorites is 'Violet Beauty', which I grow with hyacinths such as 'Splendid Cornelia' and short daffodils like 'Topolino'. *Chionodoxa* can also be grown in loose grass with other bulbs like squill and grape hyacinths.

Chrysanthemum 'Hillside Sheffield Pink'

Chrysanthemum 'Grandchild'

Chrysanthemum /
CHRYSANTHEMUM

SHAPE daisy
ROLE bold beauty or mid-border delight
late summer into autumn // front to mid-back;
containers // 12–36 in. × 12–36 in. // zones 5–9,
perennial or tender perennial

Chrysanthemums are late-season flowers that are among the last to bloom in the garden. Hardy chrysanthemums are easy plants to look after that require little care and don't call attention to themselves until they are bloom. The predominant colors are yellow, orange, rust, white, lavender, and pink, with the classic daisy-like yellow eye or with double and semi-double petals. The singles make great late-season pollinator plants. Chrysanthemums should be pinched out a few times before midsummer to keep them compact. They also appreciate a shovelful of compost each

spring or fall to keep the soil moist and well drained. I love the pink and white of the old-fashioned 'Clara Curtis'. There are some less-hardy chrysanthemums, usually called mums, that can be bought in the fall to add to beds and containers for instant floral appeal. These may survive a mild winter, but in general they are short-lived.

Cleome / SPIDER FLOWER

SHAPE loose dome
ROLE mid-border delight
high summer to autumn // mid-front to back //
24–60 in. × 12–24 in. // half-hardy annual

Cleome hassleriana, spider flower, is an easy-care, summer-into-fall-blooming half-hardy annual. The common name comes from the floral parts that stick out beyond the pink, white, violet, or bicolor petals

Cleome hassleriana

Colchicum 'Lilac Wonder'

and give the flower a spidery look. Grow these plants from seed sprinkled directly into the bed where they will germinate once the soil warms up. Tall cultivars such as the Queen Series grow quickly, making them perfect for the mid-back of the bed. Shorter cultivars like the Sparkler Series look good mid-front. Spider flowers are left alone by deer and rabbits due to their slightly skunky foliage smell and their spined stems. Use gloves when you handle adult plants. Let some of them set seed, collect and save it for next year, or shake them in place as they ripen. They are heat and drought tolerant once established.

Colchicum / COLCHICUM

SHAPE cup
ROLE tiny treasure or mid-border delight
late summer into autumn front of the border //
6–12 in. × 6–12 in. // zones 4–8, hardy bulb

Colchicum, sometimes called autumn crocus or meadow saffron, is a bulbous fall-blooming plant. Unlike the crocus it resembles, it is poisonous and unbothered by herbivores. Their chalice-shaped flowers come in a range of purples, pinks, and whites. I am partial to *C. speciosum* 'Album' and *C. cilicicum*. Hybrid cultivar 'Waterlily' has an open flower composed of many strap-like petals. Site colchicum in plantings that will hide their spring-emerging bright green leaves that die down by summer. Plant them in rich, well-drained, medium-moisture soils and do not irrigate them in summer, otherwise they may rot.

Conoclinium
coelestinum

Consolida ajacis

Conoclinium / BLUE MISTFLOWER

SHAPE loose dome
ROLE mixer
high summer to autumn // mid-front to mid-back //
12–30 in. × 12–24 in. // zones 6–10, perennial

Conoclinium coelestinum, blue mistflower, is a
self-perpetuating short-lived perennial that flowers
with puffs of periwinkle blue resembling annual flossflower in the late summer and early-autumn garden.
These plants provide a good contrast in shape and
color to daisy-shape flowers like sneezeweed and
rudbeckia. They will seed around your garden where
conditions are right and spread by underground
roots. The flowers are popular with pollinators. You
may still see them for sale by their former name of
Eupatorium. They will grow in a range of soils from
medium-wet to medium-dry and are especially suitable in a wild garden.

Consolida / LARKSPUR

SHAPE spike
ROLE mixer
late spring and early summer // mid-front to mid-back
// 24–48 in. × 12–24 in. // hardy annual

Consolida, larkspur, is a fabulous hardy annual for the
late-spring and early-summer mixed border. Its dainty
blooms, held on slender stems, rise up between later
emerging plants. The most popular flower color is a
true royal blue, but there are white and pink cultivars
too. The flower has a characteristic spur at the bottom, where the nectar is stored. The earliest blooms
are produced by seeds scattered outside in fall where
winters are mild, or in early spring in other areas.
Larkspurs need well-drained soil and grow well in
gravel gardens or raised beds. Grow them with other
cool-season annuals such as poppies, flax, and cornflowers. Pull old plants out as they fade and replace
them with warm-season annuals. Larkspurs make
excellent cut flowers, especially the tall cultivars. Look
for the old-fashioned *C. ajacis* 'Giant Imperial Mix' for
semi-double flowers in a variety of colors.

A group of double and semi-double pastel-colored *Consolida ajacis*.

Coreopsis
verticillata
'Zagreb'

Coreopsis tinctoria
in a mixed bed.

Coreopsis / TICKSEED

SHAPE daisy
ROLE mid-border delight or background
late spring to autumn // front to back; containers //
12–96 in. × 12–30 in. // zones 4–9, perennial or
hardy annual

Tickseeds produce masses of predominantly yellow daisy-like flowers that smother the plants from summer to fall. There are annual and short-lived perennial tickseeds that vary in leaf size and quality. They are all easy-care plants that are super for pollinators. In cold areas, choose the reliably hardy perennials and grow others from seed. *Coreopsis* combines well with many other flowers. Its small-scale blooms act as an integrator between neighboring plants. Deadhead old flowers to encourage rebloom and leave the last flowers on to make seeds for the birds. They are a good cut flower, and they are deer resistant.

Coreopsis tinctoria, plains coreopsis, is an annual flower with delicate foliage and is sometimes called calliopsis. It most commonly has yellow petals with mahogany bases that form a ring surrounding the dark red center, but there are several other color variations. Sow seeds in place and let your last flowers self-sow. It is a good choice for a meadow planting or weaving between perennials in a hot-colored flower bed.

Coreopsis verticillata, threadleaf coreopsis, is a perennial commonly grown in gardens for its showy mass of delicate divided foliage covered with small flowers. The most commonly seen cultivars are 'Zagreb', with bright yellow flowers, and 'Moonbeam', which blooms in soft yellow. The short cultivars can be grown in containers. *Coreopsis grandiflora*, large flower tickseed, is a short-lived perennial. Some of the most widely grown are the short semi-doubles 'Early Sunrise' and 'Sunray'. They thrive in hot and sunny places and would be a good choice for a rock

Coreopsis 'Sun Splash'

garden or the edge of a dry bed. *Coreopsis rosea*, pink tickseed, brings a different color to the genus and has been used to produce some fun cultivars for the front of a bed that are best treated as an annual in most climates. *Coreopsis lanceolata* is a short, water-wise plant that can grow in places with low-fertility, well-drained soil. Bright yellow flowers bloom in late spring and early summer on long stems, and it is easy to grow from seed. *Coreopsis tripteris*, tall coreopsis, brings the flowering year to a close with its waving stems that hold golden-yellow blooms up high. Pair it with swamp or willow-leaved sunflower for a late yellow show.

Cosmos bipinnatus

Cosmos sulphureus

Cosmos / COSMOS

SHAPE daisy

ROLE mid-border delight or mixer

late spring to autumn // mid-front to back; containers // 12–60 in. × 12–24 in. // half-hardy annual or tender perennial

Cosmos are half-hardy annuals that have summer-blooming daisy-like flowers with flat, almost translucent outer ray florets and a yellow center. There are single or double blooms in white, pink, orange, yellow, crimson, blush, and bicolors. The flowers float on long stems over slender foliage. In the garden, cosmos are great intermingling plants as they need little horizontal space and can be fitted between clump formers. Cosmos are easy to grow from seed sown inside or directly outside in the flower bed. To extend the flowering season, make a second sowing a few weeks after the first and deadhead the flowers regularly. They are a great cut flower for adding height and soft, wispy texture to arrangements. Grow them in a sunny spot in average

well-drained garden soil. Annual *Cosmos bipinnatus* is the most commonly grown and has large floaty flowers. The tall cultivars are great for the mid-back of the flower bed, where they can be supported on a fence or grown up and through other plants. Some of my favorites are the Sensation Series, with large flowers, the Seashells mix, which has rolled petals, and the shorter Sonata Series. I like to grow cosmos with dahlias and amaranth for a good cutting trio.

Cosmos atrosanguineus, chocolate cosmos, has velvety, deep red-brown bowl-shaped flowers. They are notable for their scent, which resembles chocolate on a warm day, making it a favorite for sensory gardens. It is a medium to short tender perennial that is grown as an annual in zone 6 and colder. Annual *C. sulphureus*, sulfur cosmos, has double and single flowers in sunny yellows and bright oranges. One of the most popular cultivars is 'Bright Lights', a mix that contains both colors. Combine it with brightly colored zinnias for a summer treat for you and passing pollinators.

Crambe maritima

Crambe cordifolia in bloom in a gravel garden.

Crambe / SEA KALE

SHAPE cloud
ROLE mixer
late spring, early summer to high summer // mid-front to back // 24–72 in. × 24–48 in. // zones 5–8, perennial

These bold-leaved perennial plants are good choices for a big, well-drained bed. Large, cabbage-like leaves emerge first, followed by sprays of honey-scented four-petaled flowers. *Crambe cordifolia*, heartleaf sea kale, produces sizable clouds of small blossoms and has an undeniable presence when in bloom. Its imposing green leaves take up a lot of space, so when planting, leave it room to grow. Grow it with lupines, Jerusalem sage, and mulleins. *Crambe maritima*, sea kale, has powdery blue foliage with wavy margins that looks good even before the plant produces its branching clusters of white flowers. Its leaves are eaten as a vegetable in Europe. Sea kales are suitable for growing in seaside areas where they thrive in gravelly or sandy soil, but they will grow well in average garden soil too. Try them with red hot poker and Russian sage.

Crocosmia ×crocosmiiflora 'Honey Angels'

Crocosmia 'Limpopo'

Crocosmia / CROCOSMIA

SHAPE trumpet
ROLE mid-border delight
high summer to autumn // mid-front to mid-back //
24–48 in. × 12–24 in. // zones 6–9, perennial

If you are looking for a splash of bright color in summer, try crocosmias. Their spray-like inflorescences of flared tubular trumpets are borne on wonderful arching stems above clumps of blade-like, pointed green foliage. You can find cultivars in many shades of red, orange, and yellow. They grow from a corm that needs moderately rich, moist, well-drained soil but is drought tolerant once established. These plants are salt tolerant and resistant to deer and rabbits. In some areas of the world, they are considered invasive, so check before you plant. The hardiest and most popular cultivar is the scarlet red 'Lucifer'. *Crocosmia masoniorum*, great montbretia, blooms in mid and late summer with deep orange flowers on a taller plant. Try crocosmias with dahlias and cannas for a very bold combination or with lilies of the Nile, daylilies, and red hot pokers for a colorful summer picture.

Crocus tommasinianus
'Ruby Giant'

Crocus chrysanthus
'Snow Bunting'

Crocus / CROCUS

SHAPE cup
ROLE tiny treasure
early to mid-spring // front; containers // 3–6 in. ×
1–3 in. // zones 3–8, hardy bulb

Crocus are some of the earliest spring flowers to
bloom. They have tiny cup-shaped blooms, so when
you plant crocus corms in the fall, cluster them for
impact. Flowers are mostly lilac, yellow, purple, and
white, some with bronze shadings. You can raise them
up in containers or window boxes to better admire
their intricate patterns, color variations, and scent.
They are wonderful in beds or in thin grass, but they
are a favorite target of squirrels and other animals
who will dig them up and eat them. I add a handful of
sharp grit to my planting holes to improve drainage
and deter burrowing creatures. Planting in containers
can protect them. I like to grow the early *Crocus
tommasinianus* with its slender lilac pink chalices that
can seed into lawns. This is followed by the delightful white 'Miss Vain' and the stripy purple and white
'Pickwick'. Pair them with other early-spring bulbs like
snowdrops and rock garden iris.

Cynara cardunculus flower

A stunning red dahlia

Cynara / CARDOON

SHAPE thistle
ROLE bold beauty
high summer to autumn // back of the border // 36–72 in. × 24–36 in. // zones 7–10, perennial

Cynara cardunculus, cardoon, is a slightly tender perennial with outstanding divided silver leaves and large, blue-violet, thistle-like flowers that soar up on a thick stalk. It is loved by pollinators, especially bees. Later on, cool fluffy seed heads develop. You can save seed to sow or leave it for the birds. Grow this plant for its outsized architectural leaves, which make a strong statement in a flower bed. Give each plant some space, and shelter them from strong winds. Mulch the crown for winter in areas where it is borderline hardy. Closely related to the edible artichoke.

Dahlia / DAHLIA

SHAPE ball or daisy
ROLE bold beauty, mid-border delight, or front-border treat
high summer to autumn // front to back; containers // 12–84 in. × 12–30 in. // zones 8–11, tender perennial

Dahlias are tender perennials that provide a profusion of late-season color in the garden. There is an incredible diversity of plant height, flower shape and size, and foliage color, so choose the right dahlia for your situation. There are tall background plants, mid-height ones for the center of a bed, and other short and bushy ones perfect for the front of a border or a container. Flower shapes can be round ball-like pompons, frilly anemone types, spiky-looking cactus, single daisy shapes, waterlily-like blooms, and more in an incredible range of sizes. Dahlia colors include

Cactus
dahlia

Anemone-shaped dahlia
'Totally Tangerine'

almost every hue except true blue, with single colors, bicolors, and gorgeous shaded flowers. Leaf colors range from bright green to mahogany red. If you are gardening for pollinators, choose single flowers where the pollen is visible. Dahlias are a must-have plant if you love cut flowers, especially double ones, which last well in a vase. Grow dahlias from a spring-planted tuber. Tall ones require staking, which is best done at planting time so you do not spear the tuber later. To make plants bushy, nip out the growing tips when they are about six inches tall. Dahlias grow fast, so they need regular watering and are heavy feeders. Improve the soil with plenty of organic matter, and fertilize them about once a month in the growing season. Deadhead or pick flowers to promote further blooming. Grow dahlias with canna and tender salvias for a tropical look. Combine them with zinnias and cosmos for a great cut flower patch.

Pompon-shaped dahlia
'Moor Place'

Delphinium cultivar

Dianthus gratianopolitanus 'Firewitch'

Delphinium / DELPHINIUM

SHAPE spike
ROLE bold beauty
late spring, early summer to high summer // mid-back to back // 48–84 in. × 12–30 in. // zones 3–7, perennial

Delphiniums are sigh-worthy garden occupants with tall flower spikes that tower above surrounding plants. They thrive with rich soil, adequate moisture, and cool summers. Shelter from strong winds or stake them. Cobalt blue delphiniums are the most desired, but you can also find white, pink, lavender, or light blue cultivars. Breeding efforts have produced shorter plants and others that are somewhat tolerant of hot summers. Try the New Millennium Series or the Pacific Coast hybrids. American native species, like the delicate *D. tricorne*, are not as grand but still delightful. A big enemy of delphiniums grown in moist situations are slugs and snails that nibble emerging shoots. They are ignored by deer.

Dianthus / PINK

SHAPE five-petaled
ROLE tiny treasure or mid-border delight
late spring, early summer to high summer // front to mid-front // 6–24 in. × 6–24 in. // zones 4–9, perennial, biennial, or annual

Pinks are fabulous garden plants that span the range of annuals, biennials, and perennials. Foliage is usually slender and can be silvery, blue-green, or green. Pinks are often spicily scented. The flowers tend to be true to their name in shades of pink, with additional cultivars that are combinations of magenta, fuchsia, white, or peach. The common name may not necessarily refer to the flower color, but to the frayed edges of the petal that resemble fabric cut with pinking shears.

Dianthus barbatus, sweet William, is one of my favorite cottage-garden classics, with a clustered head in maroon, white, pink, or purple that may have patterns in concentric rings on each bloom. Sweet

Dianthus barbatus
'Holborn Glory'

William is grown as a biennial that overwinters before flowering the following spring. It flowers in late spring with a dome-shaped head atop fine green foliage. This plant will grow well in regular garden soil. It looks great when underplanted with little spring bulbs like spring starflower and grape hyacinths. It makes a good cut flower, especially if picked before they are fully open. There are dwarf cultivars that look good in containers and can be used as bed edging, especially in rocky or gravelly soils.

Dianthus gratianopolitanus has a name that is longer than it is tall! Also known as Cheddar pink, this carpeting plant will spread out from the crown with narrow gray foliage. In late spring, it is covered with flat-topped fringed flowers that smell spicy like cloves. I grow several cultivars, but my favorite is 'Firewitch' with its hot pink flowers. This plant needs perfect drainage to survive and so is a great choice at the edge of a gravel path. *Dianthus plumarius*, cottage pink, is a strongly fragrant, drought-tolerant,

low-growing plant that will rebloom if cut back. There is a pretty one with laciniated petals called 'Rainbow Loveliness' that has an enchanting fragrance. I don't think there is a *Dianthus* that isn't worth growing if you have suitable conditions. Many types can be grown from seed started inside in spring or from cuttings. The plants need light and air, so do not allow other plants to flop over their foliage. Tucking their roots between rocks increases drainage, and mulching them with gravel helps keep their leaves dry.

Digitalis purpurea

Digitalis
ferruginea

Digitalis
grandiflora

Digitalis / FOXGLOVE

SHAPE spike
ROLE bold beauty or mid-border delight
late spring, early summer to high summer // mid-front
to mid-back // 24–60 in. × 12–24 in. // zones 4–8,
perennial or biennial

Foxgloves are some of the most iconic garden flowers
for a mixed flower bed or cottage-garden look. Their
vertical spikes lined with tube-like flowers that rise
above basal foliage add a touch of drama. Flowers
open from the bottom up, giving a long season of
interest. There are perennial foxgloves and biennial
ones, so read the label before you buy. The most
commonly seen biennial species is the old-fashioned
favorite *Digitalis purpurea*, common foxglove. It has
flowers in purple or white and usually has spots within
the tubes. This plant blooms alongside tall alliums
in late spring, filling the gap between spring bulbs

and summer perennials. *Digitalis ferruginea*, rusty
foxglove, has small, honey-brown, tubular flowers
arranged around tall, narrow spikes in early summer.
The upright seed heads remain attractive through the
winter. *Digitalis grandiflora*, yellow foxglove, is a short
perennial species with large, soft yellow flowers. *Digitalis lutea*, straw foxglove, is a perennial with stacks
of small, pale yellow flowers packed along its slender
stems. *Digitalis parviflora* is also small flowered and
has warm chocolaty flowers that make an unusual
color story in the garden. All foxgloves are loved by
bees and produce prolific seed. They may bloom for
a couple of years if cut back to the base after flowering.
Otherwise let foxgloves set seed and either collect
it to sow in trays or sprinkle fresh ripe seed around
the bed where you would like blooms next year. They
are not browsed by deer or rabbits because they are
poisonous.

Echinacea purpurea

Echinacea purpurea
'Green Twister'

Echinacea paradoxa

Echinacea / CONEFLOWER

SHAPE daisy
ROLE mid-border delight
late spring to autumn // mid-front to mid-back //
18–36 in. × 12–24 in. // zones 3–8, perennial

Coneflowers are great plants for the mid-section of a mixed border. Their daisy-shaped flowers have prominent central cones that are followed by architectural seed heads, which birds will perch on and peck at in winter. *Echinacea purpurea*, purple coneflower, is a popular summer garden plant with dusty pinkish-purple outer petals and a vibrant, spiky, orange cone. There are many single and double cultivars that vary in color from pale pink, cream, orange, rust, to sunset yellow. I grow *E. paradoxa* with its dark cone and yellow petals, which is the earliest to bloom in my garden. I love the wispy, long, pale pink petals of *E. pallida* on a tall and slender plant that blooms in early to midsummer. All plants in the genus have good value for wildlife and look at home in a regular flower border or in a butterfly garden. Grow them with blazing star, cosmos and tall verbena. Some coneflowers can be short-lived, so let them seed in, or renew your plantings every few years.

Echinops ritro 'Veitch's Blue'

Eremurus

Echinops / GLOBE THISTLE

SHAPE ball
ROLE mid-border delight
high summer to autumn // mid-front to mid-back //
24–36 in. × 12–24 in. // zones 4–7, perennial

Echinops ritro, globe thistle, is a clump-forming
perennial that thrives in dry to medium, well-drained,
low-fertility soil. Blue-purple or white ball-shaped
flowers add an unusual look to the sunny border.
Its silvery stems and divided spined leaves look
good as long as they don't get wet. Plant with other
drought-tolerant plants like sea hollies, Russian sage,
and baby's breath. Globe thistles have a tap root that
makes them hard to move. They are covered with
bees when in bloom and make an unusual cut flower.
My favorite cultivar is 'Veitch's Blue'.

Eremurus / FOXTAIL LILY

SHAPE spike
ROLE bold beauty
late spring and early summer // mid-back to back //
36–90 in. × 12–36 in. // zones 5–8, perennial

Foxtail lilies make a dramatic punctuation mark with
their feathery bottlebrush blooms. They are one of
the tallest vertical flowers for late spring and early
summer. Some, once established, can top out at eight
feet. They need very well-drained, rich, dry soil and
protection from wind. The fragile tuberous roots need
careful handling and planting. They are large and spidery and look a little strange when you receive them
in the mail. Give each plant sufficient space to grow
and be careful not to damage the roots. *Eremurus
robustus*, giant desert candle, is the most commonly
seen species and is available in white or pale pink.
Hybrid cultivars come in a range of colors, including

Eremurus
'White Beauty'

Eryngium
×*zabelii*

orange, pink, peach, and yellow. The tall foxtail lilies are a great addition to the back of the border, where their starry flowers twinkle down on their lower neighbors. Plants die back after flowering, so place them at the rear of a bed where you can cover the area with seed-sown annuals for later bloom.

Eryngium / SEA HOLLY

SHAPE dome or ball
ROLE mid-border delight
late spring to autumn // mid-front to mid-back // 12–48 in. × 12–36 in. // zones 4–8, perennial or hardy annual

These are plants that need good drainage and full sun. Their showy, spiky bracts and domed flower heads are a refreshing change of form that contrasts well with daisy-shaped flowers and amorphous

inflorescences. Take care when placing them, as they may be spiny and need to be away from a path. It is a prickly plant with a long tap root that makes it hard to move successfully. Most of them are fairly short-lived perennials that may renew themselves from seed. *Eryngium giganteum* is known as Miss Willmott's ghost after an English gardener who would sprinkle the seeds around when she visited friends. The silvery white bracts help this plant stand out in the garden. *Eryngium planum*, flat sea holly, has smaller-scale flowers with a bluish hue. I like the cultivars 'Blue Hobbit' and 'Blue Glitter'. *Eryngium yuccifolium*, rattlesnake master, bears its rounded flower heads high up on tall stems. It is native to the southeastern part of North America and is good for dry and gravel gardens. The annual *E. leavenworthii* is a spectacular plant with prickly purple flowers that bloom in mid and late summer. All have pollinator-friendly flowers and tend to be deer and rabbit resistant.

*Eryngium
yuccifolium*

Eryngium giganteum

*Eryngium
leavenworthii*

Erysimum
'Bowles's Mauve'

Erysimum cheiri

Erysimum / WALLFLOWER

SHAPE four-petaled
ROLE mixer or front-border treat
early spring to early summer // front to mid-front;
containers // 8 –24 in. × 6 –24 in. // zones 5 –8,
perennial or biennial

Wallflowers are easy, colorful plants to add to a spring garden. They are a classic plant of cottage gardens, and their four-petaled flowers are sweetly fragrant. They grow in extremely well-drained locations and, even as the name suggests, in dry-laid walls. *Erysimum cheiri* is grown as a biennial and may need protection during winter in some gardens. The colors are typically golden yellow, bright orange, bronzy red, and may be purple. *Erysimum* 'Bowles's Mauve' is a bushy wallflower, perennial in some climates, that produces spikes of purplish flowers above silver-green foliage

that is evergreen in mild winters. Wallflowers look good with tulips and later daffodils.

Eschscholzia / CALIFORNIA POPPY

SHAPE bowl
ROLE mixer
late spring to autumn // front to mid-front // 12–18 in. ×
6–12 in. // zones 9–11, tender perennial or hardy annual

California poppies are short-lived perennials that are treated as annuals in most climates. Their glossy, open, bowl-shaped flowers are usually orange, but there are fabulous cultivars in red, pink, watermelon, yellow, cream, and purple. Their flowers, which may be single or double, open on any sunny day. California poppies begin to flower in late spring and continue to bloom on and off in temperate climates for months.

Eschscholzia
californica

Eschscholzia
californica group

Eutrochium

Their finely dissected leaves are silvery gray. Great drainage is necessary to their survival, and they perform well in poor, dry soils. Grow them from seed sprinkled in place. I grow the bright orange straight species in a gravel garden combined with butterfly weed for an orange overload in early summer. I also grow 'Purple Gleam' in a bed with lavender. Try one of the seed mixtures for a colorful and cheery show.

Eutrochium / JOE-PYE WEED

SHAPE dome
ROLE background
high summer to autumn // mid-back to back // 24–84 in. × 24–36 in. // zones 4–8, perennial

Joe-Pye weeds are typically tall plants with large, open domes of dusty pink, purple, or white flowers. Their dramatic whorled leaves are borne along sturdy stems. They are strong growers, so plant them where they can spread out. Joe-Pye weeds appreciate moisture, growing best in medium to wet conditions. They are plants for the back of a flower bed, a rain garden, or other wild area, where they will attract numerous butterflies and bees, and later on, birds will eat the seeds. There are shorter cultivars like 'Baby Joe' that are suited for smaller gardens or the middle of a border. *Eutrochium purpureum*, sweet-scented Joe-Pye weed, can take some shade and has fragrant pale pink flowers from midsummer to early autumn. It makes a good large-scale cut flower. *Eutrochium maculatum*, spotted Joe-Pye weed, blooms in late summer and has strong speckled stems that don't need to be staked. *Euctrochium* may be listed by its older name, *Eupatorium*.

Euphorbia
corollata

Filipendula rubra

Euphorbia / SPURGE

SHAPE cloud
ROLE mixer or mid-border delight
late spring to autumn // front to mid-back;
containers // 12–36 in. × 12–24 in. // zones 5–8,
perennial or tender perennial

Euphorbia is a massive genus with many garden-worthy plants. They have unusual flower shapes with little true flowers surrounded by larger bracts. I love to grow *E. corollata*, flowering spurge, which has sprays of tiny white flowers held loosely on medium-height stems that branch at the top. It flowers in summer and gives the same impression as baby's breath in a garden bed. Mix with Japanese roof iris, anise hyssop, and pasqueflower. For a container planting or at the front of a border, try the annual *E. hypericifolia* and its cultivar 'Diamond Frost'. All spurges produce a toxic sap, so they are not browsed. Wear gloves when handling them. Avoid ones that are invasive in your area.

Filipendula / QUEEN-OF-THE-PRAIRIE

SHAPE plume
ROLE background
high summer // mid-back to back // 48–72 in. × 36–48 in. // zones 3–8, perennial

Queen-of-the-prairie, *Filipendula rubra*, blooms with fluffy pink inflorescences in summer. This back-of-the-border perennial is best in moist to wet soils and combines well with Culver's root, turtleheads, and swamp sunflower. It will spread via rhizomes to form a colony where conditions are right, so be cautious if you are planting it in a small space. Its stiff, long stems hold deeply lobed, serrated leaves. A popular cultivar, 'Venusta', has deeper colored flowers. I love it for its pink, frothy look.

Foeniculum vulgare
'Purpureum'

Foeniculum / FENNEL

SHAPE horizontal
ROLE mixer
high summer // mid-front to back // 36–60 in. ×
24–36 in. // zones 6–9, perennial

Foeniculum vulgare, fennel, is a tall, short-lived peren-nial that produces light yellow umbelliferous flowers in summer that are loved by pollinators. Fennel smells like anise and is used in cooking, so it makes a great addition to an herb border. Airy, feathery foliage also makes it valuable in a mixed bed, where it adds height and movement to the back or middle of the planting.

The delicate blooms are fabulous as a cut flower, and they are followed by decorative seed heads that can be left standing for late-season interest or harvested as an herb themselves. Fennel can produce a lot of seed, so if you don't want seedlings, remove the seed heads before they ripen. Fennel is not eaten by browsing herbivores due to its strong smell. Grow in regular well-drained garden soil. The leaves are a host plant for swallowtail butterfly larvae. Bronze fennel, *F. vulgare* 'Purpureum', has the added interest of dark foliage. This species is related to the fennel grown as a vegetable.

Fritillaria uva-vulpis

Fritillaria imperialis 'Rubra Maxima' in front of F. persica 'Ivory Bells'.

Fritillaria meleagris

Fritillaria / FRITILLARY

SHAPE bell
ROLE tiny treasure, mid-border delight, or bold beauty
early spring to early summer // front to mid-back;
containers // 6–48 in. × 3–8 in. // zones 5–8, hardy bulb

Fritillaries are a diverse group of spring bloomers that grow from fall-planted bulbs. This genus is full of some strange but interesting flowers. Most fritillaries need really good drainage, but *Fritillaria meleagris*, checkered lily, with its characteristic tessellated pattern, can take occasional wet soil, as it is naturally found in flood plains. The smallest of those that need excellent drainage is *F. michailovskyi*, with its pendulous, bell-shaped, mahogany red petals edged with golden yellow or the slightly taller *F. uva-vulpis*, with unique dusty brown and gray undertones and little yellow accents. There are large fritillaries that are good for growing in between later emerging spring perennials. *Fritillaria persica* has a spike of dark gray-tinged purple bells that look fabulous with late-flowering dark tulips. For a lighter look, try the pale greenish cultivar 'Ivory Bells'. *Fritillaria imperialis*, crown imperial fritillary, has a dramatic whorl of bright orange or yellow bell-shaped flowers at the top of its stems and a green tuft emerging from the top. The flowers are unlike anything else that you will see in a garden.

Plant fritillaries on a bed of gravel to increase drainage, and lay the bulbs on their sides in the planting hole. Look for species or cultivars that suit your climate and bloom at the height you would like. They need perfect growing conditions to perennialize, but it is worth replanting them every few years if you love their look. Be on the watch for, and remove, the bright red lily beetle that can decimate your leaves and flowers.

Gaillardia
×grandiflora
'Kobold'

Gaillardia
pulchella
'Red Plume'

Galanthus
nivalis

Gaillardia / BLANKET FLOWER

SHAPE daisy
ROLE mixer or front-border treat
late spring to autumn // front to mid-back // 12–30 in. ×
12–24 in. // zones 3–9, perennial or half-hardy annual

Blanket flowers are a genus of warm-colored composite flowers suitable for average to dry garden soil. Their bright daisy-like flowers bloom from summer through fall and have concentric rings of dark or bright red, yellow, or orange. *Gaillardia pulchella*, annual blanket flower, is easy to grow from seed, and colors will vary unless you buy by cultivar. The straight species has rangy stems that hold the flowers up in mid-border. Cultivars include the shorter double 'Red Plume' and 'Yellow Plume'. Hybrid perennial blanket flowers, *G. ×grandiflora*, have a range of vibrant flower colors and different heights. Look for the short dark red and yellow 'Goblin' or the slightly taller Mesa Series. *Gaillardia aristata*, common blanket flower, is another showy perennial choice. All blanket flowers are good pollinator plants.

Galanthus / SNOWDROP

SHAPE bell
ROLE tiny treasure
early to mid-spring // front to mid-front // 6–12 in. ×
2–3 in. // zones 3–7, hardy bulb

Snowdrops are one of the few truly winter-blooming herbaceous plants. The tough fall-planted bulbs send up pointed noses that can push through frozen or snowy soil. A teardrop-shaped bud gradually opens to reveal a tubular center surrounded by three outer petals in single flowers or a ruffle of tightly packed petals in doubles. Provide them with good drainage so the bulbs don't rot. A situation on a raised bank enables you to see into the flowers and watch the early flying insects that love this cold-weather source of pollen and nectar. *Galanthus elwesii*, giant snowdrop, has broad leaves and is taller in stature and needs a little bit more sun than the smaller *G. nivalis*, common snowdrop. Try snowdrops in your flower garden to get a jump start on spring.

Gaura lindheimeri

Gazania

Gaura / GAURA

SHAPE cloud
ROLE mixer

high summer to autumn // mid-front to mid-back //
24–48 in. × 12–30 in. // zones 5–9, perennial

Gaura lindheimeri, white gaura, is a late-blooming
perennial with airy stems that bear delicate white
flowers with touches of pink. The tall, graceful, upright
stems tremble and sway in the breeze when in bloom.
In spite of its height, it is a see-through plant that can
be sited in the center of a border. There are shorter
cultivars and some with pink flowers. White gaura
combines well with blazing star and hummingbird
mint. This plant needs really good drainage and air
circulation, and it doesn't like to be smothered by surrounding plants. Gaura grows long taproots and are
drought tolerant once established. If they are grown
in rich soil, they may flop over. They are wonderful
pollinator plants for bees. Gaura may be listed as
Oenothera.

Gazania / TREASURE FLOWER

SHAPE daisy
ROLE container

late spring to autumn // front to mid-front; containers //
6–18 in. × 6–18 in. // zones 9–11, tender perennial

Treasure flowers have vibrantly colored daisy-like
blooms. They are tender perennials that are usually grown as annuals in a container or at the front
of a raised rockery. Cultivars vary in color, but they
often have the same feature of a central dark ring at
the base of the petals. The petals may be solid or
striped in bright orange, red, pink, yellow, and white
according to the cultivar. They continue flowering
throughout the summer as long as they get excellent
drainage. Their leaves are slightly hairy, with a silvery
look to the underside, and they are tolerant of salt
spray. Not suitable for an evening garden, as the flowers close at night.

Geranium sanguineum var. striatum

Geranium 'Rozanne'

Geranium 'Ann Folkard'

Geranium / HARDY GERANIUM

SHAPE bowl
ROLE mixer
late spring to autumn // front to mid-front // 12–30 in. × 12–6 in. // zones 4–8, perennial

Geranium is a vast genus that contains the hardy geraniums, stalwarts of the flower garden also known as cranesbills for their prominent beaked seed capsules. They form mounds of foliage that mix beautifully with other garden occupants at the front or middle of the border. Their bowl-shaped blooms are borne on delicate stems that rise above good-quality leaves. Hardy geraniums come in a range of intensities in the color palette of blue, purple, pink, and white. They bloom most profusely from late spring to midsummer, with some long-bloomers that continue to flower until the fall and others that will rebloom if cut back after their first flush. Hardy geraniums are easygoing plants that will take average, moist, well-drained garden soil. Heights vary, with some compact plants and others with long stems that sprawl over and through nearby plants. Deer and rabbits tend not to bother them, as their foliage is often aromatic.

There are many good hardy geraniums from which to choose, but look carefully at the growing conditions they need, the plant sizes, and flower colors before you make your selection.

I like to grow *Geranium* 'Johnson's Blue' or 'Orion' where I am looking for a soft blue-purple, and I use purply 'Rozanne' where I need a long-blooming selection. Try *G. psilostemon,* with its taller stature and hot purple, dark-eyed blooms, or the hybrid 'Ann Folkard'. For a low-growing groundcover that can take some shade, use *G. ×cantabrigiense* 'Biokovo' with its pale pinkish-white splayed petals. My favorite is the old-fashioned cottage-garden plant *G. sanguineum* var. *striatum,* with its veined, soft pink flowers. It can be an aggressive grower, spreading via underground rhizomes, but it is easy to pull out.

Geum 'Tequila Sunrise'

Orange-flowered *Geum* growing in a container.

Fluffy seed head of *Geum triflorum*.

Geum / AVENS

SHAPE bowl
ROLE mixer
late spring, early summer to high summer // front to mid-front // 12–36 in. × 12–24 in. // zones 4–8, perennial

Avens are lovely perennial plants for the middle or edge of a mixed bed. They have bowl-shaped, hot-colored blooms with a central yellow mass of stamens that are held on fine stems well above their basal rosettes of foliage. Their leaves look good all summer long if they are given sufficient water. The flowers bloom from late spring to midsummer. Look for the bright orange 'Totally Tangerine', the scarlet semi-double 'Mrs. J. Bradshaw' and the yellow and orange 'Tequila Sunrise'. *Geum coccineum* 'Koi' is a short plant that is perfect for a medium-moisture rock garden. *Geum triflorum*, prairie smoke, has unusual nodding flowers that become fluffy seed heads and are a good choice for dry to average soils. Look for *G. rivale*, water avens, if you have a cool, wet spot.

Gillenia / BOWMAN'S ROOT

SHAPE cloud
ROLE mixer
late spring, early summer to high summer // mid-front to mid-back // 24–30 in. × 18–30 in. // zones 5–8, perennial

Gillenia trifoliata, Bowman's root, is grown for its cloud of delicate flowers resembling little dancing butterflies that hover over the mounded perennial plant. The flowers are white with a contrasting reddish base and bloom from late spring into summer with sporadic rebloom until fall. It thrives in moist, humus-rich, well-drained soils in full sun or part shade. It is a great amorphous mingler for the middle of the border and combines well with alliums, amsonia, great masterwort, and Oriental poppies. There is a lovely cultivar with light pink flowers called 'Pink Profusion'. *Gillenia stipulata*, American ipecac, is very similar but has toothed leaves and can take more shade. Both attract butterflies and other pollinators.

Gillenia trifoliata

Gladiolus / GLADIOLUS

SHAPE spike
ROLE bold beauty or mid-border delight
late spring to autumn // mid-front to mid-back;
containers // 12–36 in. × 4–8 in. // zones 7–10,
perennial or tender perennial

The tall spikes of gladiolus are used as bold vertical accents in a mixed border or grown as a cut flower. Fashions in flowers come and go over time, and gladiolus had a time when it was seriously out of favor, but they are well worth growing for their upright spears in the summer garden. Hybrid *Gladiolus*, sword lily, has showy flowers in colors ranging from green, white, yellow, orange, and red, to pink, purple, coral, and multi-colored. The individual floppy, trumpet-shaped flowers are tightly packed and open in sequence from bottom to top up the stem for an extended bloom time in the garden. The sword-shaped leaves provide a fresh contrast to mounded or airy plants. Soils should be humus rich, consistently moist, and well drained for the best show.

Most available hybrid *Gladiolus* are not hardy, so take this into account when making your selection. Tender gladioli are grown from corms planted out after the soil has warmed up in the spring. Select the largest corms you can find, as these will produce the biggest flowers. When you are planting them in spring, put them out in intervals of two weeks to extend the period of bloom. In the fall, the corms can be dug up after the leaves die back and stored in a frost-free place over winter. In areas where they might be hardy in the ground, a thick layer of organic mulch over the corms can help their winter survival, as can keeping them relatively dry during the cold months.

Gladiolus nanus is smaller and may be easier to integrate into a flower bed or container and rarely needs staking. *Gladiolus communis* subsp. *byzantinus*, Byzantine gladiolus, is among the hardiest and one of my favorites for its rich pink or magenta blooms in late spring that slip through and between other plants. It is slender compared to the hybrid gladioli, so the little flashes of brightness are just perfect. It will multiply where it is happy. *Gladiolus murielae*, sometimes listed as *Acidanthera*, is a less-hardy late-summer and early-autumn blooming flower. Its blooms have large flat faces with forward-facing tubes that emerge from their tall stems. The blooms are primarily white with a burgundy-purple eye. They have a lovely lingering scent reminiscent of vanilla mixed with powder.

Gladiolus communis
subsp. *byzantinus*

Gladiolus
'Wine and Roses'

Gladiolus murielae

Gomphrena globosa growing in an annual flower bed.

Gypsophila paniculata

Gomphrena / GLOBE AMARANTH

SHAPE ball
ROLE mixer or container
late spring to autumn // mid-front to mid-back; containers // 12–24 in. × 6–12 in. // half-hardy annual

Gomphrena globosa, globe amaranth, is a useful annual plant that grows well in gardens or containers. Lots of tiny flowers cluster together to make rounded inflorescences that rise above lower foliage. It is a good cut flower and can be used fresh or dried. Flowers are available in bright magenta, soft pink, lilac, strawberry-red, or cream. Look for the hybrid 'Fireworks' for a dependable show in warm bright pink with prominent yellow anthers. Globe amaranths are unfazed by hot weather and inhospitable sites and make a good addition to beds or containers designed for late-season interest. They look great massed together or intermingled with other annuals like celosia and zinnias. Can be grown from seed started inside a few weeks before the last frost.

Gypsophila / BABY'S BREATH

SHAPE cloud
ROLE mixer
late spring, early summer to high summer // front to mid-back; containers // 12–42 in. × 12–36 in. // zones 3–8, perennial or half-hardy annual

There are two lovely plants in this genus for flower gardens. *Gypsophila paniculata*, perennial baby's breath, is an airy mixer and weaver for well-drained, slightly alkaline soil. Its ethereal cloud of petite white flowers is borne on a haze of wiry stems. There are also pink blooms and single or double flowers. Grow this with other drought-tolerant plants like lavender and salvias. Do not smother it with surrounding plants, as it needs good air circulation. Use baby's breath as a cut flower fresh or dried in arrangements. It is considered invasive in some places in North America. *Gypsophila elegans*, annual baby's breath, is a smaller version of its perennial cousin, with little open starry flowers that are slightly larger. The plant

Rusty red *Helenium*

Yellow *Helenium* in a garden bed with purple *Verbena bonariensis* behind.

has an open, tumbling structure that is covered with floating white or pink flowers when in bloom. It looks appropriate in an informal flower bed or in containers where it mixes well with more substantial flowers. Can be grown from seed started inside and does best in a free-draining soil.

Helenium / SNEEZEWEED

SHAPE daisy
ROLE mid-border delight
high summer to autumn // mid-front to back //
12–36 in. × 12–36 in. // zones 3–8, perennial

Heleniums are easy-to-grow perennials in a range of warm-colored daisy-shaped flowers that are popular with pollinators. You may see these plants for sale by one of its common names: sneezeweed or Helen's flower. The central domed button of the flower is surrounded by a ring of petals that slightly twist and may hang down in bold colors of orange, russet, or

yellow, with some bicolors. They bloom from summer through to fall on sturdy tall to medium-height plants. *Helenium* 'Moerheim Beauty' is an old tall cultivar that has stood the test of time. The flowers have orange petals with a tinge of yellow that surround the central brown disc. A good yellow with short petals and a greenish center is 'Butterpat'. Sneezeweeds are relatively short-lived, but they set seeds that replace the parent plant. Some of the best specimens in my garden are chance seedlings. For a short plant at the front of the border, try *Helenium amarum* 'Dakota Gold'.

Helianthus annuus

Helianthus 'Lemon Queen'

Helianthus / SUNFLOWER

SHAPE daisy

ROLE bold beauty, backdrop, or mid-border delight

late spring to autumn // mid-front to back; containers // 24–120 in. × 12–36 in. // zones 4–9, perennial or hardy annual

Sunflowers are cheerful flower garden favorites. They are composite flowers with yellow outer ray florets and a central disc. The most well-known member of this genus is *Helianthus annuus*, annual sunflower, which is simple to grow from seed. Protect the young seedlings from being eaten until the bristly stems can protect themselves. Plant them in average garden soil with plenty of moisture to fuel their rapid growth. The flowers are easy to spot from a distance, with their large open faces and often statuesque height. Their bold, coarse leaves are a good background to perennials if they are planted at the back of the border. Dwarf cultivars can be grown at the front of a bed or in a large container. The traditional bright

yellow is always a favorite, but you can also find pale yellow, cream, rusty orange, and deepest red. Some highly bred sunflowers do not produce pollen and will not make seeds. This is a useful trait for cut flowers but not helpful in a pollinator garden. Look for double cultivars like the short 'Teddy Bear', the pollenless mid-height wine-red 'Chianti', and the extremely tall 'Russian Giant' with its dinner-plate-sized flowers. If you want flowers for cutting, choose a type that is multi-branched to provide plenty of blooms. Try the closely related sunflower *H. debilis* 'Italian White', with its profuse pale yellow flowers.

The genus *Helianthus* contains a number of perennial plants for late summer into fall that are also good cut flowers. *Helianthus salicifolius*, willow-leaved sunflower, has fine foliage on long stems and many yellow flowers that bloom alongside New England asters. The straight species is a tall plant for the back of the border, but there are smaller cultivars like 'Autumn Gold' that can be tucked at the front.

A dark-colored *Helianthus annuus.*

Helianthus maximiliani, Maximillian's sunflower, is a late-blooming yellow flower that suits dry or medium-moisture conditions and is an aggressive spreader for wild areas.

Helianthus angustifolius, swamp sunflower, is suitable for a wettish soil in a rain garden. It is slightly salt tolerant and is one of the last flowers to bloom.

Helianthus 'Lemon Queen' is a tall hybrid that blooms in mid to late summer with small, pale yellow flowers. This too can spread, so give it room to grow. Perennial sunflowers are terrific pollinator plants and provide seeds for birds over winter. For a lofty back-of-the-border composition, mix them with tall tickseed, silphium, Culver's root, and Joe-Pye weed.

Heliotropium
arborescens

Hemerocallis
'Autumn Minaret'

Heliotropium / HELIOTROPE

SHAPE dome
ROLE container
late spring to autumn // front to mid-front; containers //
12–24 in. × 12–24 in. // zones 10–11, tender perennial

Heliotropium arborescens, heliotrope, is a tender
perennial that is grown in most gardens as an annual.
Its vanilla-scented flowers form a flattened dome
atop pleated green leaves. The rich purple color is
most often grown, but light purple and white are
also available. To encourage a good shape, pinch
out the growing tips early in the season. Heliotropes
are wonderful grown in containers and would make
an excellent addition to a sensory, butterfly, or moon
garden, where their fabulous fragrance can be greatly
appreciated. In mild climates where heliotrope overwinters, it can get several feet tall.

Hemerocallis / DAYLILY

SHAPE trumpet
ROLE mid-border delight
late spring to autumn // front to back // 12–72 in. ×
12–36 in. // zones 3–9, perennial

Daylilies, *Hemerocallis*, are garden stalwarts that
bloom in summer and early autumn. Their trumpet-
shaped flowers come in a host of colors from reds,
oranges, corals, yellows, and greens, to creamy white.
Some cultivars have a different-colored eye, central
blotch, or stripe down their petals. Though they are
most often single, you can find doubles too. There are
tiny daylilies for the front of the border, like 'Penny's
Worth', and dramatically tall plants for the back of
the bed, like 'Autumn Minaret'. Some daylilies, like
H. lilioasphodelus, are pleasantly fragrant. They can
take some shade, so they are fine planted among

Hemerocallis
cultivar

Hesperis matronalis

taller perennials where their elongated foliage adds a different texture. Daylilies are so called because each bloom lasts for approximately one day. Some of the new cultivars like 'Happy Returns' have a much higher bud count and a longer blooming season than older cultivars, but all daylilies bloom for at least a couple of weeks.

Hesperis / DAME'S ROCKET

SHAPE four-petaled
ROLE mixer
late spring and early summer // mid-front to mid-back // 12–36 in. × 12–24 in. // biennial

Hesperis matronalis, dame's rocket, is a biennial plant that blooms in late spring and early summer, with four-petaled purple or white flowers that produce a gentle sweet scent. This is a classic mid-height cottage-garden plant that pairs well with foxgloves, pinks, and alliums and requires very little care in regular garden soil. Once you have a self-sowing patch, dame's rockets will come back every year. They are deer resistant, but bees love them. Cut flowers for arranging. Native to Europe and parts of Asia, it is considered invasive in some parts of North America.

Hibiscus
'Summer
Storm'

Hibiscus
coccineus

Hibiscus / HIBISCUS

SHAPE trumpet
ROLE bold beauty or background
high summer to autumn // mid-back to back;
containers // 36–84 in. × 24–48 in. // zones 5–9,
perennial or tender perennial

The genus *Hibiscus* contains both herbaceous and woody flowering plants, several of which are worth growing, especially if you have a moist area in your garden. Their characteristic large, open flowers with a prominent central stigma are one of the most distinctive in the garden. They bloom from summer to early fall. If the plant develops a woody base, do not cut that back in spring. *Hibiscus moscheutos*, crimson-eyed rose mallow, can form colonies where soil is damp. Its white, red, magenta, or pink trumpet-shaped flowers have a distinct contrasting blotch at the center and are sought by pollinators when they bloom from midsummer to early fall. *Hibiscus coccineus*, scarlet rose mallow, has crimson red flowers and blooms extensively if planted in sunny moist or wet sites. It is a good background plant that won't take center stage until it blooms in summer. Great hummingbird plant. Try growing hibiscus with swamp milkweed, Joe-Pye weed, and cardinal flower. They are fantastic plants for rain gardens or wet wildlife areas, but protect them from deer. For a different look and for smaller gardens, try the hybrid cultivar 'Kopper King', which has dark, coppery leaves and pinkish flowers.

Hyacinthus / HYACINTH

SHAPE spike
ROLE mid-border delight
early to mid-spring // front to mid-front; containers //
6–12 in. × 3–6 in. // zones 4–8, hardy bulb

Hyacinths, *Hyacinthus orientalis*, are excellent spring bulbs to include in a mixed bed for their delicious wafting fragrance. Their bell-shaped individual flowers are densely arranged up their stems in a column.

Hyacinthus orientalis
'Blue Jacket'

A drift of
Hylotelephium.

Colors range from the traditional light blue, powder pink, and white, through to bright pink, purple, coral, lilac, and more. Try fancy double flowers for a full look. Newly planted bulbs tend to have heavy heads that may flop over in inclement weather. After a few years, the flowers tend to become slightly less full, which makes for a better garden plant. Like most spring bulbs, hyacinths require adequate drainage and should be planted in fall. After flowering, remove the spent heads to encourage better bloom next year. My favorite cultivars include the complex pale purple 'Splendid Cornelia', the traditional 'Delft Blue', and the beetroot-colored 'Woodstock'. My spring garden would not smell the same without them. Handle the bulbs with gloves in case they irritate your skin.

Hylotelephium / SEDUM

SHAPE horizontal
ROLE mid-border delight or front-border treat
high summer to autumn // front to mid-back //
12–30 in. × 12–24 in. // zones 4–8, hardy perennial

Hylotelephium is an oddly named group of plants that used to be in the genus *Sedum*. They are tough succulent plants that will thrive in poor soil, but they must have great drainage and full sun. They can be cut back early in the spring to keep them shorter. Their flat-topped flower heads appear in late summer in shades of dusky pink, maroon, white, and greenish. They change color as they age, sometimes becoming darker, adding interest to the fall garden. 'Autumn Joy' is a tall tried-and-true cultivar that looks good in the mid-front of the border. The dark-leaved 'Matrona' is another reliable perennial, and there are even darker ones with red flowers, like 'Red Cauli', that suit a dramatic color scheme. They are good for late-season pollinators, and their stems and seed heads may be left up over winter.

Iberis sempervirens

Ipheion uniflorum

Iberis / CANDYTUFT

SHAPE clustered dome
ROLE tiny treasure
early spring to early summer // front to mid-front;
containers // 6–12 in. × 6–18 in. // zones 3–8, perennial
or hardy annual

Candytuft flowers are four-petaled and held in domes
on low-growing plants. *Iberis sempervirens*, evergreen
candytuft, is a short, spreading perennial with white
flowers that bloom in mid and late spring and may age
to light pink. Use it in rock gardens or as an edging in
beds with great drainage. It is deer and rabbit resistant.
Iberis umbellata, annual candytuft, blooms in shades of
white, purple, and pink. It does well in soils with good
drainage and is a good choice along walkways and to
fill in on sunny slopes. It is fragrant and attracts butterflies and bees, and it blooms for more than a month in
late spring and early summer. This hardy annual is easy
to grow from seed. Cut plants back after they finish
blooming to keep them compact.

Ipheion / SPRING STARFLOWER

SHAPE star-like
ROLE tiny treasure
early spring to early summer // front; containers //
3–6 in. × 3–6 in. // zones 5–9, hardy bulb

Ipheion uniflorum, spring starflower, has cute flat-
faced, six-petaled blooms in shades of pastel blues,
pinks, and pure white. Its short stems make it a good
choice for a position at the front of the flower bed or
in light grass. Blooms are sweetly scented, but the
foliage gives off a slight oniony smell that deters deer
and rabbits. I like to plant spring starflowers among
other spring bulbs like grape hyacinth and miniature
daffodils. Where they have good drainage, they will
return year after year. Try them in a container or bed
with candytuft and sweet alyssum.

Iris reticulata 'Cantab'

Iris sibirica
'Caesar's Brother'

Iris / IRIS

SHAPE iris

ROLE **bold beauty, mid-border delight, or tiny treasure**
early spring to high summer // front to mid-back //
6–48 in. × 3–24 in. // zones 3–9, perennial or hardy bulb

The genus *Iris* is named for the Greek goddess of the rainbow, and there are a rainbow's worth of colors that you can choose to plant: purple, yellow, white, and blue are well represented, with a scarcity of true reds. The characteristic iris shape is arranged in parts of three. The outer petals fall down and look like the tongue of a dragon or a panting dog. The inner three are usually elevated, but may be flat. They range in stature from short front-of-the-border plants to tall ones that suit the middle of the bed. There are types of iris that suit any soil or garden situation. Some bloom in earliest spring while others flower in late spring and early summer.

Iris reticulata, rock garden iris, and others like *I. danfordiae* are the earliest to bloom. They need good drainage and are happy in a raised bed or rock garden. Next to bloom is the medium-height *I. ×hollandica*, Dutch iris. This is a good cutting flower but will wither once its bloom is over, so hide it among other perennials that fill in later.

In late spring and early summer, many medium and tall species bloom at the same time. *Iris ×germanica*, bearded iris, needs dry soil in full sun. Rhizomes should be planted protruding slightly out of the soil, away from other plants, so that the sun can bake them. The large flowers have a prominent "beard" of stamens in the middle of the lower petals. Plants have been extensively bred to produce a broad range of colors and decorative features like ruffled petal edgings and cool patterns. Bearded iris may be strongly fragrant, with scents that range from powdery sweet to concord grape. *Iris sibirica*, Siberian iris, is better

Iris, continued

Iris ×*germanica* with blue and white ruffles.

Iris 'Black Gamecock', a Louisiana iris.

Iris domestica

suited for average garden soil but thrives with some extra moisture. The blooms are graceful, and the foliage maintains its upright presence throughout the season. Plants flower in shades of purple, blue, white, cream, yellow, and pink. *Iris ensata*, Japanese water iris, likes humus-rich, medium to wet soil. Its lower petals are much larger than its upright ones, giving it a distinctive droopy look. Flowers are typically purple and white, although other colors are available, some with intricate veined patterns.

Iris tectorum, Japanese roof iris, is gorgeous, unusual, but easy to grow in well-drained locations with some moisture. The fan-shaped sprays of leaves remain as an attractive feature even after it has finished blooming. I grow some in a gravel-mulched bed with camas that bloom at the same time. *Iris virginica* and *I. versicolor* are two native North American irises for moist or wet soils. They flower in early summer in shades of purple and blue and have yellow-centered lower petals. Both are appropriate for rain gardens. To close out the iris year, plant *I. domestica*, formerly *Belamcanda*, also called the blackberry lily. This starts blooming in the height of summer, with speckled yellow and orange flowers that produce decorative glossy black seeds in fall.

Knautia
macedonica

Kniphofia
'Brimstone'

Knautia / KNAUTIA

SHAPE button
ROLE mixer
late spring to autumn // front to mid-back // 18–36 in. ×
12–18 in. // zones 5–9, perennial

Knautia macedonica, Macedonian scabious, is an
easy-care, short-lived perennial that may self-sow. It
thrives in gravel gardens or well-drained soils where
the crowns stay dry in winter. It has low water needs.
Small, button-shaped flowers resemble those of
scabious and are held on floaty stems. Flowers may
be magenta, lavender, or burgundy and bloom profusely in early and midsummer and then intermittently
through fall. Cut the stems back after the first flush of
flowers to prolong the blooming season. The slender
plants weave between other flowers and add movement to a static planting. Grow them from directly
sown seed or buy plants. Try them with Stokes' aster
and sedum. They are deer and rabbit resistant.

Kniphofia / RED HOT POKER

SHAPE spike
ROLE bold beauty
late spring to autumn // mid-front to back // 12–72 in. ×
12–36 in. // zones 5–9, perennial

Red hot pokers, *Kniphofia*, are some of the best
vertical flowers for the summer garden. The flowering
spike is composed of many little tubular flowers that
surround the stem and open from the bottom to the
top. The foliage is a clump of long, narrow leaves.
Most red hot poker flowers are bicolored yellow and
orange, but there are also some lovely cream, light
green, red, and multi-colors. All of these flowers are
attractive to hummingbirds. Plant them where they
will receive a good amount of light, some heat, and
where the soil has winter drainage but does not dry
out completely during the growing season. They are
deer resistant. Before you buy, check their eventual
height, as there are some dwarf cultivars, like the

Kniphofia flowers are often bright orange in color.

Lamprocapnos spectabilis 'Alba'

Lamprocapnos spectabilis

Popsicle Series, that are suitable for mid-front of the bed. Larger ones need to be placed toward the mid-back or rear, like the tall, whitish green 'Lady Luck'. Bright orange *Kniphofia* combine well with crocosmia and daylilies. Pale cultivars combine nicely with blue or purple flowers like coneflowers or salvias.

Lamprocapnos / BLEEDING HEART

SHAPE heart
ROLE mixer
late spring and early summer // mid-front // 24–30 in. × 18–24 in. // zones 2–9, perennial

Lamprocapnos spectabilis is the old-fashioned bleeding heart plant that is so loved in gardens. The arching stems hold dangling flowers that resemble their common name. They usually have pink hearts and a white center, but the cultivar 'Alba' has pure white flowers. Grow in moist, well-drained soil. Bleeding hearts do best in afternoon shade in hot and humid climates. Plants may die down below ground in the summer. Combine bleeding hearts with spring bulbs and forget-me-nots for a lovely pastel picture. They are unbothered by deer and rabbits. You may know them by their former name, *Dicentra spectabilis*.

A mixed group of mixed color *Lathyrus odoratus.*

Lathyrus / ORNAMENTAL PEA

SHAPE bilaterally symmetrical
ROLE mixer

late spring, early summer to high summer // mid-front to back // 36–96 in. × 12–24 in. // zones 3–8, perennial or hardy annual

This genus contains some must-have plants for a flower garden and for cutting. The ones I would not be without are annual sweet peas, *Lathyrus odoratus*. They can be grown from presoaked seed sown directly outside into prepared soil in fall if winters are mild, or as soon as soil can be worked in spring in cold-winter areas. They can also be started inside in early spring in pots. Sweet peas are cool-season annuals that will grow nicely until a blast of summer heat stops flower production. They require good, moisture-retentive soil with plenty of compost and regular watering. There is a rainbow of cultivars, many of which have a heavenly scent. Most sweet peas are tall vines. Train their curling tendrils up twigs, pea sticks, or a fence to maximize flower production. You may need to tie them in with twine. Cut them daily once they begin to flower to prompt more flower production. I love the scented cultivars 'Cupani', 'April in Paris', and 'Spencer Mix'.

I also grow the perennial peavine, *Lathyrus latifolius*, which has a similar flower in pink or white but unfortunately does not win my heart in the same way, as it is not fragrant. It is herbaceous and will grow up a support or scramble through surrounding plants. It is a wonderful choice to cover soil where spring bulbs are dying down. Both of these are poisonous, so do not eat them.

An extensive planting of an assortment of different lavenders.

Lavandula angustifolia 'Munstead'

Lavandula / LAVENDER

SHAPE spike
ROLE mixer or mid-border delight
late spring, early summer to high summer // front to mid-front // 12–36 in. × 12–30 in. // zones 5–9, perennial or tender perennial

Lavenders are grown for their long-lasting fragrant silvery foliage and slender flowers. Delicate wands of scented summer blooms are held above bushy plants. Flowers are generally purple to blue, but may be pink or creamy white. They are a favorite flower of bees, and the honey those bees produce is a special treat. Lavender has woody bases to its stems, so do not cut back into these parts, as you risk killing it. Instead, trim stems after flowering and neaten up the straggly stems in spring once new growth has begun. The most commonly grown species is *Lavandula angustifolia*, English lavender. Look for the reliable dark purple cultivar 'Hidcote' and the slightly lighter colored 'Munstead'. Two larger French lavenders, *L. ×intermedia*, are 'Grosso' and 'Provencal'. For warmer climates, or for growing in a pot, look for nonhardy Spanish lavender, *L. stoechas*, which has characteristic "bunny ears" of several upright petals at the top of the flower.

Lavender plants need to grow on a dry sunny slope or in a raised bed. They require really free-draining, slightly alkaline soil. If you garden on neutral or acid soil, you may need to add some powdered limestone yearly. Plant lavender to allow free movement of air through the silvery leaves, and situate them near a path where you can brush against them when walking. Harvest the long stems to dry by hanging them upside down, and use the dried flowers for scenting rooms and clothes.

Leucanthemum ×superbum 'Becky'

Leucojum aestivum

Leucanthemum /
LEUCANTHEMUM

SHAPE daisy
ROLE mid-border delight
late spring to autumn // mid-front to mid-back //
12–36 in. × 12–36 in. // zones 4–9, perennial

This is a genus of cheerful white and yellow daisies.
The most commonly grown is *Leucanthemum ×super-bum*, Shasta daisy, which produces plentiful flowers
from midsummer into autumn that are held above
dark green, odorous leaves. The smell of the whole
plant can be off-putting, so don't place it in a fragrant
garden or too close to a patio. The smell does mean
that deer do not browse it. Plant Shasta daisies in soil
that drains well and does not stay wet in winter. The
tall cultivar 'Becky' is a popular, reliable, long-blooming
choice. For something a little different, look for ruffled
double cultivars like the shorter 'Snowdrift' and the
buttery blooms of 'Banana Cream'. Combine any
cultivar with salvias, sneezeweeds, and coneflowers.
Leucanthemum vulgare, ox-eye daisy, is a late-spring
bloomer suitable for meadows and wild areas in
Europe where it is native. It is easily grown from seed.

Leucojum / SNOWFLAKE

SHAPE bell
ROLE mixer
early spring to early summer // front to mid-front //
8–18 in. × 6–10 in. // zones 4–8, hardy bulb

There are two species in this genus that are grown in
gardens. The earliest to bloom is *Leucojum vernum*,
spring snowflake, that flowers with late snowdrops.
It is a short plant with little, white, bell-shaped flowers.
The confusingly named summer snowflake, *L. aes-tivum*, blooms in late spring. This is a taller plant that
does well in damp soil. It has strap-like leaves and
arching stems that support dangling white and green
flowers. Plant either of these snowflakes as bulbs in
the autumn in a wild area or around a pond, where
they will multiply if conditions are suitable. Neither is
eaten by herbivores in the garden. Grow them with
checkered lilies, later-blooming cardinal flower, and
bog sage, which require the same moist conditions.

Liatris spicata
'Kobold'

A white form of
Liatris spicata

Liatris / BLAZING STAR

SHAPE spike
ROLE bold beauty
high summer to autumn // mid-front to mid-back //
18–60 in. × 6–12 in. // zones 3–9, perennial

Blazing stars are fabulous flowers to add an easy vertical element to your display. Native to North America, there are a number of species that all share an upright habit, with little powder-puff flowers arrayed in groups up the stalk. They usually bloom in royal purple, but there are white or pink blazing stars too that add a fresh touch. Flowers open in sequence from the top to the bottom of the spike and are a butterfly magnet. They can be bought either as a plant or as a corm. Slot them into sunny beds around low-growing perennials. They are brilliant when combined with other prairie plants like blanket flower, tickseed, rudbeckia, and coneflowers. All blazing stars bloom during summer or early fall. *Liatris spicata*, dense blazing star, can take some moisture at the roots but not in winter. I use this species around my rain garden. Most of the others need good drainage while maintaining some moisture in the soil. Look for *L. ligulistylis*, *L. scariosa*, or *L. pycnostachya*, which have a similar look but vary in plant height and in the way they present their blooms. *Liatris microcephala*, smallhead blazing star, is a small-scale plant that looks appropriate in a rock garden or at the front of a border.

Lilium 'Scheherazade'

Lilium martagon 'Guinea Gold'

Lilium / LILY

SHAPE trumpet
ROLE bold beauty or mid-border delight
late spring to autumn // front to back; containers //
12–108 in. × 12–30 in. // zones 4–9, hardy bulb

Lilies are the stars of the garden when they are in bloom. They typically grow with multiple flowers per stem and may be scented. They have trumpet-shaped or swept-back curved flowers, depending on the species. There is an enormous variety of flower sizes and shapes from which to choose, along with a multitude of colors and bicolors, including red, pink, magenta, yellow, coral, orange, brown, and white. In addition, some have different-colored centers, shading, or spots. Tall flowering lilies are especially noticeable when their stems rise among and between lower plants to reveal their large flowers. Not all lilies tower above you. There are also medium-height ones for mid-border and short species and cultivars that suit container growing and small gardens. Lilies are full of nectar and attract many different pollinators. Fragrant lilies are great placed near a path or sitting area so that you can easily smell them.

There are many possible lilies to choose from, so start with popular, easy-to-grow favorites like 'Stargazer' in dark rose and white, or 'Black Beauty' with its recurved petals in rich magenta with white edges. For good white flowers, try classic 'Casa Blanca', and for white and yellow together, 'Conca d'Or'. One of the tallest and most dramatic reliable lilies is 'Scheherazade', with stems that easily clear six feet and cream-edged deep claret petals that recurve slightly. For something more delicate, try some of the species lilies like orange summer-flowering *Lilium henryi*, and late-spring *L. martagon* and its cultivars. If you like

Tiger lily, *Lilium lancifolium*

Lilium regale

Limnanthes douglasii

the look of trumpet lilies, choose *L. formosanum,* *L. longiflorum,* or *L. regale*. No matter which lily you choose, it will steal the seasonal show.

Lilies are all easy to grow if their bulbs are planted in well-drained sites where their roots can be in the shade and their leaves and stalks can be in the sun. To increase drainage, add sand or grit to the bottom of the planting hole. If you struggle to grow lilies in the ground, try growing them in large pots that you place right in among other plants when the lily is nearly in flower. Deer love to eat lilies, so plant them inside a fenced area, or spray a deer repellent on the plants. The other pest that eats lilies is the repugnant lily beetle. The adults are bright red and should be easy to spot and pick off. Also look for their eggs and black larvae, which should be removed and crushed.

Limnanthes / POACHED-EGG FLOWER

SHAPE five-petaled
ROLE front-border treat
early spring to early summer // front of the border // 6–1 in. × 6–12 in. // hardy annual

These are low-growing hardy annual plants that bear five-petaled flowers. *Limnanthes douglasii,* poached-egg plant, flowers in spring with characteristic lobed white-edged, yellow-centered flowers that gave rise to its common name. It is a perfect plant to line your paths, where it will self-sow for next year's show. It is native to western North America but will grow in most areas, producing seed and dying in the heat of summer. It can be used to surround displays of spring bulbs and looks good in cottage gardens and in pollinator areas. Poached-egg plant is lightly fragrant and attractive to bees.

Linum perenne

Annual
Lobelia erinus

Linum / FLAX

SHAPE bowl
ROLE mixer
late spring, early summer to high summer // front to mid-front // 12–24 in. × 6–12 in. // zones 4–8, perennial or hardy annual

Linum, flax, is a slender, wiry-stemmed annual or perennial plant that looks good in groups or sown among other plants to add some airiness to the bed. Try any flax flowers as an intermingler in a border or wild planting. The different species bear slightly flared or flat flowers in pale sky blue, white, or red. Grow them from seed sown in place into free-draining soils. Look for the light-blue-flowered *L. perenne*, a short-lived perennial, or the annual *L. grandiflorum*, with its red or crimson flowers that have a lovely dark eye. All are easy to start from seed. They tend to be left alone by deer and rabbits.

Lobelia / LOBELIA

SHAPE trailer or spike
ROLE container or mid-border delight
late spring to autumn // front to mid-back // 6–8 in. × 6–24 in. // zones 3–11, perennial or tender perennial

There are several lobelias for the flower garden which play different roles. They all have characteristic bilaterally symmetrical lipped flowers. *Lobelia erinus*, trailing lobelia, is treated as an annual and is most often grown in containers. Its petite flowers are usually a fresh sky blue or a pure white. Trailing lobelia grows best in cool temperatures, so in warmer climates use it for spring and fall combinations.

Perennial lobelias are best used in flower beds. Their upright inflorescences make a great counterpoint to the plentiful daisies of the summer garden. *Lobelia cardinalis*, cardinal flower, has spikes of bright, pure red flowers that are loved by hummingbirds.

Perennial *Lobelia siphilitica*

Dark and light purple *Lobularia maritima* growing together.

Grow this species in medium to moist soil like a pond margin or rain garden. They are relatively short-lived but will seed into the bed where conditions are right. *Lobelia siphilitica*, great blue lobelia, has spikes of sky blue or occasionally white flowers. It is more prolific than cardinal flower, but is easily dug up and moved. Deadhead promptly to reduce seeding in. Grow with yellow sneezeweeds and rudbeckias for a beautiful late-summer show. Tender perennial *lobelia tupa*, with its tubular red flowers, is a good choice where summers are hot. Give it good drainage and watch the hummingbirds flock to your garden. Lobelias are not favored by herbivores.

Lobularia / SWEET ALYSSUM

SHAPE cluster
ROLE mixer or tiny treasure
late spring to autumn // front; containers // 6–12 in. × 6–18 in. // hardy annual

Sweet alyssum, *Lobularia maritima*, is an ideal low-growing plant for the front of a spring flower border, where its clusters of small, four-petaled, airy flowers can spill over the edge and mix with nearby plants. It is also excellent in containers. The flowers are sweetly honey scented and usually white, but may also be pale lavender, dark purple, and occasionally pink. Sweet alyssum can be sown from seed directly outside in the spring or bought as small plants. Cut the plants back by half after flowering to encourage rebloom and produce a more compact shape. Their flowering declines in the heat of summer, but with good care and trimming, they may rebound for an autumn flush of flowers.

Lunaria annua

Developing *Lunaria annua* seed pods.

Lunaria / HONESTY

SHAPE four-petaled
ROLE mixer
late spring and early summer // mid-front to mid-back
// 18–36 in. × 12–18 in. // zones 5–8, biennial

In spring, the four-petaled flowers of honesty, *Lunaria annua*, are held on upright stems. After pollination, the flowers turn into flat seed pods that later reveal inner silvery discs, which can be used in dried flower arrangements and give rise to another common name, silver dollar. The most common flower color is purple, but there are also attractive white-flowered forms and a variegated cultivar that has white edges to its leaves. They are biennials, so sow the flat seeds in place in summer where you would like them to bloom the following spring. Use honesty among tall spring-flowering bulbs like tulips and daffodils.

Lupinus hybrid

Lupinus 'The Governor'

Lupinus / LUPINE

SHAPE spike
ROLE bold beauty
late spring and early summer // mid-front to mid-back
// 30–48 in. × 12–24 in. // zones 4–7, perennial

Lupines are a beloved addition to a late spring and early summer mixed flower garden. They bear vertical spikes of lightly scented flowers above basal divided leaves. Each spike is covered in densely packed, pea-like flowers that clothe it from top to bottom. The color range includes blue, purple, red, yellow, terra-cotta, and various bicolors. The Russell hybrids are a popular seed-grown mix of lupines that contains a variety of colors. They can be difficult to integrate into a strictly color-coordinated bed but add a charming spontaneity to a cottage-style planting. Look for the Band of Nobles Series, including 'The Chatelaine', which is pink and white, and 'The Governor' in blue and white. The shorter Gallery Series is suitable for small flower beds. Lupines do not tend to be long-lived, so renew them from seed each year. Give them a sunny, well-drained site in unfertilized soil. It is a good idea to place lupines toward the middle of the bed because after they flower, the plant does not look very neat. They are great in a garden with poppies and cornflowers.

A group of Lychnis coronaria.

Lychnis flos-cuculi 'Jenny'

Lychnis chalcedonica

Lychnis / CAMPION

SHAPE disc or dome
ROLE mid-border delight or front-border treat
late spring, early summer to high summer // front to mid-back // 12–36 in. × 12–24 in. // zones 3–7, perennial or biennial

Lychnis is a genus with several dissimilar species that are worth growing. *Lychnis coronaria*, rose campion, has low-growing silvery felted leaves similar to lamb's ears that are pretty in a bed even before their tall, thin stems emerge. The flat-faced flowers come in bright magenta, white, blush, or a two-tone combination in early summer. The magenta color is rather strident but is one of my favorites to jazz up a flower bed. These plants are either short-lived perennials or biennials, depending on your climate. I have established a grouping that seems perennial as they self-sow in place. Give them average soil with good drainage, especially in winter. Try sowing the seeds directly in the garden on some gravel where the young seedlings can get established, and then do so again the following year to keep them going. *Lychnis chalcedonica*, Maltese cross, has bright scarlet, slightly domed flower heads held high above green foliage in summer. Plant it in average to moist soils with other hot-colored flowers. Also look for *L. flos-cuculi*, ragged robin, which has pink flowers in spring, including cultivars 'Jenny' and 'Petite Jenny'. They can take more moisture than the other campions and should be placed near the front of a bed for easy viewing of their delicate flowers. All campions are suited to a cottage-garden style. *Lynchnis* is closely related to the genus *Silene*.

Lycoris squamigera

A field of Lycoris radiata.

Lycoris / SURPRISE LILY

SHAPE trumpet or loose ball
ROLE mid-border delight

high summer to autumn // mid-front // 12–24 in. × 6–24 in. // zones 5–10, bulb

Surprise lilies are not true lilies and are in their own genus. They have a strange life cycle where the leaves emerge in spring and then die down. Once the leaves have withered away and the bulbs have had a good baking, the naked flower stems rise up in late summer with a ring of trumpet-shape flowers at the top. *Lycoris squamigera* is one of the hardiest of the group, with shell pink fragrant flowers. *Lycoris radiata*, red spider lily, has a red, whiskery sphere of flowers. There are several other species and cultivars that are worth growing, including *L. sprengeri* with its incredible pink flowers suffused with blue. Try the melon to yellow-colored *L. chinensis*, golden surprise lily, that is hardy in my Pennsylvania garden in a gravel-mulched area. In cold places, surprise lilies can be grown with heavy winter mulch. Where they are not hardy, try them in containers that are brought in for winter. They are not bothered by herbivores.

Macleaya cordata

Matthiola incana 'Vintage Rose'

Macleaya / PLUME POPPY

SHAPE plume
ROLE background

high summer to autumn // back of the border //
60–96 in. × 24–48 in. // zones 3–8, perennial

Macleaya cordata, plume poppy, is a tall, dramatic addition to the back of the bed. The lobed gray-green leaves have a whitish back that flashes when the wind blows. The rounded stalks hold up large, fluffy, creamy white summer flower plumes. In some soils, plume poppies can spread aggressively by underground roots and will need dividing every few years. In poor, dry soil, they grow more slowly. If you don't want extra volunteer plants, deadhead the flowers after they bloom. I grow it in my gravel garden, where it mixes well with giant scabious and lower-growing Stokes' aster. For a different flower color, look for 'Kelway's Coral Plume', with pinky coral inflorescences.

Matthiola / STOCK

SHAPE four-petaled
ROLE front-border treat or container

late spring and early summer // front to mid-front;
containers // 12–30 in. × 8–18 in. // hardy annual or
tender perennial

If you are looking for spring flowers to add fragrance to your garden, try adding some stocks. They are nice in containers and at the front of a bed. They are especially lovely near a path or bench, and their scent tends to be strongest in the evening. This genus contains a variety of pink, white, blush, or lavender four-petaled flowers that are clustered into spiked flower heads. Grow your own from seed or buy them as small plants. They are normally grown as annuals that are removed from the bed after flowering. *Matthiola longipetala*, the night-scented stock, is great for a moon garden. *Matthiola incana*, the common stock, comes in single or double forms from pastel to rich colors. It has a spicy, sweet fragrance. If you are growing them from seed, do not pinch out the floral growing tip.

Mentha ×piperita

Mentha / MINT

SHAPE spike
ROLE container
high summer to autumn // containers // 12–24 in. ×
12–24 in. // zones 5–9, perennial

Mint is a delicious herb with edible leaves and
flowers, great for a spot by the back door where you
can quickly grab a stem for your iced tea. The small
summer-blooming flowering spikes of white or pale
purple flowers are much loved by pollinators. Mints
are aggressively spreading perennials that are best
grown in a restricted area or container to control their
roots. If you want to grow it in a bed, try sinking a large
pot of mint into the ground and removing any roots
that escape over the rim or through holes in the pot.
These stems are great as a filler in flower arrangements, and the leaves or flowers can be used fresh or
dried in cooking. They are deer and rabbit resistant.
There are many kinds of mint you can grow, but the
two most commonly available and useful are *Mentha
×piperita*, peppermint, and *M. spicata*, spearmint.

Monarda didyma
'Jacob Cline'

Monarda
bradburiana

Monarda / BEEBALM

SHAPE tufted dome
ROLE mid-border delight
late spring, early summer to high summer // mid-front
to mid-back // 12–48 in. × 12–36 in. // zones 4–8,
perennial or hardy annual

Beebalms have strong square stems that are topped
with a dome of hooded flowers. Their individual
tubular blooms are a pollinator magnet, available in
red, pink, purple, or white. They are a summer staple
for moist areas and can grow on heavy soil. They
appreciate a top dressing of organic matter once a
year to improve water retention. Place them at the
edge of a rain garden or by a downspout growing
with turtlehead and perennial lobelia. The whole plant
smells deliciously of a combination of citrus and mint,
and so is not bothered by herbivores.

Monarda didyma, scarlet beebalm, and its cultivars are widely available and very attractive to
hummingbirds. Look out for *M. fistulosa*, wild bergamot, with its tall stems and pale purple flowers, which
is good for a wild area. *Monarda bradburiana*, Eastern
beebalm, is shorter, blooms earlier, and can take a
drier position than others in its genus. All flowers can
be cut, and the dried plant is a good addition to pot-
pourri. When choosing a cultivar, look at the height
of the plant, color of flowers, but most importantly
powdery mildew resistance. This fungal disease is not
usually going to kill the plant, but it can defoliate it in
summer or cover the leaves in what looks like white
powder. To reduce mildew, plant *Monarda* where
there is plentiful moisture in the soil and good airflow.
For increased mildew resistance, look for 'Jacob
Cline', a red-flowered cultivar, and 'Raspberry Wine',
which has deep pinkish-red flowers. There are shorter
cultivars available that suit a small garden, and *M.
citriodora* is an annual beebalm.

Muscari armeniacum

Myosotis sylvatica

Muscari / GRAPE HYACINTH

SHAPE spike
ROLE tiny treasure
early to mid-spring // front; containers // 4–8 in. ×
1–2 in. // zones 4–8, hardy bulb

Grape hyacinths are easy spring flowers to grow from
fall-planted bulbs. Their minispike of tiny bells are
often cobalt blue, but there are species and cultivars in pastel blue, light pink, white, and two-tone.
Interplant them with daffodils or other spring bulbs.
They are lovely in beds or grown through grass and
are great in containers. Some species can seed into
the garden, but choice cultivars are well behaved. The
main species of grape hyacinth for sale are *M. armeniacum*, *M. azureum*, and *M. latifolium*, which are similar
in habit but vary in color. My favorites to grow are the
pale blue cultivars 'Valerie Finnis' and 'Peppermint'.
Try them in a mini spring arrangement with other little
bulbs and violets.

Myosotis / FORGET-ME-NOT

SHAPE cluster
ROLE mixer
early spring to early summer // front to mid-front //
6–12 in. × 8–18 in. // zones 3–8, perennial or biennial

The enchanting powdery blue clusters of forget-
me-nots, *Myosotis sylvatica*, are a fabulous mixer
and mingler that unifies the spring flower bed as
a groundcover beneath taller perennials like columbines and bulbs such as tulips and daffodils. Forget-
me-nots also come in a soft pink or white. All colors
have a characteristic little yellow eye. The common
forget-me-not of gardens is a self-sowing biennial.
To get a colony established, sow seed into a consistently moist, well-drained soil for several years in
a row. If they seed in too successfully, remove some
plants after they flower. They are not bothered by
herbivores. This plant may be invasive in some places.

Narcissus 'Geranium' is a fragrant daffodil.

Narcissus 'Yellow Cheerfulness' is a double daffodil.

Narcissus 'Sundisc' is a late-blooming tiny treasure.

Narcissus / DAFFODIL

SHAPE trumpet
ROLE bold beauty or mid-border delight
early spring to early summer // front to mid-back;
containers // 6–24 in. × 2–4 in. // zones 3–9, hardy bulb

Daffodils are traditional easy-to-grow spring-blooming flowers with an incredible diversity of season of bloom, plant height, flower shape, and color. Daffodil flowers tend to be yellow and white, but some have cups accented with orange, coral, red, or green. The most widely grown daffodils are crown-like trumpet shapes with small or large cups, but there are others with swept-back outer petals, multiple heads to a stem, or fully double flowers. Daffodils have a range of diverse fragrances, from heady tazetta types through to the sweet scent of jonquils. With careful cultivar choice, you can have a series of *Narcissus* in flower from early through late spring. Look for miniature flowers for a rock garden, mid-size ones for the front of the bed, and taller ones that are best toward the middle. All daffodils are easy to combine with forget-me-nots, hyacinths, and other short-statured spring flowers. Medium and small-sized daffodils are fabulous when planted in containers with other spring bloomers like pansies. They are deer and rabbit resistant.

I grow 'February Gold' for its cheerful bright yellow flowers and early emergence, followed by another dependable yellow cultivar, 'Rapture'. For a good white daffodil, try the wonderful 'Thalia', which is a reliable increaser. I love miniature daffodils like hoop-petticoat daffodil, *Narcissus bulbocodium*, with its trumpet and tiny fringe of outer petals. The final daffodil to bloom in my garden is *N. poeticus* var. *recurvus*, the pheasant's eye daffodil, which I grow in light grass combined with short bulbs.

Plant daffodil bulbs in autumn in a spot that is well-drained and not wet or irrigated. If daffodils stop blooming after a few years, they may have produced so many new bulbs that the clump is congested, and it needs to be dug and divided. They may also stop flowering if they are grown in too much shade, so dig the clump up and move it to a sunny spot. Once they have finished flowering, let the daffodil leaves wither in place so they can provide enough energy to form next year's flowers. Surround your daffodils with spring-emerging perennials like catmint and daylilies to disguise the old foliage.

Narcissus, continued

Narcissus 'Ornatus' is a
late-blooming poeticus
daffodil with a flat face.

Narcissus 'King Alfred' is
a classic early-blooming
yellow trumpet daffodil.

A yellow sweep of
Narcissus 'Rapture'.

Flowering stem of *Nepeta*.

A drift of *Nepeta* 'Walker's Low'.

Nepeta / CATMINT

SHAPE spike
ROLE mixer

late spring to autumn // front to mid-back // 12 –36 in. × 12 –36 in. // zones 3 –8, perennial

Catmints are tough perennials that are easy to grow in sunny positions. They are not fussy plants and will grow in poor soil as long as it drains. The whole plant has an amorphous quality to it, so it makes a good weaver in the flower bed. Its petite blue-purple tubular flowers are attached around the upright stems so that pollinators can easily access them. Most garden catmints have silvery foliage that combines well with other gray-leaved plants like lavender and Russian sage. Catmint makes a great companion for spring bulbs where its emerging leaves will cover the dying bulb foliage. You can plant slightly later bulbous plants like tall alliums to come up through the catmint. Their fragrant foliage is not eaten by herbivores, so use catmints to surround more appetizing flowers. Cut back the plant after the first flowery flush for a new set of blooms later in the season. There are several different species of catmint and many cultivars. My favorites are *N. racemosa*, its cultivar 'Walker's Low', and the hybrid *N. ×faassenii* 'Cat's Meow'.

Nicotiana regularly hybridizes in gardens where several different types are grown. This is a self-sown specimen.

A front view of a deep rose-pink, tubular *Nicotiana alata* flower.

The slender tubular flowers of *Nicotiana langsdorffii.*

Nicotiana / FLOWERING TOBACCO

SHAPE tube

ROLE mixer and mid-border delight

late spring to autumn // front to mid-back; containers // 12–60 in. × 12–24 in. // zones 8–10, tender perennial or half-hardy annual

Flowering tobacco has tubular blooms with flat faces that are available in a variety of colors, including white, cream, lime green, purple, and pink. Some species are sweetly scented. With simple leaves and a narrow profile, *Nicotiana* fits easily into a mixed bed, mingling between perennial groupings. It has large, slightly sticky leaves that are lower on the plant and do not obstruct your view of other flowers behind them. *Nicotiana alata*, flowering tobacco, is one of the most commonly available types. There is an interesting green cultivar called 'Lime Green'. Grow it with the slightly more lofty green flowering tobacco *N. langsdorffii*, Langsdorff's tobacco, which has slender dangling tubular blooms. *Nicotiana mutabilis*, color-changing tobacco, is a lovely tall plant that has clouds of small flowers held on narrow stems. The blooms emerge as white and then change through several shades of pink. There are hybrids between *Nicotiana* species that make good candidates for a mixed garden or a container planting. Some of the shorter ones you can buy as small plants may be listed as *N. ×sanderae,* which may not have fragrance. All have tiny seeds that can be started inside for early bloom or outside after soil has warmed. If conditions suit them, they will self-sow. They are all deer and rabbit resistant. Choose flowering tobaccos by plant height, flower size, color, and fragrance. Pollinators love these plants.

A group of white *Nigella damascena*.

Blue *Nigella damascena* with developing seedpods.

Nigella / LOVE-IN-A-MIST

SHAPE five-petaled
ROLE mixer
late spring, early summer to high summer //
front to mid-front; containers // 12–24 in. × 8–18 in. //
hardy annual

Nigella, love-in-a-mist, is one of the most sought-after hardy annuals for the flower bed. This late-spring-in-to-summer bloomer has delicate flowers with a prominent spiky green center surrounded by a ruff of finely dissected misty leaves that give rise to its common name. Whether single or fully double they make good cut flowers. Once pollinated, they produce decorative balloon-like seed pods that can be cut for bouquets or dried. It is easy to sprinkle the seeds where you would like *Nigella* to bloom. It loves cool weather and finishes blooming once heat arrives. In cool summers, you can plant a succession by sowing some every few weeks. In hot summers, replace *Nigella* in the bed with zinnias or celosia. Light and dark blue love-in-a-mist flowers are generally available, but there are also flowers available in pink, purple, and white. I like the *N. damascena* Miss Jekyll Series and also 'Oxford Blue'. Look for other interesting species like *N. papillosa,* its cultivar 'Delft Blue', with fascinating gray-blue flowers, and *N. hispanica* 'African Bride', which is a white-petaled variety with purple-black centers.

Ocimum basilicum
'Cinnamon'

Oenothera fruticosa subsp.
glauca 'Sonnenwende'

Ocimum / BASIL

SHAPE spike
ROLE mixer
late spring to autumn // front to mid-front; containers //
12–30 in. × 12–24 in. // tender perennial

Ocimum basilicum, basil, may not instantly spring to
mind as a plant for a flower bed, but it adds wonderful
upright spikes of summer flowers on a fragrant plant.
Basil is easy to grow from seed or find as a young
plant. I love to use purple-leaved cultivars such as
'Dark Opal' and the green-leaved lemon-scented basil
to add a lovely aroma to my plantings. Use the edible
flowers and leaves in salads and other dishes. Include
stems of tall-growing basil plants like 'Cinnamon',
which provide fragrance and good foliage in your
summer bouquets. Try this with zinnias and cosmos.
Basils require moist and rich well-drained soil in a
sunny, warm spot for best growth. They are frost tender, so do not plant them out until there is no danger
of cold weather. Pinch the growing tips for a bushier
plant with more side shoots.

Oenothera / EVENING PRIMROSE

SHAPE bowl or four-petaled
ROLE mid-border delight
late spring, early summer to high summer // front to
mid-back // 12–60 in. × 12–24 in. // zones 4–9, perennial
or biennial

If you are looking for a no-nonsense plant for a sunny,
well-drained spot in poor soil, consider evening
primroses. The genus *Oenothera* contains some
short-lived perennials and biennials that may seem
like long-term occupants if they seed into the bed.
Oenothera fruticosa, sundrop, is one of the most
commonly grown for its early-summer vibrant yellow
bowl-shaped flowers that bloom in succession above
low rosettes of leaves. This eastern North American
native blooms in the day, unlike the true evening
primroses. Sundrops can be a rather aggressive
spreader where conditions are ideal, so control them
by removing extra plants. They look fabulous when
planted with purple flowers like clustered bellflower.
Oenothera biennis, common evening primrose, is a

Oenothera speciosa

tall biennial plant that also has bowl-shaped scented yellow flowers borne in groups near the top of the stems. The fragrance it produces from dusk to the early hours of the morning is intoxicating. This plant looks good in a bed with annual blanket flowers, coneflowers, and rudbeckia. *Oenothera speciosa* flowers open white and then change to a lilac pink color with a white base. This is another member of the genus that can spread quickly in a garden setting. All evening primroses are perfect for a meadowy or wild area of your garden.

Origanum laevigatum

Origanum 'Kent Beauty'

Origanum / OREGANO

SHAPE cluster
ROLE mixer
late spring to autumn // front to mid-front; containers // 12–30 in. × 12–24 in. // zones 4–9, perennial or tender perennial

Origanum is a genus of often fragrant-leaved plants that are used in herb gardens, rock gardens, or at the front of beds and in containers. If they are grown well, with plenty of sun and excellent drainage, they will spread out vegetatively and may seed into the bed. Add extra gravel and grit to the planting hole and mulch with stone. Oreganos have sprays of usually purply flowers that are a pollinator treat. Their fragrant leaves deter browsing by herbivores. Some species and cultivars are edible, and others are decorative. *Origanum laevigatum* is an ornamental oregano used in flower beds for its purply flowers with darker bracts that can also be cut for bouquets. Look for the showy flowering cultivars 'Rosenkuppel' or 'Herrenhausen'. *Origanum* 'Kent Beauty' has a delicate bloom that resembles a miniature hop flower with greenish purple bracts. Grow it as an annual in cold climates or a perennial if you can give it excellent drainage. It looks best hanging over the edge of a wall or container, where the dangling bloom can be admired. *Origanum vulgare* is used in cooking, with some cultivars having better flavor than others. There is a golden-leaved form, 'Aureum', that is perfect for a bed edging. Greek oregano and marjoram are two other oreganos that are commonly grown for cooking.

Orlaya grandiflora

Osteospermum 'Whirlygig'

Orlaya / WHITE LACE FLOWER

SHAPE horizontal
ROLE mixer
late spring, early summer to high summer // front to
mid-front // 12–30 in. × 8–12 in. // hardy annual

Orlaya grandiflora, white lace flower, is a pretty, delicate, white flower for late-spring-into-summer bloom.
With its highly divided, dainty flat top, it is beautiful
both in the garden and as a cut flower. Continue
to pick its flowers and the plants will produce new
blooms until the weather becomes hot. Plant your
white lace flower among other annuals like love-in-a-
mist and poppies. Grow it from seed sown outside in
the fall or early spring.

Osteospermum / AFRICAN DAISY

SHAPE daisy
ROLE container or front-border treat
late spring to autumn // front to mid-front; containers //
8–24 in. × 12–24 in. // zones 10–11, tender perennial

African daisies are plants with colorful flowers perfect
for containers and at the front of beds in a sunny
site with good drainage. They are a tender perennial
that is grown as a cool-season annual in areas with
hot summers and throughout the summer in mild
climates. Their outer petals are in a host of colors,
including white, pink, peach, yellow, or purple, with a
contrasting central eye. The reverse of the petals may
have a different color as a surprise. The flower form is
typically daisy-like, but you can also find interesting
and unusual versions with spoon-shaped petals like
'Whirlygig'. African daisies love the sun, and the flowers close on dull days and in the evenings.

Paeonia lactiflora
'Fuchsia Dragonfly'
is dark pink with
yellow petaloids.

Paeonia / PEONY

SHAPE bowl or ball
ROLE bold beauty
late spring and early summer // mid-front to mid-back
// 24–36 in. × 24–36 in. // zones 3–8, perennial

Peonies are classic flowers that stop you in your
tracks when they are in bloom. There are three types
of peonies that you could grow: herbaceous, woody,
and an intersectional group that is a cross between
the other two. Herbaceous peonies are suited to any
flower garden and are easy to grow. If you have success with these, investigate the other types.

Paeonia lactiflora, herbaceous peony, is available
in a wide variety of cultivars, including cup-shaped
blooms that may be single, anemone shaped, or semi
to fully double. Their colors range from white to coral,
pale pink to fuchsia, and dark crimson red or maroon.
Some peonies have delicious fragrance, while others
are unscented. They are not bothered by deer or
rabbits. Herbaceous peonies make excellent cut flowers. Harvest them before they are fully open to help
them last longer in the vase. Tall plants and those
with heavy double flowers need staking. Peonies do
not like to be moved once planted, so think carefully
before you place them. They should be planted with
their shoots only a couple of inches down in the soil,
otherwise they might not flower. Do not mulch over
the peony crown but add a side-dressing of compost and a sprinkling of wood ash or similar organic
fertilizer. Help the plant to establish by picking flowers
but not foliage in the growing season for the first few
years. To reduce the spread of foliar diseases, cut the
leaves to the ground in fall and do not compost them.
If well cared for, with plenty of sun, peonies produce
more and more flowers each year and may live for
more than half a century. I would not have a garden
without these spectacular late-spring blooms.

Double pale pink
Paeonia lactiflora.

A mid-toned
pink peony.

Single white *Paeonia
lactiflora* with yellow
petaloids.

Papaver atlanticum

A light pink and white *Papaver rhoeas.*

Lilac single *Papaver somniferum*

Papaver / POPPY

SHAPE bowl or ball
ROLE bold beauty or mid-border delight
early spring to early summer // mid-front to mid-back //
12–36 in. × 6–36 in. // zones 3–8, perennial or hardy annual

Poppies are some of the most eye-catching, sought-after flowers in the garden. Look for bright red, orange, white, coral, lilac, pink, or plummy-purple petal colors in single bowl-shaped or double flowers. Annual poppies are ephemeral beauties that have enchanted poets and artists for centuries as they attempt to capture the translucent delicate beauty of their petals. There are a variety of different poppies that bloom in succession, so include several types in your garden to extend the bloom time. They are an easy plant to slot in between perennials because they need little horizontal space for their slender flower stems. Many poppies will self-sow, and they are not bothered by herbivores.

Papaver nudicaule, Iceland poppy, is a perennial that is often treated as a biennial or an annual. It flowers early in the year in fresh yellow, orange, pink, and white. *Papaver atlanticum*, Atlas poppy, is a short-lived drought-tolerant perennial with light orange single or semi-double blooms in spring and early summer that will self-sow into even the tiniest crack. *Papaver rhoeas*, corn poppy, is the traditional red poppy found wild in European fields that has been bred to include singles and doubles in red, pink, and white with contrasting centers or rims. I love the Shirley series, with a multitude of delicate pastel colorations often with a white edge. *Papaver commutatum*, ladybird poppy, has four crimson red petals with a black spot at the base of each and makes a bold statement in a garden bed. *Papaver somniferum*, breadseed poppy, is one of the stars of the early summer border, with single or double flowers and some blooms so full that they resemble powder puffs. Colors range from lavender purples through various

*Papaver
orientale
'Brilliant*

pinks, white, and dark red to almost black. I love every single one I have ever grown, but I recommend trying the white 'Swansdown' or the purply 'Lauren's Grape'. Grow them with foxgloves, mullein, and rose campion for a lovely show. For best results, annual poppies should be grown from seed sprinkled onto areas of gravel or melting snow over low-fertility soil where you want them to bloom, because they resent transplanting. Keep the area free from heavy mulch, as the tiny seeds need contact with soil to germinate.

Papaver orientale, Oriental poppy, is an easy-to-grow, clump-forming perennial that requires a rich, well-drained soil. It is a showy beauty in the early summer garden, with distinctive bowl-shaped blooms that are often brightly colored with a black base and stamens. The flowers burst from tightly packed buds, crinkles still visible in the papery petals. The divided leaves and stems are covered in soft, bristly hairs. Plants die back after they have finished blooming. To disguise their retreating leaves, plant them toward the mid-back of the bed where you will not notice their disappearance. Some of the best-known cultivars include the bright scarlet 'Beauty of Livermere', purply 'Patty's Plum', and white 'Royal Wedding'.

Patrinia
scabiosifolia

A group of
scarlet and coral
Pelargonium.

Patrinia / PATRINIA

SHAPE horizontal
ROLE mixer
late spring, early summer to high summer // mid-front
to mid-back // 24–48 in. × 18–24 in. // zones 5–8,
perennial

Patrinia scabiosifolia, golden lace, is a delicate flowering plant with flat-topped vibrant yellow flowers
held in sprays on slender stems above rough basal
foliage. In spite of its height, it makes a good candi-
date for mid-border placement because of its airy
nature. It needs good winter drainage and a rich soil
with adequate moisture. The flowers of golden lace
contrast well with purple flowers like tall vervain and
also fit in with hot color schemes. Treat them as short-
lived perennials or biennials and renew your planting
every few years from seed. Where it is happy, it may
self-sow.

Pelargonium / GERANIUM

SHAPE ball or bilaterally symmetrical
ROLE container or mid-border delight
late spring to autumn // mid-front; containers //
12–30 in. × 12–24 in. // zones 9–11, tender perennial

These popular, brightly colored flowers are easy to
grow in summer containers. They originate in warm
climates and need protection from frost. They are
commonly called geraniums, but they are a different
genus than hardy geraniums. Flowers are arrayed into
clusters of scarlet red, coral, pink, purple, white, and
orange. They are wonderful plants for containers and
need regular deadheading to keep the floral show
going. Look for trailing ivy-leaved cultivars for window boxes and zonal geraniums for larger pots. There
are a wide range of scented geraniums that smell like
mint, citrus, apple, and more. All geraniums are easily
propagated by cuttings taken in spring or summer.

Pelargonium make great container plants.

Penstemon 'Pensham Laura'

To overwinter your special cultivars, cut them down significantly before you bring them inside in the fall. My favorite geraniums to grow are 'Attar of Roses', with leaves that smell like roses, and *P. tomentosum*, which has soft, peppermint-scented leaves.

Penstemon / BEARDTONGUE

SHAPE spike
ROLE mid-border delight
late spring to autumn // front to mid-back // 12–36 in. × 12–24 in. // zones 4–8, perennial

The genus *Penstemon* contains plenty of gorgeous garden plants. They are known for their spires of flared, tube-shaped flowers containing characteristic fluffy stamens on the lower petal that are the "beardtongue" of their common name. They are a perfect mid-border delight in an array of colors including white, blue, magenta, red, pink, purple, and bicolors. Beardtongues are typically long-blooming summer plants that entice pollinators to your garden. They may be short-lived, but where they are happy, they will seed themselves into the garden. *Penstemon smallii*, Small's penstemon, is a favorite of mine. I have it growing with beebalm, catchfly, bluestar, and tickseed. *Penstemon digitalis*, foxglove beardtongue, grows in various places in my garden, where its spikes of pale purple-tinged flowers delight in early and midsummer. Look for cultivars with maroon-red foliage like 'Husker's Red'. Among the many hybrids that I covet are purple-flowered 'Sour Grapes' and reddish 'Garnet', which need low-humidity summers to thrive. Do not overwater beardtongues, and give them good drainage.

Penstemon
'Garnet'

Pentas
lanceolata

Petunia
'Lavender
Sky Blue'

Pentas / EGYPTIAN STARCLUSTER

SHAPE five-petaled

ROLE container or front-border treat

late spring to autumn // front to mid-front; containers //
12–24 in. × 12–24 in. // zones 10–11, tender perennial

The five-petaled, star-like flowers of *Pentas lance-olata*, Egyptian starcluster, are grouped together to make domed flower heads that are perfect landing spots for butterflies. These are tender perennials that are usually grown as annuals. Blooms are produced all season long and are perfect in a container with other warm-season flowers like million bells. Flower colors include pink, crimson, lavender, and white, with some bicolors. Deadhead old blooms to keep the plants looking nice and to encourage new flowers to form. Keep them watered during hot and dry weather.

Petunia / PETUNIA

SHAPE trumpet

ROLE container or front-border treat

late spring to autumn // front to mid-front; containers //
9–12 in. × 12–48 in. // zones 10–11, tender perennial

Petunias are one of the most popular easy-to-grow flowers for summer show in a flower bed. Single flowers are trumpet-shaped, with a flared opening often with a contrasting eye color. Doubles have a ruffled appearance within the trumpet. Petunias are sweetly scented, and new cultivars are weather resistant. The hybridization of this genus has produced a plethora of colors and characteristics that make the plants a long-blooming addition to a flower garden. They are listed as *Petunia ×hybrida*. Look for petunias that match your color scheme and choose by the size of their blooms and whether they are compact growers, spreaders, or cascading plants. They are especially good for container plantings or bed edging. If grown

Petunias come in a wide range of colors and can be grown together.

Phlomis russeliana

in containers, give petunias regular water and low-nitrogen fertilizer to fuel their rapid growth. Start seed indoors or buy small plants in the spring. To encourage plants to stay compact and rebloom, trim back the stems regularly and deadhead. Grow petunias with summer annuals like celosia or cascading vervain. Petunias are rarely bothered by deer, but if you have rabbits, raise your petunia plantings into window boxes or hanging baskets.

Phlomis / JERUSALEM SAGE

SHAPE vertical whorled
ROLE mid-border delight

late spring, early summer to high summer // mid-front to mid-back // 24–48 in. × 12–48 in. // zones 4–8, perennial

Jerusalem sages are magnificent additions to a lackluster early or midsummer garden. From low-growing hairy basal leaves, a whorled upright spike of flowers emerges to enliven the scene. Each encircling ring of flowers is composed of hooded blooms that are attractive to bees. *Phlomis russeliana* has tiers of medium yellow flowers and felty foliage. *Phlomis fruticosa* also has yellow flowers and gray-green, sage-like leaves, and it is slightly less hardy. *Phlomis tuberosa* has lavender-pink whorls of flowers and textured green foliage. *Phlomis cashmeriana*, Kashmir sage, has light purple flowers and is great for a dry garden. *Phlomis* flowers are an unusual addition to a vase, look lovely dried, and, if left in place on the plants, provide excellent winter interest. Most species do best in fertile, well-drained, dry or medium soil in full sun or very light shade. They are deer and rabbit resistant. Try a Jerusalem sage in a dry bed with lavender and lavender cotton or in a border with salvias and agapanthus.

Phlox subulata 'Fort Hill' spreading down a rock-garden bank.

Phlox paniculata 'Bright Eyes'

Phlox / PHLOX

SHAPE five-petaled
ROLE bold beauty or carpet
late spring to autumn // front to back // 6–60 in. ×
12–36 in. // zones 3–9, perennial

Phlox flowers have five petals with a flat face and a central eye. The genus *Phlox* contains several distinct plant forms. Starting in mid-spring, *P. subulata*, creeping phlox, blooms in shades of hot pink, lavender, and white, with several striped forms. It is a great plant for a gravel or rock garden or the front of a border where it will not be smothered by surrounding plants. Over time it will form a low-growing mat if conditions are right.

Phlox paniculata, border phlox, is an essential component of a high-summer flower garden that is a treat for you and for visiting butterflies and bees. It holds its bold clusters of flowers high above surrounding plants, releasing a remarkable sweet fragrance that lingers in the warm air. The color range has expanded from magenta-pink and white, both of which I love, to ones with contrasting eye colors, brilliant reddish pink, and soft pinky lilac. Choose your border phloxes by height and color but also by powdery mildew resistance, as the cultivars vary tremendously in their ability to withstand it. Thin out some of the stems early in the growing season, give them a site with good rich soil, and water deeply in times of drought without splashing the leaves. If you leave the seed heads on, you may find self-sown seedlings that tend to revert to magenta-pink. Late in summer, *P. maculata*, meadow phlox, blooms and attracts hummingbirds in its native North American range.

Pink *Physostegia virginiana*

A tall pale lavender *Physostegia virginiana.*

Physostegia / OBEDIENT PLANT

SHAPE spike
ROLE mid-border delight
high summer to autumn // mid-front to mid-back //
18–48 in. × 18–36 in. // zones 3–9, perennial

Physostegia virginiana, obedient plant, has late-summer spikes of tubular flowers. The obedient part of the common name comes from the ability to move the individual flowers around on the stem, where they will stay put. Gardeners joke about this plant really being the disobedient plant, as it can be a strong grower, spreading both by underground runners and by seed. However, when it is blooming in late summer and early autumn, all is forgiven because it brings a splash of bright magenta, strong lilac, or fresh white to the bed. If those colors are not bright enough for you, look for the cultivar 'Vivid'. If you want a slightly more well-behaved, white-flowered obedient plant,

try 'Miss Manners'. Native to eastern North America, obedient plant combines well with Culver's root and Joe-Pye weed. Grow it in soil with plenty of leaf mold or compost to retain soil moisture, and water new plants until they are established. They make great cut flowers.

Platycodon / BALLOON FLOWER

SHAPE bowl
ROLE mid-border delight
late spring, early summer to high summer // front to mid-front // 12–36 in. × 12–24 in. // zones 3–8, perennial

Balloon flower, *Platycodon grandiflorus*, is a fun addition to the front or the middle of a bed, where you can watch their pointed, balloon-like buds open into a star-like bowl. The unusual summer-blooming flowers are often blue-purple but can also be found

Platycodon grandiflorus

Polianthes tuberosa 'The Pearl'

in white or pink. The plants emerge from the ground slowly in spring, so leave a label next to them to make sure you don't plant something else in the seemingly empty spot. Deadhead flowers to prolong the bloom time. The plants contain a toxic milky sap, so if you cut stems for arranging, soak them for a couple of hours before use. Balloon flowers are a lovely addition to a cottage garden, where they look fabulous when combined with short border phlox. I like the cultivar 'Fuji Blue'.

Polianthes / TUBEROSE

SHAPE spike
ROLE mid-border delight
late spring to autumn // mid-front to mid-back; containers // 24–30 in. × 6–12 in. // zones 8–10, tender perennial

Tuberoses, *Polianthes tuberosa*, are among the most fragrant flowers one can grow. Their typically white tubular blooms are borne on tall stalks that arise from strap-like leaves. They flower in summer and project a heady fragrance into the garden. This tuberous perennial is not hardy everywhere and so may be grown in containers or lifted out of the ground to be stored inside in a cool, dark place for the winter. There are double cultivars like 'The Pearl' and pink ones like 'Pink Sapphire'. Grow it in rich, fertile, well-drained soil with consistent moisture in summer.

Pulsatilla vulgaris

Puschkinia scilloides var. libanotica

Pulsatilla / PASQUEFLOWER

SHAPE bowl
ROLE front-border treat
early spring to early summer // front to mid-front //
8–12 in. × 8–18 in. // zones 4–8, perennial

Pulsatilla vulgaris, pasqueflower, is a spring-blooming plant with open-faced flowers that pop up out of the ground before the leaves. The eiderdown-soft petals in purple, maroon, or cream surround the decorative yellow boss of stamens. After pollination, the petals drop off and reveal ornamental fuzzy seed heads. It is a great plant for gravel gardens as it needs well-drained soil with no plants laying over it. Pasqueflower will self-sow where conditions suit it. Plant it with purple rock cress and basket-of-gold. This rabbit- and deer-resistant plant should be handled with gloves because it produces a potentially irritating sap.

Puschkinia / STRIPED SQUILL

SHAPE star-like
ROLE tiny treasure
early to mid-spring // front; containers // 6–8 in. ×
2–3 in. // zones 4–9, hardy bulb

Striped squills are short flowers for spring that grow from fall-planted bulbs. Similar in role and appearance to glory-of-the-snow and squill, striped squill is light blue with darker blue lines that run the length of the petal. It does well planted in groups for best impact. Plant little clumps along the front of a border or in thin grass with short early daffodils and grape hyacinths for a pretty spring picture. Striped squill needs well-drained conditions and may multiply where it is happy.

Pycnanthemum muticum

Ratibida columnifera

Pycnanthemum / MOUNTAIN MINT

SHAPE cluster
ROLE mixer

high summer to autumn // mid-front to mid-back //
12–36 in. × 12–36 in. // zones 3–8, perennial

The flowers of mountain mints, *Pycnanthemum*, are white and borne in little clusters. They are not very showy, but they make some of the best pollinator plants in the garden. They have a long season of bloom, flowering on and off until frost. There are several good garden species, all of which have a tendency to spread. The plants can be kept in check by cutting parts off the edges of the expanding clump and deadheading the flowers. Try them first in a wild part of your garden before planting them in a neat flower bed. True to their common names, they have a pleasant, minty scent to their foliage that deters animals from eating them. Try blunt mountain mint, *P. muticum*, which has silvery bracts surrounding the flowers, or one of the narrower green-leaved species like *P. tenuifolium* or *P. virginianum*.

Ratibida / RATIBIDA

SHAPE cone or daisy
ROLE mixer

late spring to autumn // mid-front to mid-back //
12–48 in. × 12–18 in. // zones 3–8, perennial

Ratibidas have small, narrow, brown cones that point to the sky, with outer petals that trail down in shades of bronze, yellow, or red. They are held on delicate stems with slim leaves that weave their way in between surrounding flowers. *Ratibida columnifera*, upright prairie coneflower, is the species commonly seen for sale. Its shape is fascinating, so place it near the front of a bed where people can study its delicate details. This plant is not long-lived, so sprinkle seed around where you would like it to grow. Ratibidas thrive in well-drained soil and are good plants to add to an informal area or gravel garden. Grow them with coreopsis, rudbeckia, and coneflowers. If you like the look but want a slightly bigger plant, try *R. pinnata*, pinnate prairie coneflower, and place it at the mid-back of the border.

Rudbeckia triloba

Rudbeckia hirta

Rudbeckia / RUDBECKIA

SHAPE daisy
ROLE mid-border delight or background
late spring to autumn // front to back; containers //
12–96 in. × 12–30 in. // zones 3–8, perennial or annual

Rudbeckia contains some simple-to-grow flowers for the summer and fall garden. The classic jolly black-eyed and brown-eyed Susans have characteristic daisy-shaped flowers. They are attractive to pollinators in bloom and to birds once the seeds have formed, so plant some if your family loves to watch birds. *Rudbeckia hirta*, gloriosa daisy, or black-eyed Susan, is one of the showiest members of this group. It is easy to start from seed and can be treated as an annual, or a short-lived perennial that may live for a couple of years in well-drained soil. The other rudbeckias are usually perennial but may also be short-lived. *Rudbeckia fulgida*, black-eyed Susan, is a clump-forming plant that puts on a good show. Some subspecies and cultivars are very resistant to powdery mildew. One of the best introductions is 'American Gold Rush', which has proved to be an instant favorite for the front of the border. *Rudbeckia triloba*, brown-eyed Susan, has bristly stems and smaller-scale flowers in late summer and early fall. It may not be long-lived, but it seeds in regularly. *Rudbeckia subtomentosa*, the sweet coneflower, has cultivars with quilled petals like 'Henry Eilers' and the shorter 'Little Henry' that give a different look to the late-summer border. *Rudbeckia maxima* is tall, with stems up to eight feet. It makes a strong statement behind lower-growing plants at the back of the border where its large blue-green leaves can be displayed to good effect.

Salvia horminum

Salvia 'Wendy's Wish'

Salvia yangii

Salvia / SALVIA OR SAGE

SHAPE spike
ROLE mid-border delight

late spring to autumn // front to mid-back; containers // 12–60 in. × 12–48 in. // zones 4–10, perennial, tender perennial, or half-hardy annual

Salvia is a huge genus that contains a plethora of good garden plants. They have upright or trailing horizontal spikes of tubular flowers in blue, red, purple, white, coral, pink, orange, and yellow, sometimes with contrasting calyxes. There are different salvias that bloom from spring to fall. Perennial sages like the classic *S. ×sylvestris* 'May Night' and 'Caradonna' are stalwart late spring perennials in many areas, as is *S. nemorosa,* which blooms at a similar time. They pair beautifully with white lace flower, poppies, and yarrow.

Later in the season, try *Salvia sclarea,* clary sage, which is a biennial or short-lived perennial characterized by large, toothed leaves and a tall, candelabra-shaped inflorescence. The short-lived perennial *S. argentea* produces a spike of white flowers in summer but is grown primarily for its soft, silvery leaves. The hardy annual *S. horminum* is an old cottage-garden favorite with papery bracts in purple, pink, or white that I remember in my granny's garden. It thrives in cool weather and stops blooming in heat. Some warm-weather perennials are grown as annuals, like *S. coccinea,* scarlet sage, and its cultivars 'Snow Nymph' and 'Coral Nymph', and *S. farinacea,* mealy-cup sage, and its cultivar 'Victoria Blue'. They bloom strongly from early summer through to fall if they are started indoors and planted out after frost. Also look for the brightly colored bedding flower *S. splendens.*

Tender perennial salvias like *Salvia guaranitica,* blue anise sage, *S. elegans,* pineapple sage, which has a fruity fragrance to its leaves, and *S. leucantha,* Mexican bush sage, may overwinter if you site them in a warm microclimate and mulch heavily with dry leaves or salt hay over winter. They require a long growing season and some heat during the summer to flower well, but in good conditions you will be rewarded with arching stems resplendent with flowers in late summer and fall. In areas with hot summers, try *S. greggii,* which has profuse petite blooms in shades of red, pink, white, and purple. For a cooler summer climate, try *S. patens* with its gorgeous sky blue flowers. *Salvia uliginosa,* bog sage, has similar

Salvia, continued

Salvia
farinacea

Salvia
'Hot Lips'

Salvia ×sylvestris
'Blauhugel' (Blue Hill)

Salvia
coccinea

Sanguisorba
tenuifolia
'Purpurea'

mid-blue flowers that are held on long, tall stems, and the plant can take some moisture in the soil.

There are two salvias often grown in herb gardens. The first is *Salvia officinalis*, common sage, the edible herb. The next is rosemary, which was recently reclassified as *S. rosmarinus*. Another new member, *S. yangii*, used to be in the genus *Perovskia* and is called Russian sage. It has light blue-purple, feathery flowers and is excellent for dry sites. Every member of the genus is beloved by pollinators, with red and purple salvias being particularly attractive to hummingbirds. Rabbits and deer rarely bother salvias due to the fragrance of their leaves.

Sanguisorba / BURNET

SHAPE bottlebrush or button
ROLE mixer
late spring to autumn // mid-front to mid-back //
12–48 in. × 12–36 in. // zones 4–7, perennial

These plants are not often grown in North American gardens but deserve to be better known. They have graceful arching stems that hold the cylindrical, bottlebrush-like flowers that emerge from divided basal foliage. Burnets are great as mixers and minglers between more conspicuous blooms. They need moist, well-drained soils and will not tolerate drought. Where conditions are perfect for growth, some burnets are aggressive spreaders. Other species, especially planted in drier conditions, do not romp around the garden. Buy by flower color, which can be white, pink, lilac, or maroon, and by plant height. Also consider bloom time, which may be early, mid, or

Santolina chamaecyparissus

late summer. *Sanguisorba obtusa*, Japanese burnet, and *S. hakusanensis* are see-through plants with pink flowers that are good at the mid-front of the bed. *Sanguisorba tenuifolia* is for further back in the border, where you can admire its elegant form and late-summer flowers in dark pink or white. *Sanguisorba officinalis* is probably the easiest to find, with dark crimson blooms in late spring and early summer.

Santolina / LAVENDER COTTON

SHAPE button
ROLE mid-border delight
late spring, early summer to high summer // mid-front to mid-back // 18–24 in. × 24–30 in. // zones 6–9, perennial

These are classic plants for dry soils in a sunny location. The finest plants I have ever seen were growing in southern France in well-drained alkaline soil. Recreate these conditions in your garden by planting them on a hot, sunny slope, mulch with gravel for increased drainage and heat retention, and add a little lime if your soil is acid or neutral. Choose from the silvery-leaved *S. chamaecyparissus*, or the green-leaved *S. rosmarinifolia*. Both plants have cute yellow, button-shaped flowers in summer. Their delicately divided, aromatic foliage is not eaten by deer or rabbits. The plants are partially woody at the base. Do not cut into this and trim the herbaceous foliage in spring after growth has started. Lavender cottons combine well with the upright spires of lavender. Add in other plants like sea holly or pinks, as they make good bedfellows. The leaves are an important evergreen, or ever-gray, addition to a bed.

Scabiosa atropurpurea 'Beaujolais Bonnets'

Scabiosa / SCABIOUS

SHAPE button
ROLE mixer
late spring, early summer to high summer // front to mid-back // 12–36 in. × 8–24 in. // zones 3–7, perennial

Scabious, also known as pincushion flower, has hemispherical flowers with slightly frilled larger outer florets. The common name comes from the way the anthers stick out above the flowers and resemble pins stuck into a pincushion. Blooms are held on wiry stems above divided foliage, so it makes a great plant to mix among more substantial plants like yarrow or betony. The most common flower colors are lavender purple or creamy white but may be pink, blue, purple, or crimson. Scabious need really good drainage, a sunny spot, and slightly alkaline to neutral soil. The perennial *S. caucasica* is not long-lived but is wonderful at the front of the border or in a gravel garden.

Look for 'Fama Blue' or 'Fama White', with larger-than-average flower heads. Try *S. ochroleuca*, which forms a floating mass of creamy flowers in summer. *Scabiosa graminifolia* is a short plant for the front of a well-drained border or a rock garden. It has grassy foliage and pretty pale lilac flowers. *Scabiosa atropurpurea* is fragrant and is sometimes sold as sweet scabious. I like the dark-flowered cultivar 'Black Knight' and the raspberry-pink 'Beaujolais Bonnets'. Plants are sold as annuals, but they might survive a few winters with some protection and dry soil. Grow scabious from seed sown in place or started indoors, and all are great cut flowers that last well. Deadhead faded blooms regularly to prolong blooming.

Scilla bifolia

Silene armeria

Silene regia 'Prairie Fire'

Scilla / SQUILL

SHAPE star-like
ROLE tiny treasure
early to mid-spring // front; containers // 3–8 in. ×
2–6 in. // zones 2–8, hardy bulb

These are easy-to-grow, hardy spring bulbs that require little care once they are planted. Their star-like flowers are sometimes white but are normally blue. They are tolerant of a wide range of conditions and are perfect at the front of a bed or in a low-maintenance lawn where grass is thin. Pair them with other little spring bulbs like grape hyacinth or spring starflower, or use them to underplant daffodils. All squill will seed in if conditions are suitable. *Scilla bifolia*, *S. mischtschenkoana*, *S. sardensis*, and *S. siberica* all bloom in early to mid-spring, and *S. litardierei* blooms later in spring and is a little taller. They are planted in fall and should be clustered together for best impact in the garden.

Silene / CATCHFLY

SHAPE five-petaled cluster or dome
ROLE mixer or edger
late spring, early summer to high summer // front to
mid-front // 12–24 in. × 6–12 in. // zones 5–8, perennial
or hardy annual

The genus *Silene* has a number of garden plants that are closely related to *Lychnis*. *Silene armeria*, garden catchfly, has rosy pink flowers that self-sow, especially in graveled areas. This species has the potential to be invasive in some places, so check before planting. There are several other worthwhile plants, including *S. regia*, royal catchfly, and *S. virginica*, fire pink, that both have reddish flowers, attract hummingbirds, and are native to North America. They need well-drained soils that contain some moisture. *Silene asterias*, cherry drumsticks, is an unusual plant that has spherical reddish magenta blooms held above low foliage. *Silene caroliniana*, sticky catchfly, is a good low-growing edger to a natural area or a medium to dry rock garden.

Silphium
perfoliatum

Silphium
laciniatum
flowers

Silphium / SILPHIUM

SHAPE daisy
ROLE background
high summer to autumn // mid-back to back //
30–120 in. × 12–36 in. // zones 3–8, perennial

Silphiums are tall plants for the back of a border. Some of the species tower over your head and are not for the timid gardener. They have yellow daisy-like flowers that attract bees and butterflies. I love *Silphium perfoliatum*, which forms an impressive stand by summer. It colonizes an area by underground roots and makes a good deciduous screen. The common name of prairie cup plant comes from the way that its sandpapery leaves clasp around the stem and collect rainwater. Goldfinches and other birds sit on the leaves to drink the water and peck at the seed heads. There are several other silphium species worth growing. Look for *S. laciniatum*, the compass plant, which orients its leaves with respect to the sun, and *S. terebinthinaceum*, prairie dock, with huge architectural lower leaves and soaring tall stems that can reach up to ten feet. *Silphium* make excellent plants for wild gardens, at the back of a border, and large spaces.

Solidago rugosa
'Loydser Crown'

Solidago rugosa
'Fireworks'

Solidago / GOLDENROD

SHAPE feathery spike
ROLE mid-border delight
late summer into autumn // front to back // 12–48 in. ×
24–36 in. // zones 3–9, perennial

Goldenrods, *Solidago*, are a huge genus of late-blooming, easy-to-grow perennials. Yellow golden-rod flowers are held in feathery spikes, in clusters, or along branching stems. The blooms are rich in pollen and nectar and are covered in late-season insects. Choose your goldenrod by its height and shape, but be aware that most spread aggressively. Look for varieties such as 'Fireworks', whose flowers live up to its name, and the compact cultivar 'Golden Fleece', with fluffy flowers held on a shorter plant.

Dig and divide clumps every few years to reduce the width. Cut off a portion of the seed heads before they can seed around the garden, but leave some for the birds. Goldenrods are well suited to a wild garden or meadow and are a classic fall pairing with purple asters. They are deer and rabbit resistant.

Stachys byzantina flowering spike.

Stachys officinalis 'Hummelo'

Stachys / LAMB'S EARS OR BETONY

SHAPE spike

ROLE mid-border delight or edging

late spring, early summer to high summer // front to mid-front // 12–24 in. × 12–24 in. // zones 4–8, perennial

This genus contains two distinct plants that are both good in the garden, lamb's ears and betony. They are reliable growers in positions with well-drained soils and are drought tolerant once established. *Stachys byzantina*, lamb's ears, has velvety-soft simple silver leaves that look great at the front of a flower bed. In summer, they send up a whorled vertical flower stalk, with little pinky purple blooms that are loved by pollinators. They are an excellent choice for a sensory garden.

Stachys officinalis, betony, is sometimes listed as *Betonica officinalis*. It is also a neat plant for the front of the border, where their green, slightly lobed leaves look fresh all season long. In late spring and early summer, the upright columnar flowering heads shoot up above the leaves, with magenta or pink blooms that cling to the stalk. The cultivar 'Hummelo' is a new garden classic. There are also lovely cultivars like 'Summer Romance' and 'Pink Cotton Candy' that have lighter pink flowers. Remove the flowering stalks of both types of *Stachys* after blooming. They are rabbit and deer resistant.

Sternbergia lutea

Stokesia laevis 'Peachie's Pick'

Sternbergia / AUTUMN DAFFODIL

SHAPE cup
ROLE tiny treasure
late summer into autumn // front of the border //
6 in. × 3 in. // zones 6–9, hardy bulb

Just when you think your bulbous plants have finished for the year, up pop the chalice-shaped, bright yellow *Sternbergia lutea*. Although they are not in the same genus as the spring-blooming daffodils, they are a similar egg-yolk color. Plant them in a gravel-mulched area or rock garden where their bulbs will get a good summer baking. They should not be irrigated during the summer. In autumn, after the flowers bloom, strappy green leaves come up and persist throughout the winter. They are deer and rabbit resistant.

Stokesia / STOKES' ASTER

SHAPE daisy
ROLE front-border treat
late spring, early summer to high summer // front to mid-front // 12–24 in. × 12–24 in. // zones 5–9, perennial

Stokes' aster, *Stokesia laevis*, is one of my favorite underused perennials that is well worth including at the front of the border or in a gravel garden. It has large, round, slightly fluffy, flat-faced summer flowers in colors from periwinkle blue to dark purple and creamy white. The long-blooming flowers are held on shortish stems above a low-growing rosette of elongated, white-veined leaves. This is an easy-care plant that grows best in well-drained soil that is not waterlogged in winter. It may gently self-sow or can be divided in spring. Plants are not bothered by rabbits or deer, and butterflies love them. Choose a named cultivar for best results. Some, like 'Color Wheel', change color as the flower ages. Stokes'

Symphyotrichum oblongifolium 'Raydon's Favorite'

aster makes a good cut flower. Grow with sea hollies, Macedonian scabious, and lavender for a drought-tolerant summer-flowering garden. They are native to the southeastern United States.

Symphyotrichum / ASTER

SHAPE daisy
ROLE edging, mid-border delight or background
late summer into autumn // front to back // 12–60 in. × 12–36 in. // zones 3–8, perennial

The hard-to-pronounce genus *Symphyotrichum* now contains the North American species that were divided out of the genus *Aster*. They are sometimes called Michaelmas daisies. They produce masses of small, purple, pink, lavender, or white daisy-shaped flowers with yellow centers that give great flower power in the garden from late summer through frost. The best cultivars last for weeks, with new flowers replacing the fading ones. When they are in bloom, they are often abuzz with pollinators and make good cut flowers. Some of the most popular and reliable species and cultivars are the low-mounding *S. oblongifolium* 'Raydon's Favorite', with purply-blue flowers, and *S. novae-angliae* 'Harrington's Pink', a bright rose-pink New England aster that I love. *Symphyotrichum ericoides* 'Snow Flurry' is a short but wide plant for the front of a raised bed that smothers itself in small white flowers in fall. *Symphyotrichum lateriflorum* 'Lady in Black' also has white flowers combined with dark stems and pink flower centers. It is worth trying out some other members of this genus, all of which make excellent pollinator plants. Tall plants can be cut back by about a third in late spring to keep the ultimate height and spread smaller. Asters are great in a wild garden or a flower border and are deer resistant. Buy plants by looking at their ultimate height, flower color, and resistance to foliar diseases. Combine asters with annual salvias, zinnias, or goldenrods.

*Symphyotrichum
novae-angliae
'Harrington's Pink'*

Tagetes tenuifolia

Tagetes patula

Tagetes / MARIGOLD

SHAPE daisy or dome
ROLE edging or mid-border delight
late spring to autumn // front to mid-back; containers //
6–48 in. × 6–24 in. // half-hardy annual

Marigolds are easy-to-grow half-hardy annuals that are staples of a cheery summer garden. Their flowers are bright yellow, creamy yellow, orange, or rusty red, with flowers of a single color or with contrasting stripes and circles in singles, semi-doubles, and double ball-shaped cultivars. They originated in Central America, so they are lovers of a sunny spot in any regular garden soil. The whole marigold plant has a characteristic pungent smell that deters deer from eating them.

French marigolds, *Tagetes patula*, are bushy plants that are best for the front of the border or in containers like a window box, where they need plenty of water. French marigolds are a companion plant that is used as a pest deterrent. *Tagetes tenuifolia*, signet marigold, has a delicate, wispy look. I like the cultivars 'Tangerine Gem' and 'Lemon Gem', which I grow in my herb garden as an edging. *Tagetes erecta*, African marigolds, are tall plants that look good in the mid-border and produce plentiful flowers for cutting. They are the only marigold I have found to be sometimes susceptible to rabbits. Try creamy yellow 'French Vanilla' as a change from the predominant orange and bright yellow cultivars. All marigolds can be started inside from seed or purchased from a nursery. To produce more flowers, pinch the growing tip of young plants and then cut and deadhead flowers all summer.

Tanacetum vulgare

Tanacetum parthenium

Tanacetum / FEVERFEW, TANSY, OR PAINTED DAISY

SHAPE daisy or button
ROLE mixer or mid-border delight
late spring to autumn // mid-front to back //
18–48 in. × 12–24 in. // zones 4–8, perennial

There are three main garden plants in the genus *Tanacetum*: tansy, feverfew, and painted daisies. These plants all have aromatic bright green divided foliage that looks great from spring to fall. They are not bothered by deer or rabbits, so use them around plants that herbivores will eat. They are suitable for an herb garden or a wild area.

Tanacetum parthenium, feverfew, has small, white, daisy-shaped flowers with yellow centers that are borne in profusion at the top of their stems in late spring through summer. Its fresh blooms combine well with yarrow, oregano, and pot marigold.

Tanacetum vulgare, tansy, is a mid or tall height plant, depending on its growing conditions, with flowers that appear in summer and continue to bloom into fall. It has little yellow button flowers with no ray florets that are great in the garden and as a cut flower. It can be an aggressive spreader and may seed into the bed, so divide every few years and deadhead blooms. In some areas, tansy is considered an invasive plant. *Tanacetum coccineum*, painted daisy, is a hardy flower with yellow centers surrounded by crimson red, fuchsia pink, or light pink petals. It is a front or mid-border plant that blooms from early to midsummer.

*Thalictrum
aquilegiifolium
*'Nimbus Pink'

Thalictrum
'Black
Stockings'

Thalictrum / MEADOW RUE

SHAPE cloud
ROLE mixer
late spring to autumn // mid-front to back //
24–72 in. × 24–30 in. // zones 4–8, perennial

Meadow rues are light, wispy plants with ethereal flower heads that are great planted at mid to back of the bed, where they take up little horizontal space relative to their height. The divided leaves are an attractive counterpoint to more solid foliage in the garden bed. They grow well in a plant-packed flower bed because their leaves can take being partially shaded by surrounding plants. *Thalictrum* flowers vary in form from single or double blooms to fluffy flowers with dangling stamens. Depending on the species and cultivar, they may be purple, white, pink, yellow, or greenish cream. There are meadow rues that bloom in late spring and others for summer. Heights vary from mid-border *T. aquilegiifolium* and Nimbus Series through to the skyscraper-tall cultivar 'Elin'. I like *T. delavayi* 'Hewitt's Double', with masses of multi-petaled lilac-colored flowers, the easygoing *T. rochebruneanum*, and the yellow-flowered *T. flavum*. Give them all an extra shovelful of compost when you are amending your flower bed, as they perform best with a moisture-retentive soil. Meadow rues are not eaten by deer or rabbits.

Thermopsis
villosa

Thymus serpyllum
'Pink Chintz'

Thermopsis / CAROLINA LUPINE

SHAPE spike
ROLE bold beauty or background
late spring and early summer // mid-back to back //
48–60 in. × 24–36 in. // zones 3–9, perennial

Carolina lupine, *Thermopsis villosa*, has spires of
yellow, pea-like flowers attached to tall flower stalks
that have upright, divided foliage similar to blue
false indigo. Flowering in late spring, this easy-care
perennial should be more widely grown, as it looks
great in flower, produces interesting seed heads, and
the leaves continue to look great until frost. They are
drought-tolerant plants with a long taproot, so plant
them in the correct place, as they are hard to move.
They are not troubled by herbivores or pests. There
are a number of other species of *Thermopsis* that you
could grow. Try Carolina lupines in gravel gardens or
wild areas with coneflowers, yarrow, and poppies.

Thymus / THYME

SHAPE cluster
ROLE tiny treasure
late spring and early summer // front; containers //
2–6 in. × 4–18 in. // zones 5–8, perennial

Thymes are some of the best fragrant, low-growing
flowering plants for the front of the border or for containers. They bloom in spring with miniature purple,
pink, and white flowers that are loved by bees. Grow
them in lean, inorganic soil with no added fertilizer, and
incorporate extra grit or stones into the soil and as a
mulch to improve drainage. Most people know thyme
as a culinary herb, but there are numerous creeping
ones that are grown for their decorative appearance.
Plant thyme in dry gardens, gravel gardens, or herb
gardens where they get good air circulation and will
not be crowded by neighbors. *Thymus vulgaris*, common thyme, is short and upright and provides leaves
for cooking. *Thymus serpyllum* is a popular species
of creeping thyme. To create a thyme carpet, place
plants between gravel-laid paving slabs or boulders.
I am especially partial to the low cultivar 'Elfin'.

Tithonia
rotundifolia

Triteleia laxa
'Queen Fabiola'

Tithonia / MEXICAN SUNFLOWER

SHAPE daisy
ROLE background or mid-border delight
high summer to autumn // mid-back to back //
48–96 in. × 24–36 in. // half-hardy annual

Tithonia rotundifolia, Mexican sunflower, has large, rich orange, daisy-like flowers that are borne on long, slightly fuzzy stems. It is a warm-season annual, so sow seed directly in the garden where it is to bloom in late spring, or start the plants inside earlier. It is one of the best lofty plants for late summer and early fall. If you garden for butterflies, this is a must-have flower to feed the last monarchs and swallowtails of the season. Keep deadheading the spent blooms to prolong flowering, and let some of the last ones go to seed for the birds to eat or collect them to sow next year. Plants have hollow stems, so shelter plants from strong winds or stake them. There are shorter cultivars like 'Fiesta del Sol' that suit small spaces and make good container plants. 'Yellow Torch' has flowers that are a melon-yellow color. I combine Mexican sunflower with other tall plants like amaranths, cosmos, and dahlias.

Triteleia / TRIPLET LILY

SHAPE loose dome
ROLE mixer
late spring and early summer // front to mid-front //
12–18 in. × 6 in. // zones 6–10, hardy bulb

The perky blue, white, or pink star-like flowers of *Triteleia laxa* are arranged in loose, open hemispheres that rise on slender stems in late spring and early summer. Triplet lilies perform best in an area with good sun and excellent drainage, so add extra grit or sand when planting. Triplet lilies do best with dry winter conditions and inorganic mulch. Plant the corm-like bulbs in fall in a rock garden, gravel garden, or at the top of a bank. I have a lovely patch of them growing among creeping phlox and pinks. I also have them growing among salvias, catmints, and yarrows in a cottage-like planting. This plant was previously called *Brodiaea*, and it may still be listed that way in catalogs.

Tropaeolum majus

Tulbaghia violacea

Tropaeolum / NASTURTIUM

SHAPE trumpet
ROLE mixer or container
late spring to autumn // front to mid-back //
12–48 in. × 12–36 in. // half-hardy annual

Tropaeolum majus, nasturtium, has trumpet-like flowers that are born on low-growing plants with beautiful round leaves. The flowers bloom in colors of orange, scarlet, yellow, magenta, or cream. Grow these cheerful hardy annuals from large, round seeds. They do best in free-draining infertile soils, otherwise plants tend to make more leaves than flowers. In hot weather, nasturtiums will decrease flower production, but if you have kept them watered, they should rebloom profusely in fall as the weather cools. Some cultivars are clumpers that do well at the front of a bed or in a container. Others have climbing or trailing stems that look great in hanging baskets, sprawling between plants in a border, or clothing a fence if you train their growing stems upward. There are cultivars with variegated leaves, like 'Alaska', and some, like the dwarf 'Empress of India', that have darker foliage. All parts of the plants are edible, with a peppery taste, so they can be thrown into salads or used to decorate your plates as long as they are grown without pesticides. Nasturtiums make nice short-stemmed cut flowers. Check the underside of leaves to make sure that there are no blackfly. If you find them, wash them off with water or squash them.

Tulbaghia / SOCIETY GARLIC

SHAPE star-like
ROLE mixer
high summer to autumn // front to mid-front; containers // 12–24 in. × 12 in. // zones 8–10, tender bulb

In colder regions, the slightly tender *Tulbaghia violacea*, society garlic, makes a wonderful container plant that can be brought inside for winter. It is loved in warm gardens for its violet clusters of tubular flowers that flare at the ends. It blooms in summer on narrow stems above strappy foliage. Grow it in an herb garden, in pots, or in a well-drained, sunny rock garden. I grow a variegated form whose leaves add interest to a collection of potted herbal plants. Society garlic has an odor that is not as strong as true garlic but still deters pests and herbivores. It thrives in Mediterranean climates.

Tulipa turkestanica

Tulipa 'West Point'

A red-and-white flame tulip.

Tulipa / TULIP

SHAPE cup
ROLE bold beauty or mid-border delight
early spring to early summer // front to mid-front;
containers // 6–30 in. × 3–4 in. // zones 3–8, hardy bulb

Tulips are some of the most delightful blooms of spring, with their iconic cup-shaped flowers in every color except blue. Species tulips are the closest to the wild tulips from which garden cultivars have been bred and are most likely to perennialize. Some of my favorites are *Tulipa clusiana*, with its alternating petal colors and slender form, *T. turkestanica*, with its multiple small white and yellow flowers that mingle well with other spring plants, and *T. humilis,* with its charming coloration and diminutive form.

Typical garden tulips are much larger and bloom in mid and late spring. You can grow them as annual bedding or container plants and then remove them to make way for your summer plantings, or choose long-lived cultivars, like Darwin hybrids, that will return year after year. To extend the show, include some early, mid-season, and late types. If you choose a color-coordinated scheme, they will look good together even if bloom times overlap. Tulips come in different forms, including doubles, multi-stemmed, and lily-flowered. I love the scented orange lily-flowered cultivar 'Ballerina', the exuberantly colored parrot tulips, and the classic cultivars 'Prinses Irene' and 'Couleur Cardinal'.

Even though they have the potential to be long-lived, tulips rarely last more than a handful of years in the garden. To help them return in subsequent years, allow the foliage to completely die down before removing it, and try some of the smaller species tulips, which tend to return for several springs. They are extremely attractive to burrowing and browsing animals, so their top growth needs to be protected from deer and rabbits by physical barriers or pungent sprays. Plant large garden tulips at least eight inches deep in extremely well-drained soil, and add gravel to the bottom of the planting hole to help with drainage. Their bulbs will rot in wet soil, so do not automatically irrigate them. Small tulips look good grown in window boxes or containers. Large tulips add magic to a spring border.

A collection of mid-spring garden tulips.

Verbascum
chaixii
'Sixteen
Candles'

Verbascum
phoeniceum
'Violetta'

Verbascum chaixii
'Album'

Verbascum / MULLEIN

SHAPE spike
ROLE bold beauty or mid-border delight
late spring to autumn // mid-front to back // 24–108 in.
× 12–30 in. // zones 5–8, short-lived perennial or biennial

Mulleins are a wonderful addition to a mixed bed because of their upright flowering spikes clothed with bowl-shaped flowers in yellow, white, purple, or pink. Some mullein plants make a single spike that acts as an architectural focal point. Others have a branched, candelabra-like presence. The foliage is basal, so despite their total height, they can be planted in the middle of the bed. The different species vary according to their eventual height and the fuzziness of their foliage. *Verbascum chaixii*, nettle-leaved mullein, and *V. nigrum*, dark mullein, have green, slightly leathery, textured leaves. They both produce tall stems of flowers, often in white or yellow with dark centers. Hybrids like *V.* 'Southern Charm' flower in ranges of dusty-rose and pale apricot. *Verbascum phoeniceum*, purple mullein, is best grown in very well-drained soil and tends to be short-lived. Look for the cultivar 'Violetta', which has vibrant purple flowers. *Verbascum*

bombyciferum is a tall, dramatic biennial with soft yellow flowers borne on a fuzzy, silvery-haired plant. *Verbascum olympicum* is the tallest type and has green leaves and a large torch of yellow flowers. Mulleins can be purchased as small plants or grown from seed. They are biennials or short-lived perennials, so renew your stock regularly by sprinkling seed around. They do well in medium to well-drained soils and can tolerate low fertility. Grow them in gravel gardens, cottage gardens, or regular flower beds. They may need staking if grown in overly fertile soils. They tend to be left alone by deer and rabbits. Some of the mullein species can be aggressive seeders or are listed as invasive in some areas.

Verbena bonariensis

Verbena ×hybrida

Verbena / VERVAIN

SHAPE dome
ROLE mixer or edger

late spring to autumn // front to mid-back; containers // 6–42 in. × 12–24 in. // zones 7–9, perennial or tender perennial

Two main types of vervains are commonly found in gardens. *Verbena bonariensis*, tall verbena, is a short-lived perennial or annual, depending on your climate. Even in cold areas, it can self-sow in place, perpetuating itself in any well-drained soil. The purple domed inflorescences are borne on long, rough, square stems, which makes it a great mingling plant that blooms from early summer to frost. This plant can be combined with other mid-height plants like foxgloves, bearded iris, and cosmos. It is attractive to pollinators and is not eaten by deer or rabbits.

There are a number of low-growing or trailing vervains that make excellent plants for containers or bed edges. *Verbena ×hybrida*, hybrid trailing vervain, is a short tender perennial that is grown as an annual. It forms low-growing or cascading mats. Cultivars are available in a wide range of colors, including red, purple, white, mid-pink, and various bicolors.

Vernonia lettermanii
'Iron Butterfly'

Vernonia noveboracensis

Vernonia / IRONWEED

SHAPE fluffy
ROLE mixer or background
high summer to autumn // mid-back to back //
30–84 in. × 24–36 in. // zones 5–9, perennial

Vernonia noveboracensis, New York ironweed, is a tall plant for the back of a bed. These majestic plants are known for their small, fluffy, purple flower heads clustered at the ends of tall stems that are covered from base to tip with good-quality mid-green leaves. Their tufts of flowers attract monarchs at the summer's end. Grow it in moist to wet soils. A shorter ironweed with soft, thread-like foliage, *V. lettermanii* 'Iron Butterfly', is suitable for dry or rocky soils. *Vernonia* 'Southern Cross' is a hybrid ironweed that is shorter than some of the species and has fine foliage. They all work well in flower borders, rain gardens, or in wild areas.

Ironweeds bloom late in the season and so make a perfect combination with goldenrods, asters, and border phlox for summer-into-fall interest.

Veronica ×media
'First Love'

Veronicastrum
virginicum
'Lavendelturm'

Veronica / SPEEDWELL

SHAPE spike
ROLE mid-border delight
late spring, early summer to high summer // front to
mid-front // 12–30 in. × 12–24 in. // zones 4-8, perennial

The most popular garden speedwells are narrow,
spike-flowered, summer perennials that are great for
mid-border, with flowers in blue, pink, purple or white.
Veronica longifolia and *V. spicata*, spiked speedwell,
have tiny flowers that open from the bottom of their
flowering spires upward. Look for the blue-flowered
'Royal Candles', the white flowers of 'Icicle', or the reddish pink 'Red Fox', also called 'Rotfuchs'. The upright
blooms combine well with the horizontal flowers of
yarrow and the diffuse flower sprays of catmint. Plant
speedwells in moist but well-drained soils. They are
deer and rabbit resistant and attractive to butterflies.
Deadhead them after flowering.

Veronicastrum / CULVER'S ROOT

SHAPE spike
ROLE background
high summer to autumn // back of the border //
36–72 in. × 24–36 in. // zones 3–9, perennial

If you are looking for a dramatic vertical accent for
the back of the border that blooms in late summer,
consider *Veronicastrum virginicum*. It rises up with
whorled leaves and a central spike surrounded by
multiple other bottlebrush-like flowers, which makes
the whole inflorescence resemble a white, light lavender, purple, or slightly pink candelabra. Grow Culver's
root in moist soil for maximum height alongside
Joe-Pye weeds and turtleheads. Look for the popular
cultivars 'Fascination' and 'Lavendelturm', sometimes listed by the English name 'Lavender Towers'.
Culver's root plants take a couple of years to establish
themselves and attain their full height, but they are
worth the wait. They are perfect for rain gardens and
pollinator-friendly plantings.

Veronicastrum
virginicum
'Album'

A carpet planting of
Viola ×wittrockiana

*Viola
×wittrockiana*

Viola / VIOLETS, PANSIES, AND JOHNNY-JUMP-UPS

SHAPE bilaterally symmetrical
ROLE tiny treasure
early spring to early summer; late summer into autumn // front; containers // 6–12 in. × 6–12 in. // zones 3–9, perennial or hardy annual

Violas, or violets, are short plants that are a welcome addition to the cool-season garden. The edible flat-faced flowers come in a cheerful range of colors and multi-colors and can be eaten in salads or candied to decorate cakes. Pansies and the smaller Johnny-jump-ups are annuals or biennials. *Viola ×wittrockiana*, garden pansy, has a larger flower than the perennial violas, and is a lovely spring and fall addition. Choose your favorite colors and tuck them in as a temporary addition. The smaller *V. tricolor*, Johnny-jump-up, is great to tuck in between other plants in a flower bed where they may seed themselves into your garden. The perennial *V. odorata*, sweet violet, has been loved in gardens for centuries. The specific epithet *odorata* means "fragrant." If you gather a little bunch of them or get down on your hands and knees, you can smell their honey-like scent. Plant any violas at the front of a flower bed or in containers.

Xerochrysum
bracteatum
'Sunbrella Red'

Xerochrysum / EVERLASTING DAISY

SHAPE daisy
ROLE mid-border delight
high summer to autumn // mid-front to mid-back;
containers // 12–36 in. × 6–18 in. // zones 8–10,
tender perennial

This everlasting daisy, or strawflower, has been known by several Latin names but is currently called the tongue-twisting *Xerochrysum bracteatum*. The flower makes a great addition to a sensory garden, as the outer petals feel almost like paper, and the open centers resemble a tiny soft cushion. The flowers are available in a lovely range of colors, including yellow, orange, red, pink, and white. They are great for fresh or dried flower arrangements and will retain their shape and color. Pick the bristly-petaled flowers while in loose bud, as they will continue to open. Dry them by hanging them upside down in a cool, dry, shady place. Grow this plant from seed sown in normal garden soil after the last frost, or start it indoors.

Yucca filamentosa
'Color Guard'

Zephyranthes
candida

Yucca / YUCCA

SHAPE spike
ROLE bold beauty
high summer // mid-front to mid-back // 36–72 in. ×
24–36 in. // zones 5–9, perennial

Yucca filamentosa is one of the most indestructible
flowers you can grow in a garden. I am a convert to
the easy-care drama of the variegated forms like
'Color Guard', which has yellow centers to its basal
rosette of elongated leaves. One of its common
names, Adam's needle, is an apt descriptor, as its
leaves have a sharp tip, so do not plant it near a path
or a bench. Instead, site it where you can admire its
architectural presence and tall, cream-colored, summer flower spike composed of bell-shaped individual
flowers. Yuccas can be grown in dry areas, coastal
gardens, roadside gardens, or in a place with poor
soil. Deer and rabbits avoid this plant.

Zephyranthes / RAIN LILY

SHAPE cup
ROLE tiny treasure
late summer into autumn // front; containers //
4–12 in. × 2–6 in. // zones 7–10, bulb

Rain lilies, *Zephyranthes*, are an unusual choice for
a flower garden, as some of them only bloom after
summer rains. Their grassy foliage emerges first and
nicely frames the crocus-shaped flowers that arrive
later. Several species are native to warm parts of
the Americas, but in colder climates they do well in
containers that are brought inside and kept quite dry
during the winter. Where they are borderline hardy,
try them in a rock or gravel garden. They require a
well-drained spot to thrive. Choose rain lilies by cold
hardiness and by flower color. *Zephyranthes candida*
has a white flower, *Z. robustus* is pink, and *Z. citrina* is
bright yellow.

A mixed planting of *Zinnia elegans*.

Zinnia marylandica 'Zahara Starlight Rose'

Zinnia / ZINNIA

SHAPE daisy
ROLE mid-border delight

late spring to autumn // mid-front to mid-back;
containers // 12–36 in. × 12–24 in. // half-hardy annual

If you are looking for a colorful addition to a summer flower patch, grow some zinnias. There is a wide range of vibrant red, orange, yellow, pink, magenta, fuchsia, and creamy white colors. If you want something different, look for novel bicolored flowers. Flower shape varies, from the cactus type to little buttons and medium-sized discs. The single flowers are daisy-like with an obvious center, the semi-doubles have extra rows of petals, and the doubles are like pompons. Pick flowers for arrangements, and deadhead regularly. Pollinators love zinnias, and birds love to eat the seeds at the end of the season. Tall ones are best at the back of a border or as a cut flower, whereas the short-statured ones make a fabulous container plant or bed edging. The key to success with zinnias is to choose disease-resistant plants, as they can get foliar diseases like leaf spot or powdery mildew. Keep the roots, not the leaves, of the plants well watered during dry spells, and space them out to allow good air circulation. Zinnias are easy to start from seed planted right into the ground after the soil has warmed up, or they can be started indoors if you have a short growing season. Many of the cultivars used in a cutting garden are *Zinnia elegans*. I have many favorites, but if in doubt I go with the tried-and-true 'Benary's Giant' for tall plants, 'Cut and Come Again' for mid-height flowers, and then 'Dreamland' or 'Thumbelina' for compact specimens. *Zinnia marylandica* and *Z. haageana* are good choices for containers. Combine them with celosia, cosmos, and marigolds for an annual garden that looks good outside and provides cut flowers all summer long.

Various brightly colored *Zinnia elegans*

A personal assemblage of salvias, zinnias, mountain mint, coneflower, crocosmia, and lily of the Nile among other flowers in a private garden.

You have had a chance to really get to know individual flowers and their qualities. These are the building blocks of your flower bed design. In the following chapter you will decide where to plant them, look at inspirational gardens to get ideas for your own, and learn how to assemble aesthetically pleasing groups of flowers.

Laying the Groundwork for Your Flower Garden

Location, Inspiration, and Design

Your flower garden is a place where you can be yourself and relax year-round. Life is often serious, so it is lovely to have an outlet where you can just enjoy yourself for a while. I think of my flower garden as a playground. What a brilliant way to spend a day: outside, playing with my flowers. Even now, I get excited at the prospect of planning a new garden. But before I get too carried » away, I remind myself of a few essential practical considerations. Choosing the garden location and outlining the shape and size of the flower bed is the first step. Once that is decided, I can move on to plant selection, design, and planting.

Choosing a Location to Grow Your Flowers

You may have some idea where you are going to plant your flowers, but before you put a shovel into the ground or lug your garden containers to their final positions, take the time to consider some practical and aesthetic aspects of situating your garden.

FINDING SUITABLE GROWING CONDITIONS

As you consider placement, you may picture an entirely new area or a fresh look for an existing space. Wherever you plan to site the bed, make sure that the conditions are right for the flowers you want to grow. Most garden flowers grow best and produce the most blooms in an area with full sun, usually defined as six hours or more of direct sunlight each day. In the northern hemisphere, a south-facing bed gets the most light, whereas in the southern hemisphere, a north-facing bed will be the sunniest. Take note of things that could block sunlight: trees, shrubs, hedges, walls, a house, hills, or banks that surround the garden. If you have between two and six hours of sun a day, you have part sun, also called part shade, and will need to choose a different set of plants. Fewer than two hours of sunlight is considered full shade, and these conditions also have their own plant palette.

Sun-loving flowers will grow with fewer than six hours but maybe not as vigorously as they would with full sun. Stems tend to elongate as they reach for light, and the plants produce fewer flowers. Dappled sunlight from overhead trees can produce more shade than you realize. Two or three hours of dappled shade might equal about one hour of direct sunlight, but it is a more unpredictable amount than if the sky were open above the garden. To get more light to your flowers, site a new bed farther away from any shade-producing object, which also lets more precipitation reach it because trees and the eaves of your house can block rainfall as well as sun. Evaluate whether you could trim a few overhanging branches to let in a little more sun. Get professional help if it is a large tree or if you are not

The *Alstroemeria*, Peruvian lily, and queen-of-the-prairie in this bed do well with some afternoon shade.

sure what to do. When planting a new woody plant, make sure it isn't on the sunny side of your flower garden.

A partly sunny area is often sheltered, cooler in the summer, and allows you to grow a wider diversity of plants than you can in full sun alone. Within a fully sunny garden, you may still have spots shaded by tall plants or a structure. These are a few plants that could be tucked into those places.

Anemone ×hybrida, Japanese anemone

Astrantia major, great masterwort

Digitalis purpurea, common foxglove

Filipendula rubra, queen-of-the-prairie

Gillenia trifoliata, Bowman's root

Lamprocapnos spectabilis, bleeding heart

Lychnis coronaria, rose campion

Scilla siberica, Siberian squill

Symphyotrichum cordifolium, blue wood aster

Viola odorata, sweet violet

Another consideration, but one not usually taken into account, is the heat produced by the sun. The hottest time of the day is late afternoon. This can be desirable or not, depending on your situation and the plants you plan to grow. If you live in a warm or hot climate, some flowers will perform better if they are in morning sun and afternoon shade rather than blazing heat at the end of the day, which can burn and dehydrate them. In a cool climate, the warmth of the afternoon sun may be welcome.

These gloriosa daisies and blanket flowers are perfect for a sunny bed.

The soil for your flower garden is of vital importance for good plant growth. Soil is the medium in which your plants' roots grow. They anchor themselves in it, and it provides the water and nutrients they need for growth. The geology beneath your house and garden makes up the inorganic matter in your soil and influences its pH (soil acidity or alkalinity). At the soil surface, the subsoil is mixed with organic matter that falls from trees and other plants to form topsoil, a fertile mix that is perfect for most flowering plants. Before you start your garden, look carefully at the topsoil in your bed. You may already know if you live in an area of heavy clay or loose sandy soil. Clay-based soils are easily identified because they are hard to dig, the soil is heavy, and if you look closely and rub it between your fingers it has tiny particles. The benefits of this soil type are that it is nutrient rich and great for plant anchorage. The downsides are that it gets waterlogged after heavy rain and is as hard as a terracotta pot when it dries out. Sandy soil is the opposite. It has large, grainy particles that you can feel between your fingers. It drains really well but is low in nutrients, as they wash away with water. When you look and feel your garden soil, you may not have one of these extreme types of soil. Soils that are a mixture of clay, sand, and silt are referred to as loams. This is a desirable soil type for flower gardening.

Whatever your soil type, there are flowering plants that will suit it. If you are amending the soil, try to prepare it a season before you want to plant. The easiest way to improve topsoil as you prepare to grow garden flowers is to add lots of compost and other organic-rich materials to the surface of the soil. Organic matter improves water-holding capacity, drainage, and available nutrients. Clay soils become more open in structure and sandy soils hold on to water and nutrients for longer with these additions. Another possible soil addition is small-scaled stones such as grit or gravel. My favorite is the insoluble grit that is used to help chickens with their digestion. I use it as a top dressing on pots and beds and mixed into soil to help improve drainage, especially in heavy clay. Grit or other chipped stone is necessary if you are growing rock garden plants that require free-draining mineral-rich soils.

Water is essential to establish new plants in your garden. Think about how you will get enough water to your new plants' roots during their first season or two of growth in the soil. The amount of water you will need to add depends on the plants you choose, the way you plant them, and your climate. If you want to grow annuals, they will need to be watered throughout the year, so they should be within easy reach of your hose.

SIZE, SHAPE, AND ARRANGEMENT OF YOUR FLOWER BEDS

Flowers like these rudbeckias and spider flowers grow well when gathered together into a bed.

Garden flowers are normally grown clustered together into beds or borders that allow you to efficiently pre-pare and improve the soil. Beds may be any shape or size that suits the location and surroundings. Island beds are those that can be viewed from all sides, with lawn or paths around them. Elongated beds beside a path or fence that are longer than they are wide are often described as borders. They may be single or set out symmetrically on either side of a driveway or walkway.

Once you have decided on the position of the bed, you can consider its size and shape. One of the main determi-nants of bed size is how much space you think you can plant and look after. The amount of energy, time, and money needed to prepare the bed, purchase plants, and tend to it throughout the year increases with the dimen-sions. If you are just beginning your adventures with flower gardening, it is best to start with a little area. You can expand a petite jewel of a flower bed later if you find that you can easily take care of it. If you are an experienced gardener, you will know how much space you can look after in the time you have available.

Another important factor is that you need to be able to reach every plant in the bed without stepping on the soil. Every time you step into a bed, you squash the air needed for root growth out of the soil. Make the bed no wider than you can reach. An island bed, where you can access plants from all sides, can be wide. If you want to create an even wider bed for greater impact or to match the scale of the surroundings, provide yourself with strategically placed stepping-stones.

A narrow, elon-gated bed runs along the outside of a fenced garden.

Formal and Informal Flower Beds

Flower gardens can be arranged in a formal or informal manner or a combination of the two. Bed shape and layout indicate where the garden falls on the formality spectrum. Formal beds are square, rectangular, or otherwise strongly geometric in shape. They are often situated near the house and fit in with its architectural lines. They may be arranged in symmetrical pairs or as a pattern of beds. One formal arrangement is four even beds with a cross-shaped path running between them. This traditional four-square design dates back hundreds of years but is still popular today, particularly for enclosed flower, herb, or vegetable gardens. Another favored formal arrangement

Straight paths and symmetrical plantings are characteristic of formal gardens like the herb garden at the Pennsylvania Horticultural Society garden at Meadowbrook Farm.

Informal flower beds like this one in a private garden may have flowing, intermingled plantings.

gardens with few straight lines that you want to follow, where there are undulations in the landscape, or where an informal style is desired. Amorphous beds are used in larger gardens and in gardens that border the countryside or wild areas. You can combine formal and informal beds in the same garden.

Formality or informality is found not only in the outline of the beds and how they are placed but also in how flowers are arranged within the beds. In a formal planting scheme, plants are lined up in rows, set out in regular blocks, or arranged in other neat patterns. Plantings may be symmetrical within a bed or mirrored across adjacent borders. Extremely formal gardens require trimming and nipping to keep them looking tidy. The beauty of these gardens comes from the overall orderly impression of the patterns.

Informal planting has a relaxed look, with intermingled combinations or loose drifts grown from irregularly placed plants or scattered seeds. Plants are used in abundance to produce an overflowing look, and paths meander between the flowers. These are sometimes called naturalistic, which means they emulate scenes found in nature. Naturalistic gardens fit easily into casual lifestyles and busy schedules. Their relaxed look requires little maintenance if they are thoughtfully planned and planted. Most planting schemes fall somewhere between formal and informal, with elements of both in their beds.

is a matched set of borders that face each other across a swath of grass or a path. Gardens in urban settings tend to have elements of formality, as they are influenced and bounded by rectilinear buildings. Beds can follow the buildings' lines and be edged by materials that coordinate with their surroundings.

Informal beds are rounded, vaguely oval, or fluid in outline. They fit into

Your flower bed can be any shape that you like. It may be dictated by your overall garden, your house, or other existing trees, paths, and structures. A simply shaped bed often looks better than a complicated one. A straight-edged square or rectangular bed could line a linear path or driveway. Curved beds can be used where existing structures prevent straight edges or along sinuous paths. If a bed adjoins a lawn, it is a good idea to keep the edges as straight as possible to make it easy to mow without inadvertently clipping your flowers. Another way to simplify bed maintenance is to line the edge with stones, bricks, or other hard materials. You can use these to slightly raise the soil level in the planting bed to improve drainage, or place the stones flush with the lawn to allow easy mowing.

If you are not sure where to place your flower bed, put it where you can enjoy seeing it every day: next to outdoor seating, anywhere you walk past, or in a place you can see from a prominent window or door. Perhaps you'd like to see it from where you have your morning cup of tea or coffee or take your evening meals. You will get maximum enjoyment from flowers if they are somewhere that you will interact with them daily.

Flowers can also be grown in pots or other containers. This method allows you to garden on paved surfaces where there is no soil. It is also useful where the soil is poor quality or the wrong type for what you want to grow. Fill the pot with a potting mix that suits the plants. Unleash your creativity with your choice of pots and how you arrange them. Containers look dramatic gathered together around a door, near a seating area, or on a deck or patio. Most flowers in containers require frequent watering, so cluster them near an outdoor tap to save water and effort.

top A front-of-the-border planting with creeping thyme, sea thrift, love-in-a-mist, and white lace flower.

above A rectangular stone trough container with yellow and purple viola is perfect next to a door.

MAKING A GARDEN FOR YOU AND YOUR FAMILY

Set yourself up for success by creating a garden that works for you and your family. Gardens can be a personal expression, an extension of your house, a playground, a place for hobbies, a relaxing area, an entertaining space, and more. As you develop your flower garden, think about how you and your family use your outdoor space. Maybe for you it is a lovely place to sit or walk, to be out in nature, and do your gardening. The main reason people grow flowers is to beautify their garden, so contemplate which flowers are beautiful to you. Include flowers that smell lovely, are edible, or appeal to any of your senses. You might consider flowers for wildlife, or the ecological benefits that your garden could provide. Whatever flowers you choose, make sure they suit your needs and wants.

Think about who you are making this garden for. If you have children or dogs, they will probably be playing in the garden, so choose plants that are friendly for them. Kid-proof plants also have to be strong, as I found out when my border was constantly in use as a soccer goal. I chose plenty of tough flowers to use in front that were fairly indestructible but still pleasing to my eye.

It is a good idea to plan for somewhere to sit near your flower bed. A garden is a lovely setting to have an outdoor dining table where you can take tea or have

Include a place to sit so you can relax and observe your flowers at different times of the day.

a meal with friends. Placing an inviting chair or bench gives you a destination when you walk out into your garden. You can take a book out there or just day-dream for a while and watch the flowers, insects, and birds. At that moment, you are in and among your flowers and part of the garden, not a mere observer. There is the likelihood that you will not sit for long, because you will spot a little something that needs taking care of, but that is part of the pleasure that your garden is giving back to you.

PATHS FOR ACCESS AND ENJOYMENT

My garden is an integral part of my life, and I love to check on it daily. It is only then that I get the whole experience of bud to flower and flower to seed head. I tend to rush into the garden after work regardless of my footwear, so paths keep my feet dry while providing access. Paths govern the way that we experience our gardens.

Paths are both utilitarian, allowing you to get to the garden whatever the weather, and part of the overall aesthetic look. The lines of a path lead your eye into the garden as you explore it. A straight path leads you to an area quickly and tends to speed up your walking pace. A curved path forces you to slow down and watch your step as you look at the flowers. Plants located in the nook of a curve are viewed from several sides as you walk, so plant these areas with favorite flowers.

Path material is also important. The surface has to be safe to walk on and not slippery in damp weather. Choose stepping-stones or chipped stone to provide traction. Both options allow rainwater to filter into the ground. Some of the simplest materials to use are gravel, wood chips, or a basic grass path.

A path through an herb garden provides easy access to smell the flowers.

Visitors really appreciate paths because they offer clues about where to walk for the best views. Provide interesting plants, vignettes, or objects to lead people around your garden. Walk along the path one way and then back the other way to check how flowers look from both directions. Small gardens or ones that center on a lawn don't require paths.

The width of a path affects how fast you walk and how you interact with the surrounding plants. If you want to use your paths for strolling, make them wide

from left Line your path with flowers like lamb's ears, betony 'Hummelo', and sweet alyssum.

This dry-laid stone path draws visitors through a gravel garden, which features California poppies.

enough that plants can tumble over the edges without impeding your pace. Wide paths also allow you to walk with someone and share the special experience of being in a garden. A broad path is a good choice for utilitarian paths, like from a garage or sidewalk to the door where you might be carrying packages. In contrast, I have a garden with a deliberately narrowed path that lets only one person at a time pass down it. The surrounding plantings are fragrant herbs that release scent as you brush by them. There is a sense of safety and enclosure as you are engulfed by flowers. You can really take the time to smell them, touch them, and observe them up close. If your planting beds abut a path or patio, make sure there are no spiky plants that could injure people.

The final type of path is the one only you know exists. In a wide bed or border, set up an inconspicuous and narrow path toward the rear. You can use it to get to all parts of your flower bed to smell a bloom, pull a little weed, or pick a flower without stepping on aerated soil. By providing a way to get into the heart of the bed, you are increasing your chances of interacting with your garden and enjoying it from a new perspective.

HEDGES, WALLS, AND FENCES

Hedges, walls, and fences provide extra privacy, protect from prevailing winds and browsing herbivores, and can make a nice backdrop for your flower borders. They might run along your garden's perimeter or surround a smaller area within it. Aesthetically, a flower bed can look lovely against the green of a hedge or backed by a fence, which can also help support tall plants. Fences or walls are great protection from animals who might otherwise devour your plants. Keeping them out of an enclosed area allows you to grow plants they would normally eat. If there is a hedge behind a flower bed, leave a couple of feet between the planting and the hedge to reduce root competition and give you room to trim the hedge and work on tall plants at the back of the border.

The hedge in this garden provides a backdrop that showcases fall flowers.

If you garden where there is a strong prevailing wind, think about adding protection for your flower bed. A certain amount of air circulation through plants is good, as it reduces fungal disease, but too much wind can be destructive. Most flowers grow on slender stems, and strong blasts can snap off their heads or blow entire plants over. A fence, wall, or hedge can be a wind break to shelter plants from the worst damage.

I am very fond of an enclosed garden. Perhaps it is because I grew up in England, where they are very popular, or maybe it is the romantic notion of a secret garden. Even a slightly hidden bench where you can rest and take in the sights and sounds of your garden becomes your own private haven. You feel a sense of seclusion, where flower fragrances are amplified and bird songs are clearer.

Looking for Flower Garden Inspiration

The idea for your flower garden may come to you out of the blue as an idle thought when you are flicking through sumptuous garden pictures or as you wander around a friend's garden. Existing gardens can act as the catalyst for your own flower garden thinking. They provide the inspiration to get your creative ideas flowing.

As you learn about flowers and flower gardening, visit as many gardens as you can. What you are looking for is that flash of a thought that you can then bring home and use to guide your choices. Your garden will not be the same as any that you see, but it may combine little things from each. If I go on a garden visit and learn one new plant or get a great idea, it makes my day. Mind you, what is better than spending the day in a garden?

Stroll around your neighborhood to see what other people are doing in their yards. Go on private garden visits organized by local gardening groups. They are a delightful treat where individual garden owners welcome you through their gates to see their own patch of ground. Local garden tours are particularly useful because you will probably be able to grow the same flowers in your own garden. It is also a way to meet like-minded garden people who can give you advice and maybe even some plants. Gardening is definitely all about plants and plant appreciation, but a lot of joy comes from sharing it with the wider community of gardeners.

Public gardens are also very helpful places to go as you continue gathering your garden thoughts. Walk around until you find one or two areas that you like the most. Concentrate on these sections and work out what you like about them. Public gardens are a good source for practical information because flowers are often labeled with their names, and garden staff might be able to answer questions. You can visit the garden several times during the year to see how its flower beds change and take plenty of photos for reference. Keep a record of your thoughts about the visits in the same place as your flower wish list. Jot down anything that might help you improve your present or future garden. Your garden-visit notes might even be a place to doodle—whether or not you can draw. You can also start a visual file of flowers and garden styles that appeal to you.

In addition to your in-person visits, keep browsing images of inspirational gardens. Note any flowers or features you are repeatedly drawn to, as these are likely to bring you pleasure in your own garden. You are identifying things that you like, even if you are not sure why you are drawn to them. Pay attention to configurations, combinations, and colors that consistently catch your eye. You may not have thought about your garden preferences before, but you can hone your tastes by immersing yourself in garden possibilities and taking good notes.

opposite Visiting the private gardens of knowledgeable local gardeners can help you envision what is possible in your own garden.

from left Artistic public gardens like Chanticleer in Wayne, Pennsylvania, can be marvelously inspiring when you are developing your own flower garden.

While you cannot recreate the total effect of a public garden, find combinations like this red poppy and white lace flower to try at home.

The personal flower garden you develop over time will reflect your interests, passions, and personality. There are many styles and themes of flower gardening to use as inspiration for your own creation. You can choose to pursue one particular style or make a combination of several. Look through the following examples to get an idea of possible types of flower gardens.

COTTAGE GARDENS

Cottage gardens are a traditional European informal garden style that originated as a practical solution to limited growing space. The gardens that surrounded these little houses were packed with everything the cottage dwellers needed, including vegetables, flowers, herbs, and fruit. The hallmark of this garden style is the constant parade of flowers that emerge and bloom throughout the growing season within a relatively small space. Every available inch is packed with plants, from bulbs to perennials to annuals, and herbs and vegetables, which are perfectly at home alongside the flowers. Self-sowing annuals and biennials are the glue that binds these gardens together, as they tend to proliferate throughout the space and provide unity and visual continuity.

Classic cottage-garden plants such as hollyhocks, foxgloves, delphiniums, and roses are beloved by proponents of this style. These flowers don't grow well everywhere in the world, so to keep the overall look and feel of this style, adapt the plant palette to your climate. For example, where summers are cool, delphiniums are one of the glories of the garden. Here in the hot and humid summers of the mid-Atlantic coast of the United States, delphiniums are hard to establish as a perennial. I love them, but instead I choose to grow lots of the annual blue larkspur, which has a similar, though less grand, look.

There are many places around the world where you can visit a cottage garden. You may even own a cottage yourself and have, or would like to have, this charming style of garden. It is still a practical solution for today's small gardens and can be scaled up to fill larger areas.

In addition to classic hollyhocks, foxgloves, and delphiniums, these plants are lovely choices for a cottage garden: *Aquilegia vulgaris*, columbine; *Campanula*, bellflower; *Dianthus barbatus*, sweet William; *Geranium*, hardy geranium; *Lathyrus odoratus*, sweet pea; *Lupinus*, lupine; *Papaver*, poppy.

from left Cottage gardens, like this one, are characterized by closely planted flowers that may self-sow, including verbascum, goldenrod, and hollyhock.

Annual poppies mix and mingle with perennials like betony and lupine in this cottage-style planting.

Plant plenty of flowers you can use for cutting, like these vibrant red lilies and dahlias.

opposite You can dedicate a separate space for growing cut flowers, or you can harvest from your borders.

CUT FLOWER GARDENS

I love to grow plenty of flowers to cut and enjoy in vases in my house. I enjoy cutting flowers from my beds as I stroll around the garden, but for big bouquets, I have a dedicated cutting garden that I can raid without denuding the rest of my borders. It is also a real treat to be able to give them away to friends and family. A bunch of flowers from your garden is always an appropriate gift, whatever the occasion. Growing cut flowers provides us with pleasure in our daily lives, indoors and out.

If you want to grow cut flowers in your garden, they can be incorporated into your regular flower beds, or you can grow a separate row or two specifically for cutting. Growing cut flowers in rows makes it easy to look after them and pick them. They can be in any sunny spot and would be perfectly happy alongside your vegetables. Wherever you plant them, water them well while they are in active growth, and make sure that the soil is full of good organic matter. Harvest flowers regularly and deadhead the old blooms to prolong flowering time.

Annuals are some of the best plants to use for cutting, as they bloom for several months once they have matured. Bulbs and perennials also provide flowers at different times of the year. Any plants you grow for cut flowers should produce plentiful blooms that last for a few days in a vase. As you choose flowers for your bunches, look at the flower shapes and colors carefully. If you have a lovely mixed flower garden, cutting flowers from it will produce fantastic arrangements.

These beautiful flowers will be sure to enhance your cutting garden and delight anyone who receives a bunch from you: *Achillea millefolium*, yarrow; *Antirrhinum majus*, snapdragon; *Celosia argentea*, celosia; *Centaurea cyanus*, cornflower; *Cosmos bipinnatus*, cosmos; *Dahlia*, dahlia; *Narcissus*, daffodil; *Paeonia lactiflora*, peony; *Rudbeckia hirta*, black-eyed Susan; *Zinnia elegans*, zinnia.

from left You can create an entire planting of annuals grown from seed, like this swath of cosmos, zinnias, and sunflowers.

A bright carpet bed of orange zinnia, red geraniums, *Pelargonium*, and canna.

A GARDEN OF ANNUAL FLOWERS

Annuals are the quickest and most colorful flowering plants you can grow. Though they live only one year, they tend to be inexpensive to grow yourself from seeds or buy as small starter plants. They need plenty of sun, water, and nutrient-rich soil to make lots of flowers in a short period of time. Depending on the height, shape, and color of the plant, they can be used for different purposes in the garden. An advantage to growing annual plants is that you can choose one group of flowers this year, then change them out for different ones in the same place next year.

Annual flowers are sometimes used in public parks and municipal plantings to produce colorful patterns. Each block of the design is filled with multiples of one flower in a bold color to create an eye-catching and vibrant seasonal garden. This style of gardening is called carpet bedding for its resemblance to a colorful patterned area rug. We can use bedding annuals in a similar way in our own gardens if we want some brilliant color for the summer.

A version of a stinze planting with white and blue flowering bulbs in grass around an old crabapple tree in my garden.

FLOWERS IN GRASS

If you are looking for other places to grow flowers in your garden, think about adding some into existing grassy areas. This is a way to increase the flowery impression of your garden without adding more beds.

One of the easiest ways to add early-season joy to the garden is to plant masses of spring bulbs. Bulbs are perfectly at home in flower beds, but if you add an overabundance of them into the beds, there is no room to plant later-blooming flowers. Instead, plant some bulbs into the grass and then allow them to naturalize. In the Netherlands these delightful flower-spangled patches surround old manor houses and are called stinze plantings.

To make your own stinze planting, select an area of weak lawn grass that will not outcompete the flowers. If necessary, remove small bits of grass as you plant. Choose bulbs that will emerge early in the spring before the grass starts its summer growth. Plant lots of bulbs of one type for a soothing and peaceful effect among the green of the grass, or mix various types together to make shape and color choices that please you. Careful selection can produce a succession of bloom from early to late spring. Leave the grass uncut until the bulb foliage has died down.

These bulbs are a good way to liven up a dull grassy area next spring: *Anemone blanda*, Grecian windflower; *Camassia*, camas; *Crocus*, crocus; *Fritillaria meleagris*, snake's head fritillary; *Galanthus nivalis*, common snowdrop; *Ipheion uniflorum*, spring starflower; *Muscari*, grape hyacinth; *Narcissus poeticus* var. *recurvus*, pheasant's eye daffodil; *Puschkinia libanotica*, striped squill; *Scilla bifolia*, alpine squill.

Blue grape hyacinths, *Muscari latifolium* and *M.* 'Peppermint', Grecian windflower, and white glory-of-the-snow planted in grass.

WATER-WISE FLOWER GARDENS

We each garden with certain climate, weather, and soil conditions. If we understand our environment and choose plants that suit it, we will need less time, money, and resources to take care of our gardens. One of the most important things to consider is precipitation. Plan your garden to efficiently use all the rain that falls, and consider how much additional water you have available. If you match the moisture requirements of the plants to the amount of rainfall you naturally receive, you may not need to water them at all after their initial establishment.

Water is required for plant growth because it makes up a high percentage of each cell. Thirsty plants like tender perennials and annuals require frequent watering, as they put on fast growth in a relatively short period of time. Plants grown in containers, hanging baskets, and window boxes tend to need regular additions of water because their roots are in a finite volume of soil. If you want to garden within the limits of your natural rainfall, carefully chosen herbaceous perennials and many bulbs need far less water than annuals. Consider growing plants that are well adapted to your area, like tried-and-true, easy-to-grow perennials that will tolerate a wide range of garden conditions.

All plants need water to develop their root system, but how much they need depends on the plants you choose and where and how you plant them. Your aim is to select those that will love living in your garden. Some plants do well in wet soil, while others need dry soil with really good drainage. Once perennial plants make nice deep roots, they should pretty much be able to look after their own water needs. This is ecologically sustainable and will be less work for you.

Drought-tolerant combination of perennial rattlesnake master, yarrow, and giant yellow knapweed.

Whatever your current climate, it seems we all have to be prepared for more weather extremes and extended periods of drought in the future. Planning ahead and thinking about gardening for erratic rainfall makes sense. One of the best steps is to choose drought-tolerant plants from the beginning. This works if you live in an arid climate, would like to grow flowers in an area that is extremely dry, such as a bed that is a long way from an outdoor water source, or if you don't want to water your garden much at all. These are all good reasons to choose plants that can grow with little to no additional water.

Drought-tolerant plants come from different regions of the world. They have evolved to grow in areas of low or irregular rainfall and actually fail to thrive if grown with an irrigation system or in wintertime soggy soil. Some may be able to tolerate a year-round lack of rain, while others need water at specific times in their growing cycle. If you want to grow a drought-tolerant plant that requires drainage, the planting bed may be raised above ground level to help direct water away from the roots, and rocks, gravel, and grit can be added to the soil.

One popular style that doesn't require a lot of water is a gravel garden. The soil is topped by a few inches of attractive chipped stones or small pebbles. Using gravel as a mulch keeps the underside of the foliage dry and reduces rotting. It also insulates the soil from temperature extremes and keeps it moist. Aesthetically, gravel has a clean look that provides a good backdrop to show off plants.

Sea hollies like *Eryngium planum* 'Blaukappe' are great choices for a low-water-use garden.

Another way of gardening with low water use is a rock garden, sometimes called a rockery. This type is also mulched with stone, and large rocks are included around the perimeter and within the bed, often half buried into the ground to increase drainage. Most of the plants traditionally used in rock gardens are short carpeting plants that hate to be smothered by leaves or organic mulch. They are often from arid areas or steep mountain slopes that are covered by snow for long periods and where any rain or meltwater drains away quickly. Little bulbous plants are a great addition to a rock garden, as they need dry conditions when they are in their dormant phase. Use low-growing plants to creep over gravel and garden edges and to soften the look of the stone.

Whether you are creating a rock or gravel garden or simply want to take a water-wise approach to gardening, these drought-tolerant plants offer a range of flowers and foliage: *Achillea millefolium*, yarrow; *Armeria maritima*, sea thrift; *Asclepias tuberosa*, butterfly weed; *Baptisia australis*, blue false indigo; *Echinops ritro*, globe thistle; *Eryngium planum*, flat sea holly; *Gaura lindheimeri*, white gaura; *Hylotelephium spectabile*, sedum; *Iris* ×*germanica*, bearded iris; *Salvia yangii*, Russian sage.

My Gravel Garden at Northview

The Gravel Garden at Northview is planted with a wide variety of drought-tolerant flowers like yucca, Macedonian scabious, lavender, and butterfly weed.

Many years ago, I became interested in what flowers I could grow without additional water in my Pennsylvania garden, Northview. I try to minimize the amount that I water because it comes from a well. There is a finite amount available, and I have family members that need water too!

I designed a garden area with carefully chosen plants I thought would do well without water, and I mulched it with gravel. I wasn't sure what would grow, but I was determined not to rescue plants if they wilted. I haven't watered

that garden in nearly two decades. It has been an interesting experiment in trusting plant research and my instincts. Because it is a full-sun garden that doesn't get watered, I also looked for plants with silvery gray foliage that reflect heat and light, keeping the plants cool. The garden has been an incredible success, with some plants really surprising me with their fabulous performance. Some, like lavender and pinks, I had struggled to grow in my normal flower beds but thrived in these conditions. Other plants became so aggressive they had to be pulled out.

Plants grow more slowly in my gravel garden without additional water, but their growth is stronger, so I rarely need to stake anything. The whole area needs little attention apart from removing fallen autumn leaves and editing out overzealous self-seeders. The plants that have done best in that garden have extensive root systems that quest for water, making them self-sufficient.

TOP TEN FLOWERS IN MY GRAVEL GARDEN

Aurinia saxatilis, basket-of-gold

Cephalaria gigantea, giant scabious

Dianthus gratianopolitanus, Cheddar pink

Eschscholzia californica, California poppy

Lavandula angustifolia, English lavender

Lycoris squamigera, surprise lily

Phlox subulata, creeping phlox

Pulsatilla vulgaris, pasqueflower

Santolina chamaecyparissus, lavender cotton

Stokesia laevis, Stokes' aster

FLOWER GARDENING IN DAMP PLACES

In the same way there are plants adapted to growing with very little water, there are perennials that flourish in damp to wet soil. These plants naturally occur in swamps, bogs, and streambanks. If you have a low-lying area that collects water, make the most of it by choosing moisture-loving flowers, or you can deliberately create such an area at the base of a downspout or wherever water puddles in your yard. This is called a rain garden, and it should help reduce runoff that would otherwise flow into storm drains. If you are creating one on a slope, surround the depression on the downhill side with slight banks to retain the water while it sinks into the soil. Choose plants that do well in damp soil but can cope with drying out between storms.

To set your rain garden up for success, start with these moisture-loving choices: *Asclepias incarnata*, swamp milkweed; *Chelone lyonii*, pink turtlehead; *Eutrochium*, Joe-Pye weed; *Filipendula rubra*, queen-of-the-prairie; *Helianthus angustifolius*, swamp sunflower; *Hibiscus moscheutos*, swamp mallow; *Iris versicolor*, blue flag; *Leucojum aestivum*, summer snowflake; *Lobelia cardinalis*, cardinal flower; *Monarda didyma*, scarlet beebalm.

from left Plants like red cardinal flower and pink border phlox appreciate sites with moist soil and are planted lower on a rain garden slope than thread leaf mountain mint and blazing star.

Iris 'Jenny Joy', a hybrid of *I. virginica* and *I. versicolor*, grows well in a waterside bed.

To encourage pollinators to use your garden, plant plenty of nectar-rich flowers like this purple coneflower.

GARDENING FOR POLLINATORS

As you garden and spend time looking closely at flowers, you will see different insects, some of which you may never have noticed before. When you take photos of flowers, enlarge them to get a peek into the world of tiny insects that are benefiting from the pollen and nectar at your floral buffet. As gardeners, we can do our part by providing habitat and planting a wide array of flowers that will bloom from late winter through spring, summer, and fall. I feel passionately that we should be growing more flowers to support pollinators and encouraging others to do so too.

Most animal pollination is carried out by insects, particularly bees. Bees are foraging insects that look for food from flowers to feed themselves and their young. As bees wriggle into a flower to get nectar, pollen sticks to their bodies. The bee then buzzes to another flower of the same species, carrying the pollen. When it lands, some of the pollen is wiped onto the flower's female part, and pollination occurs. Though bees are some of the most prolific pollinators, a huge variety of other pollinators visit our gardens day and night. Each one has a specific role to play in your garden and favors certain flowers. There is great joy to be found in learning about flower-pollinator interactions.

Animal- and insect-pollinated plants tend to have showy flowers. Their beautiful, intricate blooms attract pollinators and also make them compelling to humans. They produce sticky pollen that attaches to the pollinator for transfer. Without pollinators, these flowers cannot reproduce. It is literally a matter of life or death for them to be in bloom when their preferred pollinator is on the wing. Flowers have evolved shapes that make pollination efficient when they are visited by their favored pollinators.

You can make your garden into a floriferous oasis once you understand the life of a pollinator. Imagine that you are a butterfly or a bee flying over a garden, looking for food. From a distance you see blocks of color and distinctive shapes. When you fly in lower, you can make out signals from the flower that it is ready and open for business. Floral fragrances waft in the air, attracting you closer. Special patterns on the flowers show you where to land for a sweet nectar treat.

Bees

Flowers favored by bees tend to be blue, purple, yellow, white, and orange and are substantial enough for bees to land on safely. A big bumblebee needs a big, strong flower, whereas little sweat bees can pollinate many sizes of flower. You may be able to identify a honeybee or a bumblebee, but a wide range of other bees live in the ground or in decomposing wood, and we rarely see them apart from when they visit a flower. Some bees are solitary, and others form social groups, as is found in a honeybee hive.

A bumblebee visits a yellow perennial sunflower, covering itself with pollen.

Bees are well suited to the job of transferring pollen because their bristly bodies attract it electrostatically, and it sticks to their hairs. Bees collect the excess pollen into sacs on their back legs by rubbing their legs over their bodies. When the pollen sacs are full, the bees return to their nests to empty them. Bees are faithful feeders that work a patch of flowers, increasing pollination rates. We can help them by planting multiples of the same flower in our gardens.

Start out with some of these top choices for attracting bees: *Borago officinalis*, borage; *Echinacea*, coneflower; *Liatris*, blazing star; *Monarda fistulosa*, wild bergamot; *Penstemon*, beardtongue; *Pycnanthemum*, mountain mint; *Veronicastrum virginicum*, Culver's root.

Butterflies

Adult butterflies are some of the most iconic garden insects and have elaborate, colorful patterns on their wings. If you want to encourage them, plant yellow, blue, orange, white, or pinky purple flowers. Look for those with a flat or sturdy flower surface where butterflies can land safely before flitting to the next bloom. They use taste and smell to identify suitable plants. Adults feed by unrolling

A black butterfly feasts on the nectar in a coral salvia flower.

their long, tongue-like proboscis and sucking the sweet nectar out of the flower. Pollen doesn't stick easily to their bodies, so they are less efficient at pollination than bees.

Butterflies have several stages to their life cycle, so include plants in your garden to feed and shelter eggs, caterpillars, and chrysalises in addition to flowers for the adults. Adult female butterflies lay eggs on specific host plants. The eggs hatch into caterpillars, which eat the leaves before pupating. I was horrified to hear from a gardener who loved butterflies that she had squashed all the caterpillars in her herb garden. She had not realized they were juvenile butterflies. It is worth tolerating a few holey leaves to have butterflies feeding from your flowers. Just grow a few extra plants! Some examples of caterpillar host plants are milkweeds for monarchs and dill and fennel for swallowtail butterflies.

Introducing a selection of these plants will support butterflies at their different life stages: *Asclepias*, milkweed; *Eutrochium*, Joe-Pye weed; *Hylotelephium*, sedum; *Phlox paniculata*, border phlox; *Symphyotrichum novae-angliae*, New England aster; *Tithonia rotundifolia*, Mexican sunflower; *Verbena bonariensis*, tall verbena; *Zinnia*, zinnia.

Hummingbirds

Hummingbirds are the predominant pollinating bird in North America. They are superlative flyers that can dart from flower to flower, spreading pollen with their bills and bodies. If you are lucky enough to garden where you have these magnificent flying jewels, do everything that you can to encourage them. There is nothing like sitting near a patch of your favorite hummingbird-loved flowers and hearing them whizz past to sip nectar while hovering in flight. The flowers that attract hummingbirds are usually bright red, yellow, or orange, as birds can see these colors. They tend to be tubular in shape, with nectar hidden deep in the bottom of the flower where only the narrow bill and tongue of these birds can access it. Hummingbirds see colors in the ultraviolet range and can perceive combinations of colors that we cannot. I wish that I could see what they see when ultraviolet is mixed with yellow or green. It sounds like a psychedelic world that would blow our minds, but it is one that helps the hummingbirds perform their aerial acrobatics.

These flowers are excellent starts for your hummingbird-friendly garden, with plenty of color choice in each genus: *Agastache*, hummingbird mint; *Aquilegia*, columbine; *Kniphofia*, red hot poker; *Lobelia cardinalis*, cardinal flower; *Monarda didyma*, scarlet beebalm; *Phlox maculata*, meadow phlox; *Salvia*, salvia.

Supporting Other Pollinators

When gardening for pollinators, the best thing you can do is maximize the number and types of flowers you grow to encourage a plethora of pollinators, including beneficial flies, wasps, beetles, and moths. There are hundreds of flies that pollinate flowers, some of which mimic the characteristic stripes of bees and wasps to confuse predators. Wasps mostly have smooth bodies and are inefficient pollinators, but they contribute to the garden ecosystem by controlling the populations of other insects. Include some flowers that open up after sunset to attract pollinators on the night shift, such as beetles and moths. Beetles are attracted to strong, spicy, or fetid smells and open-faced or bowl-shaped flowers that allow easy access. Moths are closely related to butterflies and have similar preferences in flower shapes. Night feeders are often drawn to white or light-colored flowers with a sweet scent and lots of nectar.

GARDENS TO ENGAGE THE SENSES

Walking through a flower garden in full bloom is a multi-sensory experience. Sight is the first sense we use to engage with a garden and often the dominant one. We observe its style, layout, and composition, as well as the flower shapes, colors, and forms. The next thing we take in is often fragrance. Auditory experiences include listening to the rustling of plants and the sounds of birds or insects. You can use your sense of touch to discover what different plants feel like. Each of us experiences gardens in our own unique way. As you muse about

top Bright red flowers like this cardinal flower are favorites of hummingbirds.

above Goldenrod soldier beetle, a beneficial insect, on a yellow rudbeckia flower.

your personal flower garden, decide which senses are important to you and use that information to help you choose plants.

Floral Fragrances

Flower fragrance brings me great pleasure, and I plan for it in every garden space. But my dad has a terrible sense of smell, so whether a flower is fragrant or not is less relevant to him. He and I fall at the two extremes, so think whether smelling a flower is something that is important to you. If you are not sure, or have not really considered this aspect of gardening, start sticking your nose into every flower you pass and sniffing. Just watch out for insects.

There is an incredible range of fragrance types found in the floral world, but we have relatively few words to describe the nuances of garden smells. We tend to use general words like flowery, fruity, citrusy, or spicy. Or we take words from other flowers, and say that one flower smells a little bit like a lilac, lily, rose, or gardenia. This is tricky, as you must already be familiar with those smells before you can make comparisons.

Pick a posy of sweet peas to bring into your house and enjoy.

Those who create perfumes have a very keen sense of smell. Coupled with this, they train their nose and their memory to differentiate and recall fragrances. If flower scent interests you, try to increase your fragrance literacy. Continue to smell flowers and refine your floral palate. Describe what you are smelling in as much detail as possible. It takes practice, but it is an enjoyable way to occupy yourself. You might not like all floral scents equally, so plan to include only the ones you most enjoy smelling. I met someone who didn't like the scent of lavender because it had negative connotations for him, whereas it is one of my favorite plant fragrances. Scents are highly linked to memory, so include flowers that remind you of happy events and beloved people and places. Highly scented flowers such as tuberoses and old-fashioned sweet peas have been grown in flower gardens for centuries. These plants look beautiful but are sometimes grown just for their distinctive scents. When you buy plants, read the descriptions carefully or purchase a flowering plant when it is in bloom so that you can smell it.

Fragrance is an elusive quality. It evolved in flowering plants to attract pollinators. Some flowers are difficult to smell up close; their scent wafts unexpectedly into your nose as you are walking through the garden. The flower is pumping out its characteristic smell to draw in pollinators. The plant uses energy to produce its fragrance, so it is only released to coincide with the feeding patterns of their preferred pollinators, and at other times they are scentless. If a plant wants to attract night-flying insects, it projects its scent starting in the evening. If it is attracting day flyers, then that is when it releases its smell.

Lemon beebalm, *Monarda citriodora*, has a delightful citrusy smell when touched.

If you enjoy building a garden bed with fragrance in mind, put these plants at the top of your wish list: *Dianthus plumaris*, cottage pink; *Erysimum cheiri*, wallflower; *Heliotropium arborescens*, heliotrope; *Hyacinthus orientalis*, hyacinth; *Lathyrus odoratus*, sweet pea; *Lilium regale*, regal lily; *Narcissus jonquilla* and cultivars, jonquil; *Paeonia lactiflora*, peony; *Phlox paniculata*, garden phlox.

An Evening Garden

Some of the richest and most evocative floral fragrances are released from dusk onward. As the air cools at the end of a hot summer day, flowers that attract moths and other night-flying insects emit their fragrances. If you have been on a warm tropical holiday, you might remember the night air being laden with pleasant smells. In a temperate garden it is difficult to achieve that same intensity of olfactory experience, but there are tropical and night-scented flowers you can grow near a patio or terrace to approximate those heady nights. If you tend to use your garden in the evenings, include night-scented white or light-colored flowers that are visible in low light and call it your evening, night, or moon garden.

If I were creating an evening garden, I would choose fragrant or light-colored cultivars of the following flowers: *Agapanthus*, lily of the Nile; *Cosmos bipinnatus*, cosmos; *Gladiolus murielae*, Abyssinian gladiolus; *Iberis umbellata*, annual candytuft; *Lilium longiflorum*, Easter lily; *Lobularia maritima*, sweet alyssum; *Matthiola longipetala*, night-scented stock; *Nicotiana alata*, flowering tobacco; *Oenothera biennis*, common evening primrose; *Petunia ×hybrida*, petunia.

White and light-colored fragrant flowers like this border phlox and lily are excellent choices for an evening garden.

Edible Flowers

Using our sense of taste in the garden tends to be associated with vegetable growing, but there is no reason our flower gardens cannot also be a place of harvest. Traditional gardens did not make the same differentiation between decorative and productive gardens that we do today. Plants were fitted in wherever there was room to squeeze them.

Plant edible flowers such as peppery nasturtium, violas, calendula, and daylilies to toss into salads, decorate your cakes, or garnish your plates. Blue borage flowers, rosemary, or mint flowers and leaves can be added to your drinks. Try freezing flowers in ice cubes for a floral touch. Make sure these flowers and herbs are grown without pesticides or herbicides, and never eat a plant you are unfamiliar with, as some garden flowers are poisonous.

Growing some of these plants will keep you stocked with edible flowers or leaves for a tasty addition to meals and drinks: *Agastache foeniculum*, anise hyssop; *Allium schoenoprasum*, chives; *Borago officinalis*, borage; *Calendula officinalis*, pot marigold; *Foeniculum vulgare*, fennel; *Mentha ×piperita*, peppermint; *Ocimum basilicum*, basil; *Salvia officinalis*, common sage; *Tropaeolum majus*, nasturtium; *Viola tricolor*, Johnny-jump-up.

Try growing edible flowers like these chives.

A Floral Herb Garden

Herbal plants for scent and taste are one of my special passions, as they add so much to a flower garden. The first garden I ever designed was an herb garden for my mother when I was sixteen. It was planted with culinary herbs and situated near the kitchen so that the plants were easy to grab for a dish. I have been fascinated by herbs and the role they play in cultures around the world ever since. Each place in the world has its favorites, and growing them can be a way to bring your own heritage and culture into your garden. I love to grow English thyme, rosemary, and sage. You may have other favorites that you use in cooking or that remind you of your childhood.

The Herb Society of America defines herbs as plants "for use and delight," which opens the gate to any number of plants that can be added to your floral herb garden. Herbs were the backbone of a flowering garden in the past, as they were harvested for home remedies and many other household uses. You can grow herbs in a dedicated place or integrate them into another flower bed. They are perfect plants for containers, and you can plant one herb per pot or make a container herb garden. Herbs' scented foliage and flowers release aromatic oils into the air on a sunny day for a delightful treat when you walk near or sit close to them. These fragrant oils are a deterrent to browsing herbivores that search for food using their noses, so intersperse herbal plants between others that tend to

Lavender cotton and lavender are good companions for a drought-tolerant herb bed.

get eaten in your garden. It will not necessarily prevent all damage, but it can minimize it by confusing the browsers' sense of smell.

Herbs are decorative in the garden, even if you don't want to cook with them. Include dill or fennel for their airy foliage and the disc-like see-through flowers that wave above their leaves. Sage and oregano are a great addition to the front of a bed and will spill over a raised edging. Trim them back and use the leaves in cooking. Herbs, especially silver-leaved ones, are easy to grow in a sunny spot and don't require much water once established.

Lavender cotton is a more unusual, nonedible herb that brings silver foliage and yellow flowers to the herb garden palette. Drought-tolerant herbs like lavender require well-drained soil and will die if they are irrigated too much in the summer. Plant flowering lavender alongside a path so you brush into it and release the aroma into the air. Creeping thyme also needs great drainage, so plant it in gravel or between paving slabs for fragrance under your feet. All herbs are great pollinator plants.

The Tactile Flower Garden

We may not set out to use our sense of touch when appreciating our flower gardens, but we are used to the utilitarian handling of plants as we place them in the soil, tend them, or cut them back. If we pick a bunch of cut flowers, we handle them as we arrange them in a vase. Using our sense of touch is a great way to enhance our garden experiences.

Part of the pleasure of flower gardening is that you are working with an assortment of stimulating new surfaces and textures. If you would like to explore your garden using your sense of touch, choose a plant to investigate. Stroke the stem, leaves, and flower with your eyes closed, otherwise it is hard to concentrate just on what you are feeling. As you learn more about identifying plants by touch, these tactile cues will remind you of the last time you met the flower and what it is. Words for visual texture often apply to what the flower feels like. Shiny petals like those of California poppies are silky smooth. Dull, nonreflective flowers may feel rough or sandpapery. An echinacea's petals are coarse, and the cone in the middle is prickly. Others, like flossflowers, feel like tiny powder puffs. Be cautious of spiny plants, like some sea hollies.

Some public gardens have installed sensory planting areas where the flowers are meant to be touched and handled. A few practical tips from these gardens

from left The flower heads of this burnet are fluffy and fun to touch.

The densely packed orange-red flower head of this cockscomb celosia is surprisingly soft.

are to situate the plants in a raised bed or in tall containers so anyone can easily reach them, incorporate only plants that are nice and safe to touch, and make sure they are sturdy enough to withstand frequent handling. Include flowers and plants that emit fragrance once touched, such as scented geraniums and herbs. Use as many senses as possible to investigate a flowering plant so that it sticks in your memory.

To start your own sensory garden, try these plants for a variety of textures: *Anethum graveolens*, dill; *Celosia argentea*, celosia; *Eschscholzia californica*, California poppy; *Hylotelephium spectabile*, sedum; *Phlomis fruticosa*, Jerusalem sage; *Salvia argentea*, silver sage; *Stachys byzantina*, lamb's ear; *Thymus serpyllum*, creeping thyme; *Verbascum*, mullein; *Xerochrysum bracteatum*, strawflower.

The bowl-shaped flower of this poppy amplifies the sound of the beneficial pollinators inside.

Sound in the Flower Garden

We don't tend to think of flower gardens as soundscapes, but they are alive with gentle noises. Go out to your garden on a sunny spring or summer morning and listen. Once the sun has warmed the flowers, pollinators begin their day. Not only are the plants rustling and whispering in any little breeze, but the flowers are a hub of activity for the insect world. Sit still and listen. Birds are singing or calling to each other, bees are buzzing, and if you are lucky maybe a frog or two is ribbiting. As the gardening year progresses, take a moment every now and then

to stop and listen. Each season brings its own flower garden sounds. A change in the plant palette brings new noises, insect activity, and bird song. If you are an auditory learner or a musician, like one of my daughters, your ability to listen to and analyze sounds brings immense pleasure. Listening to a garden can be a gateway into a new appreciation for flowers and their cohabiting wildlife.

As you think about your future flower garden, include aspects of gardens that sometimes get left out of our strongly visual culture. The garden is one place where you can stretch your sensory capabilities and enrich your experience of the world right outside your door.

How to Choose Which Flowers to Buy for Your Garden

When you design your garden, you can amalgamate everything that attracted and inspired you and combine them to create your ideal flower garden. You can mix and match the styles you like and the senses you want to prioritize. Moving forward, you can further refine your flower wish list to tie in with your preferred garden style.

Once you have found a place in your garden for your flower bed and thought about some possibilities, it is time to decide on the plants that will grow there. You are looking for plants that meet two criteria: they should be ones that you would love to grow and that would also flourish in the particular growing conditions of your garden.

PRIORITIZING YOUR WISH LIST

A good starting point is your flowery wish list. While you are not required to keep such a list, your notes will be very useful to organize your thinking at this point in flower bed design, especially if you divided the list by seasons. Of the plants that you love, think which ones will do well in your garden. Those plants will form the basis of your new bed, and you will choose secondary flowers that go well with them. You are converting your wish list into your buying list, which you can take with you as you go plant shopping.

To refine your wish list, put stars next to your most desirable plants. Begin with your favorite season, starring the absolute must-have plants you can't live without; call them your personal five-star plants. Then find one, two, or three bold beauties for each season. These are the central plants in your garden recipe around which your seasonal combinations will revolve. After you have chosen the stars of each season's combinations, look for the supporting cast members: background plants, mid-border delights, weavers and mixers, front-border delights, and tiny treasures. No matter the role that the flowers will play in the garden, I make sure that I include a variety of shapes in my chosen color scheme.

Once you have finished one season, move on to the next. Bear in mind that some of your flowers will be long blooming and may keep flowering across several seasons. Become an astute observer of the total plant. Look at flower characteristics and the qualities that the entire plant brings to a flower bed. This method works for me, but you can put your beds together in whatever manner you wish. You need to make thoughtful decisions to make an effective and beautiful flower garden.

SELECTING PLANTS THAT WILL THRIVE

There are plenty of plants that you could technically grow, but the key to a great, full-looking, floriferous garden is to discover the ones that will thrive, rather than merely survive, in your unique conditions. Find them by looking carefully at their stated hardiness zones, sunlight needs, soil, and water requirements.

When I go through my wish list, I inevitably put five stars next to every foxglove. Here, I combine one with yarrow and speedwell.

If their wants match the growing conditions found in your garden, your plants will have a good chance of growing vigorously and producing plenty of flowers.

You cannot change your climate. You receive a certain amount of rainfall and have particular maximum and minimum temperatures, seasonal humidity, wind patterns, daylight lengths and intensities. Choosing plants adapted to your local conditions gives you the best chance of success without much intervention from you. If in doubt about what to plant, look at local gardens and talk to people in nearby garden centers for advice about what will do well in your region.

It is easy to check whether a plant will be able to withstand the winters in your garden if you know its hardiness zone, which is found in the plant's description and on its label. Heat and humidity tolerance is less straightforward. Some perennials that flower beautifully all summer in areas with mild summer temperatures will struggle to grow at all in places that have hot summer nights.

Annuals and tender perennials can be grown in any zone, but for maximum flower-growing success, choose ones that are adapted to your summer heat levels. If you have cool summers, you can grow hardy annuals for months but may struggle to grow some of the tender perennials or annuals from warmer climates. If you garden where summers are hot, add in heat-tolerant half-hardy annuals as soon as summer kicks in.

opposite If you are unsure about your conditions, start your garden with easy-to-grow flowers like this bright pink double lily.

from left Blue Japanese roof iris and camas can both grow in the same conditions found in this bed next to a waterfall.

Red valerian grows well in the dry, alkaline soil at the base of a stone wall.

The amount of precipitation and when in the year it falls is another factor that you cannot control. If you want to be an environmentally friendly gardener, choose plants suitable for your local rainfall patterns. Good plants to look for are those that are native to your region. These plants have adaptations that suit them to grow in your particular climate without too much extra care.

The final practical consideration is matching plant choice to soil, the medium that anchors and provides for your garden plants. The soil that suits the widest range of flowers contains sufficient water, air, and nutrients needed for healthy growth and is often referred to as moist but well drained. If the needs of a specific plant you want to grow are not met by the soil you have, it will grow weakly and may become susceptible to attack by pests and diseases. Whatever your initial soil conditions, you have a choice to grow plants that suit your existing soil or to amend it over time. Most people do a combination of the two: work with what they have and also make the soil better by amending it. Be aware that soil near new houses may be filled with rubble or debris and can need additional preparation.

THE PLANT-PACKED FLOWER BED

If you have a limited amount of space to plant and wish to create a long-lasting flowery display, many different plants have to live together in close quarters. A plant-packed bed has a full and lush look that allows you to create some fabulous intermingled flower and plant combinations. The various flowers' foliage covers the soil, keeping their roots cool and moist and reducing weed seed germination.

There are several strategies you can use to get this plant-packed look. One of the simplest ways is to create a mixed flower garden of plants with different life cycles. Perennial plants and hardy bulbs are the longest-lived plants and become the framework of a mixed flower bed. Fleeting occupants like biennials, annuals, and tender plants will come and go with the years. If you want this type of bed, make sure your list includes plants from each group in order to provide continuity of bloom.

You might wonder how to combine these types into a flower bed that has finite space. To maximize the flowers you can grow in one bed, it is important to choose plants that can coexist without overwhelming their neighbors. When plants grow, they compete in the flower bed above ground for sunlight and below ground for soil nutrients, water, and physical space as they contend to make their flowers visible to passing pollinators. The plants you put in the same bed have to be either good permanent companions or temporary

A plant-packed combination with white lesser calamint, peach dahlias, blue flossflower, and yellow coreopsis.

additions that you plant and then remove during the course of the year. You might use both strategies within your bed to increase floweriness.

There are some flowering plants that grow so enthusiastically in their preferred garden conditions that they may be labeled as aggressive or euphemistically referred to as "strong growers." They tend to take over entire beds and so are not good partner plants for more slow-growing flowers. Take a moment to think about whether you want to include these in your flower bed, as they will need active management and division as they grow. It is a strange fact that a particular plant can be a super grower in one garden yet be hard to establish in another. It takes some trial and error to find the plants that have the right growth rate for your garden.

One way to increase the number of plants you can grow in a fixed area is to carefully plant them on top of each other in the soil. Typically, new perennials will take two or three years to reach their full size. As the perennials grow, add annuals or tender perennials and bulbs that will fill the gaps until the perennials grow wider. Annuals can even be tucked in above the root zone of perennials. Bulbs can be slotted in easily between existing perennial clumps because they take up little horizontal space in the bed. The largest bulbs are planted deepest in the soil with tiny ones above them. Annuals and bulbs can be repeated throughout the bed to coordinate the overall look, or they can be included in designated planting pockets. You may like this combined look so much that you deliberately leave planting spaces between perennials to rotate in new plants or allow the annuals and biennials to self-seed.

Blue triplet lily, *Triteleia laxa*, blooms in early summer and is interplanted with lesser calamint, which flowers later.

Provide a backdrop for a herbaceous flower garden using a rose like the fragrant pink 'Ispahan' in combination with another woody plant like elderberry 'Black Lace'.

Woody Plants, Roses, and Vines

To add additional flowers to your garden, consider planting some flowering trees, shrubs, roses, or vines to add to the floral show. Some of these plants are large and are best situated as a backdrop at the rear of a bed or adjacent to it. Large, woody plants have long, questing roots that may deplete soil moisture in your bed if they are planted too close.

Woody plants are beyond the scope of this book, but some of my favorite smaller ones include *Clematis*, clematis; *Clethra alnifolia*, summersweet; *Deutzia gracilis*, slender deutzia; *Gelsemium sempervirens*, Carolina jessamine; *Hydrangea*, hydrangea; *Itea virginica*, Virginia sweetspire; *Lonicera sempervirens*, coral honeysuckle; *Rosa*, roses; *Sambucus nigra*, elderberry; and *Spiraea*, spirea.

THE LARGER IMPACTS OF YOUR FLOWER GARDEN

As you ponder your future flower patch, you will undoubtedly dwell on its aesthetic qualities, but don't forget that what we do in our garden matters to our local and global ecosystems. We can use the little pieces of land around our houses in an

environmentally aware manner. The plants we add will absorb carbon dioxide from the air, filter stormwater, and support wildlife. As we choose plants, we can include those that are native to our area or that will need little extra input from us. An environmentally savvy garden can be incredibly beautiful.

Native plants, those that naturally occur in your region, contribute to local food webs and other animal-plant interactions. Nonnative plants, if thoughtfully chosen and not invasive, add to the general ecology of your garden and may flower when native plants are not in bloom. Think of your garden as a miniature ecosystem that provides food and habitat for birds, pollinators, and other beneficial insects. Avoid using pesticides and herbicides because they indiscriminately kill not only a target pest, but also a broad range of both beneficial and benign insects, which goes against the ethos of encouraging nature to use your garden. Your garden could be an important link in local wildlife corridors for migratory birds and insects.

One of the most important factors that guides my flower choices is the benefit to wildlife. It gives me great delight to provide a home for all kinds of birds and insects. I took their presence for granted until the last few years, when the numbers of obvious key species of butterflies and bees plummeted. To someone who has gardened in the same place for over two decades, the decline was shocking. The photographs I have taken for documentation and enjoyment over that time are a record of the dwindling numbers of invertebrates that visit my plants. I have always loved gardening for the beauty my garden gives to me, my family, and other visitors, but I am now convinced that I must also be a garden steward who provides food and habitat for any animals that visit or live here. I make a point to plant flowers that provide pollinators with nectar and pollen and am growing more species that are broadly native, not just to my area, but to the United States of America. With climate change, the species from our own area may not be heat tolerant enough in the future.

top Include late-season flowers like this sedum to provide nectar for migrating monarch butterflies and other wildlife.

above It is important to grow host plants to support early life stages of beneficial insects. Milkweeds like this one are essential to feed monarch caterpillars.

Bringing Your Flower Garden Together

The old expression that beauty is in the eye of the beholder holds true in flower gardens. Each gardener has to decide what they like best. The overarching idea of combining flowering plants into a bed or border is that blooms can be admired on two levels: as individual specimens and as part of a beautiful overall impression. By siting your flowers in close proximity to each other, they can grow through, among, and between neighboring plants to produce a better picture than any one of them would do on their own. It is in the intermingling of plants and the juxtaposition of shape and colors that the magic of mixed gardening happens. It is more than loving one particular flower; it is seeing the possibilities that exist to create living pictures now and, as plants grow and change, over time.

Many different flower shapes are growing together, including daisy-like yellow coneflowers, vertical blazing star, and ball-like sea hollies.

As you bring your ideas together to design your own flower garden, you need to think about which aspects of plants and flowers are most important to you. Usually there is a balance between aesthetics and function. You may be very interested in making a garden for butterflies, a cutting garden, or maybe a fragrant garden. Whatever your theme, make sure that the plants you choose suit your conditions, and then you can work on making it gorgeous.

Everyone has their own ideas of what is lovely and what is not, but there are certain principles of design that can guide you as you think about how to create your own glorious flower garden.

COMBINING FLOWER AND INFLORESCENCE SHAPES

One of the essential aspects of gardening is getting to know details about different flowers that you could grow. As you learn more about possible plants, you will start to recognize them by their flower and inflorescence shapes. You will begin to see which ones you think look fantastic when planted next to each other. Feel free to study groupings in gardens and photos to see what other gardeners have successfully combined. You could choose flowers to plant near each other that are very similar in shape, but then the bed as a whole looks humdrum because there is no contrast. The liveliness of a flower bed is provided by the disparities between adjacent flowers.

Add excitement to your garden bed by growing a combination of different flower shapes. Here, a selection of blazing stars, mullein, crocosmia, and hare's ears glows in the late evening light.

Diversity and Harmony

The main flower and plant characteristics to consider when assembling plants in a flower bed are their sizes, textures, colors, and over-all forms. For a garden to look cohesive, the plants you choose should share some common features. Similarities help plants to seem as if they belong together and look harmonious. Conversely, if every plant in a bed looks like its neighbors, the effect can be bland. To enliven a plain border, add some spice by choosing new flower forms, shapes, scales, and colors. To make the whole bed into a fabulous and uni-fied composition, you have to balance visual unity and harmony with the variety needed to make your flower bed exciting.

Repetition and Massing Versus Variety

While a certain amount of contrast is neces-sary in a flower bed, too much leads to a mud-dled appearance. The remedy for a disjointed garden is to repeat certain flowers or groups several times in the bed. If you love lots of different flowers, it is easy to purchase one of each type, but planting many single speci-mens all together in a bed creates a collection, not a thoughtful garden composition. At the opposite extreme, you could decide to fill a whole bed with only one type of plant. Like a field full of sunflowers, a mass planting of one flower is spectacular when in bloom but then leaves behind a swath without flowers that is hard to disguise. Instead of having one large mass, include multiple smaller groupings of the plant in several places.

Whatever you repeat should be something obvious that catches your eye, usu-ally a specific flower or a group of flowers that has a strong form or color. Too much repetition of an unusual shape can reduce its effectiveness. Take one of the most obvious inflorescence shapes: spikes and spires. A selection of upright

forms in a flower bed is fabulous when used to break up the mounded look of lower-growing garden flowers. If there are too many uprights flowering at once in close proximity, they lose their uniqueness, and your bed looks like a spiky forest of flowers. If, on the other hand, they are carefully and selectively placed, they are spectacular. Instead of choosing lots of spiky forms, you can combine one or two with a good horizontal flower, or maybe a ball shape interspersed with some smaller cloud-like flowers. This varied composition looks good with just three or four flower choices and can be repeated several times in the bed.

You don't have to repeat it evenly, but if there is a good rhythm to the repetition, it looks pleasing. For example, you could divide the bed along its length into thirds or fifths and place the key groups at these lines. You can then add in other flowering vignettes for the remaining seasons. To keep your repeated groupings from looking too formulaic, you can change the numbers of each component flower in the different areas of the bed.

from left Repeat dramatically shaped flowers along a bed to create visual rhythm and harmony. Here, the vertical spires of a foxglove, *Digitalis lanata*, are used among Macedonian scabious, with plume poppy behind.

Spherical inflorescences, like those of these alliums, are another good choice to repeat in a flower bed.

How I Learned to Buy in Threes

When I was a much younger gardener and still learning which plants would grow well in my new garden, I had a visit from a well-respected gardener who asked me why I only had one of each particular plant. I had never really thought about that. In my mind, I was going to experiment and save money by propagating the ones that I liked and did well for me. Thinking back about that garden, it probably looked very uncoordinated. As I matured as a gardener, I kept her words in mind and deliberately repeated plants in my beds to produce a less fragmented look. I thought more about what each flowering plant looked like both on its own and in the broader picture.

Paring down the plant palette in a garden also makes choosing plants easier, as I can find one that I like, buy multiples, and put it in several places.

Buying three of one kind of plant works well when you are planting up an informal flower bed. Three plants when combined in close proximity can be placed at the corners of an imaginary triangle. The triangle can be any shape, and eventually the plants will grow together to make a pleasing irregular drift. For larger groupings, stick with odd numbers of plants to help the groupings flow through the bed.

Focal Points, Scale, and Balance

A claret red hibiscus is an obvious focal flower combined with the smaller blooms of border phlox.

Each flower bed should have one or two bold beauties to act as focal points. They catch the eye with their spectacular form, brilliant color, or large plant, flower, or leaf size. Not every plant in the bed can be the biggest and boldest, otherwise there is no contrast. A big plant looks especially large when it is situated next to a tiny plant or one with little leaves or flowers. Using contrast of scale provides excitement, and this concept also applies to flower size. For example, there are a lot of hemispherical daisy-shaped flowers to be found in gardens throughout the year, particularly in late summer into autumn. Normally, putting two flowers of the same shape next to each other might be boring, but by choosing a large-scale flower like a coneflower and pairing it with a small-flowered aster, you get enough contrast for it to be compelling.

Relatedly, any plant that takes up a large space tends to have a strong visual weight. These plants might have large-scale, undivided leaves and may also be tall and broad, giving them a dense presence in the bed. If you have multiple weighty plants situated at one end of a bed, the whole composition looks unbalanced. Either move some of them or group other medium-sized plants together to visually counterbalance the weighty ones. You could also situate the heavy-looking plants toward the center of the bed or one-third of the way along, which gives a nice rhythm and flow.

opposite See-through plants like globe amaranth 'Fireworks' and tall verbena can be placed from the front to the mid-back of a bed.

The flowers of this pink burnet float on long stems and sway in the breeze.

Movement and Layers

As you begin to think about where in the bed you might position each plant, you may be tempted to line up the flowers strictly by height. If you place all the tall plants at the very back, followed by a row of mid-height ones, and then step down to short ones in a band at the front, you will be able to see all your plants, but the composition may look static. To create a freer style with visual movement where your eye can dance and swirl around a bed, pull a few plants out of their height band and into the next layer of the bed. Look for slender and see-through plants that you can tuck between shorter ones to break up their ranks. Add bulbs and self-sowers to inject a bit of height change and form that brings liveliness to your bed. Also include a few plants whose height is due to long, airy flower stems arising from low, basal foliage. These add real movement to the bed as the flowers wiggle and shake when the wind blows or a bird perches on a stem. Other animated flowers are the umbellifers, like fennel or dill, and any thin-stalked flowers like cephalaria, columbine, cosmos, burnets, and Japanese anemones.

The size of dense drifts of perennials like these coneflowers and summer-blooming alliums should be in proportion to the overall dimensions of the flower bed to avoid overwhelming a small space. Vast swaths of one type look dramatic when in flower but may be uninteresting after they finish blooming.

opposite Large groups of one type of flower are called drifts. Match the size of the drifts to the scale of the bed. Here, a patch of blue scabious intermingles with hardy geranium in front of a group of yellow red hot poker plants and the seed heads of angelica at the back.

Grouping Plants in Drifts

Plant group size is directly related not only to the overall bed dimensions but also to the bulk and presence of the plant. Small-scale tiny treasures will need to be in a large group to help them stand out. Medium-sized mid-border plants should also be clustered together, otherwise the overall look of the bed will be spotty. Large plants have their own presence in the bed, so they can be planted singly, but they may be repeated for continuity.

The shape of the grouping makes a difference to the look and style of a flower bed. If your bed is formal in style, you will want to make the groups even and symmetrical. Use plants in blocks or other geometric shapes that coordinate with the bed outline. An informal bed is better planted with groupings that intermingle and overlap, akin to a jigsaw puzzle of randomly sized interlocking pieces. Another way to think about planting informally is to create waves of flowers that run diagonally to the front of the bed. Elongated groupings with sinuous edges are referred to as drifts, and like waves, they are irregular in size and shape and give motion to your design. Plan your drifts so they are visible from your most frequent vantage point.

from left This pale yellow lily combines easily with blue larkspur.

The white of Miss Willmott's ghost, *Eryngium giganteum*, shines out against the deep pink of beardtongue 'Garnet'.

A highly contrasting combination of orange and purple pleases some gardeners. If you like the look, try tall verbena and butterfly weed.

opposite This bed combines yellow, purple, and white: royal purple clustered bellflower, white lace flower, yellow sundrops, light purple Jerusalem sage, and alliums.

COMBINING FLOWER COLORS

Color contributes to pleasing combinations, especially when considered with plant habit, form, shape, and leaf texture. Color can be used to enliven a planting scheme or harmonize it across diverse shapes. There are many ways that you can choose a color scheme, and you may already know what you like. If in doubt, start with your favorite color as the anchor, and let the rest come in as they will. Alternately, eliminate your least favorite color or colors from your plant palette. Restricting your choices by this simple method immediately gives you a framework for planning.

If you want to use color as the primary factor that influences your plant choices, check that it is feasible to have your preferred colors year-round. Purple, white, and yellow flowers are easily available throughout the year, whereas others are less common at certain times. Consider the colors of your plants' leaves and the bed's background when you are planning your design. Flower colors look very different against the fresh green backdrop of a hedge compared to their appearance in front of a house wall or fence.

Colors of Flowers Throughout the Seasons

Certain flower colors predominate at different times of the year, and one flower bed might go through color transformations from spring to summer and again into fall. In late winter and early spring, many of the flowers are white, yellow, and lavender purple. As the weeks go by, the garden fills with a multitude of pastel colors. Blue, dark purple, pink, yellow, and white flowers are all well represented. A true red doesn't appear until the bright red tulips emerge in mid-spring.

In late spring and early summer, there are plenty of yellow, blue, white, pink, and purple flowers, but orange and red are still hard to find. Flower colors in the height of summer are bright and cheerful, with a lot of choice of what to grow and combine, from one end of the rainbow to the other. You can easily stamp your personal color choices onto your summer garden.

By late summer and into fall, the palette veers to classic autumn colors. There are burnt oranges, purples, maroons, deep pinks, many yellows, plus some white and cream flowers to lighten the scene. These flower colors pair well with autumn leaves to finish the flowery year.

from left A hot color combination of gloriosa daisies, crocosmia, scarlet beebalm, zinnias, and hummingbird mint.

A cool color palette of allium and salvias is very restful.

It is possible, though difficult, to make a garden that is solely composed of plants blooming in one flower color. I would recommend incorporating at least one more color to make your garden compositions more interesting and inviting. If your wish list selections have leaned toward a particular color, think about adding another color or two. Start with your favorite flower in your preferred hue and then select a few others that will carry out your new color scheme. Hot colors of red, yellow, and orange are vibrant and energize a garden bed, especially if they are saturated. Cool colors, on the other hand, particularly pastels, give the garden a peaceful and gentle feeling and blend together. Combining any hot color with any cool color will provide contrast, especially if the two colors are intense.

Each color in your flower garden does not have to be present in equal amounts. If you have three colors in your chosen palette, pick one that will be most abundant, a secondary one that will be present in smaller amounts, and the final one as an accent. If your palette includes both hot and cool colors, it is a good idea to let one of them dominate the scheme. In general, a touch of a hot color is enough to offset the presence of a greater number of cool-colored flowers. If you are only working with hot colors, it is a good idea to use a greater amount of medium or pale hues with splashes of strongly colored flowers. For highly contrasting flower combinations, try orange with blue, red with green, or purple with yellow.

Adding white to any color group gives freshness to the composition. Large, solid white flowers are refreshing in the evening but can be glaring on a sunny day. Lacy and delicate white flowers are a good choice to add airiness and help other plants mix together. If you have red and blue in a bed, try adding some white or cream. Adding pale flowers lightens up a classic yellow and blue combination. To add complexity and depth to any planting, include a few flowers that are at the deepest end of your chosen color selections. You might add touches of dark burgundy to red color schemes or a little midnight indigo to a purple bed. If you are very interested in color, seeking out refined combinations will add to the pleasure of gardening. Subtle pairings can be made by choosing flowers suffused with similar color details. You could try a lily with a blushing throat near cosmos with a delicate pink edging. Another spring combination would be a jolly golden trumpet daffodil and a little purple-and-yellow Johnny-jump-up combined with a rock garden iris that has yellow freckles.

White lilies add coolness to a bed of red cardinal flower.

When choosing for color, it can be difficult to know whether a prospective flower is precisely the shade that you want. One way around this challenge is to make selections in person when plants are in flower. If you are thinking of dividing or moving a perennial from one area of your garden to another, you can pick one of its flowers and walk around the garden until you find another flower that combines well with it before moving the plant.

COLLECTING PLANTS IN VIGNETTES

One of the easiest ways to design a flower bed is in sections instead of all at once. If you choose a set of plants that look fabulous together, bloom at the same time, and complement each other, this practically guarantees beautiful compositions.

Begin with an early summer palette, as there are plenty of plants available and the weather is usually good for planting. Think about plant functions, habits, heights, leaf textures, as well as flower shape and color. Choose your favorite flower to serve as the seasonal highlight. Bearing in mind all the qualities of this plant, choose two or three additional flowers that look fabulous together, bloom at approximately the same time, and are suitable for the middle of the border. At least one of these plants should be a bold beauty. Add a tall background plant and a few tiny treasures for the front of the border. Finally, bring your composition

Think of flowers in groups of three to five that bloom at the same time to repeat in your beds. Rattlesnake master, pale coneflower, and blazing star make a sweet trio.

together through repetition of one or two weavers and mixers that may have an abundance of cloud-like floaty flowers or amorphous inflorescences.

Once your perennial base for early summer is decided, consider some annuals and tender perennials to come on later in the season and another set of perennials that fills each role during the height of summer. Choose your favorite flower for this season and add a couple of flanking companions. Pick a few taller plants for the back of the border, as well as a few new front-of-the-border treasures. To round out the growing year, make sure to include some fall plants, including one or two for the background, a few for mid-border, and one or two short plants to bloom alongside any already blooming front-of-the-border flowers. Finally, don't forget early and mid-spring. Include a set of hardy bulbs, spring-blooming perennials, and early annuals to complete the flowering cycle.

SEASONAL FLOWER COMBINATIONS

Once you understand the process of combining plants into groupings for each season, you can start to develop your own garden. Below are some possible plant combinations arranged by season suitable for a bed with full sun and average, decently drained garden soil.

from left A cool palette for early summer of blue larkspur, chartreuse hare's ears, and feverfew.

A colorful bed in the height of summer could include dark dahlias, blue delphiniums, dark orange marigolds, red salvia, purple giant hyssop, and verbena.

An example for early summer might include a ball-shaped tall allium as your bold beauty, with an upright perennial salvia and a horizontally flowered yarrow as the supporting cast. The weaving plant that links the bed together might be a hardy geranium or a some slightly more substantial catmint. Between groups there could be scattered hardy annuals like larkspur or poppies. If you wanted to add a bit of fun and floral glitter, you could tuck in a couple of foxgloves and bearded irises. Along the front you might choose sweet alyssum as an edging. At the back, you could have a blue false indigo.

For the height of summer, you could have lilies, border phlox, and penstemons paired with airy hummingbird mints or lesser calamint, with some dwarf flossflower as an edging. Choose some Joe-Pye weeds, tall sneezeweeds, or Culver's roots for the back. Try taller summer-flowering annuals like cosmos, zinnia, or spider flower in drifts, and add tender perennials like gladiolus.

For late summer into fall, large-flowered dahlias might be your bold beauties, with New England asters, Mexican bush sage, and Japanese anemones in the mid-border between drifts of color-changing tobacco plant. Prostrate heath asters, Japanese onion, and low-growing sedums could be at the front of the border, with perennial sunflowers, Tatarian aster, or New York ironweed as background plants. With any luck, your summer annuals and tender perennials will still be going strong well into fall to complete this flowery picture.

For early and mid-spring, choose a selection of tall and short hardy bulbs to come up between your later-blooming plants. Mix them with some early hardy annuals and a few spring perennials and biennials. For example, you could choose a tall and a short daffodil that you like for their colors or fragrance. Add in a fritillary for a different flower shape and a few low-growing foamy plants like basket-of-gold or forget-me-not, with upright wallflowers. Tuck in any little bulbs that you like, as they take up very little space. There are few tall plants to add at this time of year, but I leave space for later emerging background plants to fill in. You can take combinations or progressions from these examples or simply use this method as you put together your own flower garden.

The next phases of creating a flower bed that pleases you are installation and maintenance. In the following chapter you will learn practical tips to help you get your plants in the ground and look after them as you continue to develop your garden over time.

opposite A cool fall combination of blue and purple asters, pink and white cosmos, pale yellow perennial sunflower, and mauve Joe-Pye weed.

Putting Your Flower Garden Together

Preparing, Planning, Planting, and Maintaining

It is well worth investing in thoughtful preparation and planning of your flower bed. The time and energy that you put in now will result in good soil, a pleasing bed shape, and healthy, vibrant flowers. Once the plants are in the ground, regular maintenance will keep them thriving. »

Preparing

Planting or renovating a flower garden is one of my favorite things to do. It is a lovely mixture of physical activity and creative endeavor where I am out in the fresh air, thinking about plants, getting exercise, and delving my hands into the earth. I carefully prepare my soil, as it is the heart of a successful flower garden. No matter how eager I am to get flowers in the ground, I do not skip this vital step. If possible, I prepare the flower bed the fall before I plan to plant in spring to allow time for the soil to settle.

When I first moved to my garden, I dug my flower beds to two spade depths, a technique called double digging that you may still see mentioned in older gardening books. Needless to say, after this back-breaking work, I had a very aching gluteus maximus! Turning and mixing the soil interferes with the complex interrelationships between the organisms and microorganisms that help sustain the life in soil and the growth of plants. I have since moved on to a less intensive method of bed preparation that minimally disturbs the delicate soil structure. No-dig methods of preparing a bed rely on soil organisms to aerate and incorporate organic matter into the topsoil. Making a bed without digging is a win-win situation that saves you time, energy, and injuries while creating a "happy" soil.

Many new flower beds are made in existing lawns. The soil in these areas is often compacted from years of lawn mowing, walking, and other uses. Compacted soil lacks the air spaces that plants need to get their roots down into the ground. You can punch holes in the soil with a long-tined garden fork or you can take a hands-off approach and just let the soil organisms do the work for you.

If you are making a flower bed in a lawn, you can either take off the turf grass or smother it and leave it in place to rot down. Mark out the area of the future bed using sticks, string, flags, stones, logs, or landscape paint. Keep the bed outline as simple as possible by smoothing sharp angles and creating curves or straight lines that are easy to mow around. Check the widths of any remaining grass paths and leave sufficient room for water to drain away and for people to enjoy your garden. Walk away from the bed and look at it from all angles. Make sure it is big enough to see from your preferred vantage points but not too large to manage. You can enlarge it in a year or two if you like.

The exact method of lawn removal will depend on how aggressive your grass is, your time frame, and your preferences. One option is to slice off the grass using a sharp spade held parallel to the soil surface. Then you can either remove and compost the turf or flip it over to decay in place with the soil facing up. If you have a longer lead time and are preparing the soil for plant installation in a season or two, the easiest way is to leave the lawn in place and build up on top of it to maintain your existing topsoil. Use thin cardboard like cereal boxes or a stack of about five to ten sheets of newspaper. Lay it in overlapping layers like shingles on a roof to smother the grass. Wet it down as you go and use stones or logs to hold it in place. Choose a calm day, as this process is difficult in windy weather.

previous (clockwise from top left) A trio of orange flowers: California poppy, Mexican sunflower, and cosmos 'Bright Lights'.

opposite Preparing your soil is essential in order to grow beautiful flowers like dahlias, cannas, tall verbena, and fennel.

You can convert part of your lawn into a colorful flower bed by removing the turf and amending the soil.

On top of this grass-smothering layer, build up your bed by adding loose, well-rotted organic matter like compost, green waste, leaf mold, or aged manure. You can include some topsoil in this mix. You will need to add enough material to raise the bed up by about three to five inches. Look for local products that are free of weeds, pests, and contaminants such as pesticide residue, which can linger in manure. Do not include nonrenewable materials like peat moss. If you are making a big garden, it may be more economical to get a bulk delivery of a local material. Adding to the top of the soil creates a slightly elevated bed that will sink over time as the organic matter is broken down by decomposers and incorporated into the soil beneath, aerating it. The organic matter increases the water-holding capacity of the soil to make the kind of moist, well-drained soil that most garden flowers prefer. Each year you can top your bed up with more organic material. If you are making a gravel garden, you still need to remove weeds and turf, but instead of the organic additions, put down several inches of pebbles or gravel. As you lay out your planting area, make sure that you don't compact the soil. Soil aeration is vital to good root growth, and you don't want to undo all the hard work of your soil organisms.

In Case of Dire Weeds

If you have dire weeds in the area where you want the bed, there are several possible techniques to try. Most will take some time, so you will need to plan ahead. You may be tempted to cover the area with landscape fabric, but this is usually counterproductive, as it only suppresses weeds for a couple of years before soil builds up on top and a new crop of weeds develops.

You can cut everything to ground level and then keep mowing it for a season before smothering the area with newspaper. Another method is to solarize the bed, using the power of the sun to kill the weeds. If you are preparing the area in summer or fall for planting next spring, clear away as much above-ground growth as you can and then tightly pin down clear plastic over the bed. This acts like a little greenhouse and heats up the area beneath. It is not the prettiest thing to look at, but it is an easy way to kill turf, weeds, or a pervasive ground cover. I have used this method to turn a thistle patch into a flower bed. It may take a while, and you will not necessarily kill all the plants beneath, but you will significantly weaken them. If the area for your flower bed is covered in vines or invasive shrubs, clear the top growth and pull up the roots. Try to minimize soil loss or disturbance and runoff, especially if the land is sloped. Do everything that you can to keep your topsoil for your new planting.

Even the loveliest flower bed may need clearing out and rethinking after a few years if certain plants are taking up too much space or your favorite flowers have died out. You can work around the existing plantings, moving a few perennials, dividing others, removing the ones you don't like, and adding new ones. Or you can completely clear the bed: dig the plants out, renew the soil, and then rearrange, replant, and refresh.

If you are redoing an old garden, the first thing to do is take stock of what is growing there now. If you planted it, you might be familiar with the flowers. If you just moved house or have recently taken up gardening, you may not know what everything is or whether you want to keep it. Do your best to identify the plants, and call a gardening friend if you need help. Make a list of all the flowers and their heights, shapes, and colors. Divide your list into the ones you want to keep in the bed, those you like but want to move, those that are worth giving away, and those that need to go on the compost heap. Be careful when you dig: some plants, like spring bulbs, may be hidden below the ground if you are looking at the garden in summer. The only way to identify everything is to wait for a full calendar year, though you can start at any time.

The best time to do the removal and replanting is in spring or autumn. If you do it in the heat of summer, the plants will need special attention to recover. The ones you are saving should be dug with as big a root ball as possible and stored in a shady area until you are ready to replant, ideally within a few days. Put them into pots or old cardboard boxes, or wrap them up with lots of newspaper to keep them moist. Don't forget to water them well if they will be out of the ground for more than a day or two. Clumps that are too large will need to be divided before placing them back into the bed. If you discover that there are lots of weeds in the bed, you may need to wash the soil off the roots of the plants you are replanting.

If the bed is a weedy mess, start at one side of the area and work your way across consistently. If you have weeds that are woody plants and vines, they need to be pulled out by the roots or they are likely to regrow. If your prospective garden bed has obviously aggressive spreading plants in it, look carefully at them. If they have long, questing roots, they will probably be back in that bed even after you think you have pulled them all out. It pays to know what they look like for future removal. As you work in the bed, assess the soil and how it looks. An old flower bed is often depleted of organic matter, so add compost or leaf mold into the holes as you replant and add more as a top dressing.

If you are renovating an existing flower bed, first choose which plants to keep and which ones to remove. In this bed I decided to keep the catmint, poppies, and dame's rocket and remove most of the rest.

Raised beds that are at least six inches tall can have significant benefits: they are easier to tend and provide the good drainage that many plants need. Additionally, elevated flowers are easier to see and examine in detail. Even raising the bed a few inches is beneficial for most flowers. Plants' crowns—where their roots meet their above-ground growth—need to be kept dry, especially during a wet winter, or they may rot. Beds that are above grade are almost essential if you want to grow plants with silver-colored leaves or ones labeled rock-garden plants. Give them the sunniest area of the bed and do not overwater them. To increase drainage further, include some gravel or grit in your planting mix or add it as a mulch. A raised flower bed can simply be a pile of soil that is used to create a bank or berm. These mounded bed types have more presence in a garden and are a useful way to divide two garden areas or define a space. Each side of the berm will have slightly different environmental conditions, with the flowers on the sunny side coming out about a week or so before those on the shadier side.

A distinct edge gives a finished look to your flower bed. You can define it by cutting around the shape with a sharp spade. Dig a shallow V-shaped ditch to demarcate the outline and keep grass out of the bed. One of my English grandfathers spent hours each week cutting his neat grass edges. I thought that I would do the same thing here in Pennsylvania, but my grass is super aggressive and spreading, unlike his delicate lawn. What I have done is make physical barriers out of stone to outline most of my beds, whether they are at soil level or raised. If you want the final flower bed to be flush with the ground, add a flat mowing-strip of bricks or stones sunk into the lawn that you can mow right over.

Raised edgings retain the soil in the bed and can be aesthetically pleasing, especially if you use materials that tie in with the overall look of your garden. Source local, natural materials like stones, bricks, or wood. I have seen creative edging made of upside-down wine bottles, oyster shells, and metal, all used to good effect. My new favorite raised beds are made from agricultural water troughs with holes drilled in the bottom. They are high enough that I don't have to crouch to access my plants and appreciate them, and rabbits have a harder time eating from them.

Perhaps the most interesting raised bed in my garden is one made out of a pile of old rotting logs that I didn't know what to do with. One of my sons-in-law suggested that I make a *Hügelkultur*, the German word for "hill culture." I covered the logs with old wood chips, soil, and leaf mulch, to make a planting medium. As the logs have rotted down

This white lace flower is growing in a raised bed created by drilling drainage holes in the bottom of a metal farm trough.

over the years, they have produced a moist and fertile environment where flowers have flourished. To turn it into a flower patch, I used seed that I collected, flower seed mixes, and transplanted divisions of perennials from other parts of the garden. It is now a great pollinator habitat, and the plants have grown with very little intervention or attention. The only thing I have had to do is weed and edit out plants that became too aggressive.

There are some situations where it is best to lower your planting bed to capture all available moisture. This method is used if you are designing a rain garden, a garden for water-loving plants, or if your climate is very arid. Various cultures around the world use this time-honored agricultural practice of lowering planting beds to catch rainwater because it allows you to grow plants that normally grow in regions with higher rainfall. If you have a bank or hill, plant

My *Hügelkultur* is a wild-life haven with several birdhouses.

the drought-tolerant plants at the top and the water-lovers at the bottom where water puddles. Look at the water needs of your chosen plants before you decide whether to raise or lower your flower beds.

Planning

The types of plant you can add to your garden depends on the season you are establishing it. Spring and fall are the best times to plant because the air temperatures are not too extreme, and the soil is warm enough for roots to grow. Spring and early summer are often when gardeners install their gardens, as there is a wide variety of plants available. You can plant perennials and cool-season annuals followed by tender perennials and warm-season annuals after the last frost. If your planting day is in summer, it is best to plant half-hardy annuals and wait until fall to plant perennials and spring-flowering bulbs, which can easily be slipped between other plants. If at any point your desired perennial is not available, you can fill in with annuals until you find it. Winter is the time for indoor planning that you can then implement in the spring. If you are making a new garden, it will probably not be planted all at once. Most gardens are developed over time. Part of the joy you will find in gardening is altering and amending your garden as you get new ideas.

When you are starting a flower bed from scratch, it may be difficult to know how many plants you need. I work out approximately how many square feet there are in the bed to know how much space I have to fill. Next, I break my bed into four zones: back, mid-back, mid-front, and front. Finally, I sort my completed

opposite A layered bed, like this one packed with cheerful annuals, has a selection of tall, medium, and short plants to give a pleasing fullness.

plant list by season and write in the described widths of each plant. Depending on the size of your bed, you might only need to buy one or two large plants. You are likely to need multiples of medium or small plants for each grouping.

Beginning with the tallest plants, I work out approximately how many I have room for along the back of a border, or in the center of an island bed. If I am adding in tall annuals, I leave room for them between groupings of perennials. Then I move on to the middle of the bed, which I usually divide into mid-front and mid-back. This area is typically wider and needs more plants than either the front or back zones. Work with your wish list groupings of three or more plants for each season and repeat them along the bed. Calculate how many times you can repeat this combination along the middle of the bed while still leaving room for your other seasonal arrays. I tend to devote more space to the plantings of early and midsummer and use fewer repetitions for spring and fall. I make sure to leave space for planting pockets of tender perennials, annuals, and bulbs. Finally, I think about the shortest plants that take up approximately six to nine inches each. I run my tape measure along the front and work out how many edging plants will fit.

Once you have a good idea of the plants you want to buy or grow for your flower garden, you may have to narrow your list according to what plants are available. Pick them out yourself to ensure they are strong, healthy specimens. Find more options by looking at online retailers and catalogs that will ship plants. If in doubt, start with a few perennials the first year and fill in with annuals as you see what your flower bed looks like and what things grow well. In the following years you can adjust and add more perennials.

Planning on Paper

Gardeners who prefer to plan on paper can draw out a map of their bed. Make it as accurate or approximate as you like. It is a fun way to while away winter evenings thinking about spring planting. If this sounds appealing to you, one of the easiest ways to plan is to use a different base map for each of the four flowering times of the year. You can do this as overlays using tracing paper. A different approach is to cut out pieces of paper to represent each plant or grouping of plants and move them around on your base map. This allows you to visualize the number and possible configurations of your plants. The cutouts can be rearranged until you are satisfied and then glued in place. Either method has its limitations, as it is all but impossible to accurately represent on paper the way your plants will grow together in your garden. Plans can be a good tool for some people, but they are not a necessary precursor to a great flower garden.

When installing a new bed, try to get as many plants together as possible on planting day. Look at your seasonal groupings for the entire year, and try to source them all or block out spaces in the bed where they will be added later. Once you have assembled all the plants that you can find, it is time to arrange them in your bed. My recommended method for designing with flowers is to place them out on the soil and move them around as needed. After you have configured them the first time, walk away from the bed, look at the placement from different angles, and then make adjustments. You will see whether you need to acquire more or make alternate plans. You may also decide to fill in empty spots with annuals that you can switch out or replace with perennials next year. After placing your plants, it is a good idea to take photos of the bed or sketch out a rough labeled map as a record. Keep a running list of the cultivars and numbers of plants that you have so you can refer to it in the future.

Planting

I feel rather like a plant hoarder in the days leading up to the big planting, trying to think of ways to hide my new purchases from my long-suffering husband, who already thinks I have a plant-collecting problem! I keep them moist and shaded so they are not stressed, and assemble my planting supplies, including good digging tools and soil amendments like compost, before I start.

I like to gather my plants and tools together before taking them to the planting area.

I use the spacing distance recommended on the tags as a guideline, but I tend to plant closer than it says on the label if I want a full display right away. For example, if the suggested spacing is two feet, I might place plants of the same type within a group at eighteen inches. This gives an abundant look to the bed, and the plants quickly intermesh. Spacing them farther apart leaves bare soil where weeds will grow. I know that I will likely need to dig and divide them after a few years, but then I can use the extra plants elsewhere. I leave gaps between one plant group and the next so I can plant some bulbs and annuals in these planting pockets.

I set out the potted plants and place them in the positions where I think they might go. I use stepping-stones or wooden boards placed on the soil to avoid compaction. The first plants that are put out are the tallest ones for the back of a border or the center of an island bed. Large individual plants are placed singly if they have enough presence of their own. After that, I arrange mid-size plants in the central part of the bed. Each seasonal group gets put out close together. The groupings can vary in the number of each plant and how they are set out. Groups can be stretched along in diagonal drifts, or elongated triangles that run from front to back of the bed. I repeat trios for each of the other seasons and copy these

A newly planted flower bed showing how to group perennials while leaving enough room for them to grow. In the early years of this bed, annuals were added to fill the empty spaces.

combinations along the bed. I finish up with short perennial plants at the edge in large groups so they have impact. I leave the plants in their pots until all the plants are placed to my liking. This allows me to rearrange them as many times as I like. Only then do I go back in and plant from the back of the bed forward.

If you are adding new plants to an existing flower bed, follow a similar procedure of placing the pots, standing back, and checking their placement before planting.

POTTED PLANTS

Before planting your newly purchased flowers, plunge them into cool water to rehydrate them if the potting soil is dry. If possible, choose a mild, overcast day in spring or fall for planting, and water the bed the day before. Dig each hole two to three times the width of the plant pot and at least as deep. To remove the plant from the pot, hold the bottom in one hand and place the palm of your other hand on top of the soil with your fingers on either side of the stem base. Flip the whole thing upside down and ease the plant out of the pot while supporting the root ball. Inspect its roots. Hopefully, the potting medium will be full of roots but not congested. Release the roots from the root ball and shake off any loose potting medium. If the roots are entangled or are poking out of the holes in the pot, you may need to cut several vertical slashes into the root ball to release them before planting.

Stand the plant upright in the hole so that the crown is at the same level as the plant was in its pot. Spread out the roots and backfill with topsoil mixed with plenty of compost or leaf mold. Using your fingers, press down on the surface to make sure the roots are in contact with the soil. You can leave a little soil rim a few inches away from the plant that will help to trap water when it gets irrigated if you garden in dry conditions. Water the plant thoroughly to make sure all large air spaces are removed from the soil. Be sure to add the new plants to your list and map. You can also insert their nursery labels into the ground next to the plants to help you remember their names.

BULBS, CORMS, AND TUBERS

Bulbs, corms, and tubers are planted in one season and then emerge at a later time. Dig a hole that is two to three times the height of the bulb. Sprinkle a little slow-release organic bulb fertilizer or bone meal into the soil at planting time.

A collection of fall-planted bulbs, including crocus, glory-of-the-snow, snake's head fritillary, squill, and grape hyacinth. Measure the height of the bulb from base to top and place them in holes two to three times their height with the pointed tip up.

If you want to increase drainage in wet areas or for rot-prone bulbs like lilies or tulips, place a layer of fine grit in the bottom of the planting hole. Sit the base of the bulb on the grit with the pointed end up and any little shriveled roots facing downward. If you are not sure which is the top or bottom, lay it on its side. Small bulbs or corms like crocus can be planted together in one broad hole as long as they do not touch. Large bulbs such as allium or crown imperial fritillary should be planted singly.

To create an abundant spring display, use a layered planting method to pack different-sized bulbs into a small area such as a container or a bed. Dig your mixed planting hole to the depth needed by the largest bulbs you will be planting and place them in the bottom. Add a shallow layer of soil until the resulting depth is correct for the smaller ones and then plant them on top, avoiding the places where you placed the biggest bulbs. Backfill with soil and press it down. If you plan to treat tulips as bedding or cutting annuals to be removed after flowering, they can be planted close together and intermingled with smaller bulbs like grape hyacinth or short daffodils. If you are planting tulips that you want to come back for several years, plant the bulbs at least eight inches deep with sufficient space between them.

Summer-flowering bulbs, corms, and tubers are planted after all danger of frost has passed. Dahlias are planted into a hole about six inches deep and covered by an inch of soil, with a stake inserted at planting time. They should not be watered until you see a shoot emerging. Gradually fill in the hole with loose soil as the stem grows. Plant gladiolus corms in batches about a week or two apart to produce a succession of blooming times. Tuberoses, cannas, and many other tender perennials should only be planted outside once the soil has warmed up or they may die.

GROWING FROM SEED

Starting flowers from seed is one of the most satisfying and economical ways to populate your garden. Seeds are produced through sexual reproduction when pollen is transferred from one flower to another. The new offspring share similar traits and characteristics with its parents, but there are sometimes surprises! Plant breeding takes this process and deliberately crosses plants with attractive traits to produce fun new cultivars. When planted in the right conditions, the seed germinates and grows into the next generation of that flowering plant.

You can tell that the seeds of this milkweed are ready to harvest because the seed head has burst open and the seeds have darkened in color. If you don't collect them, the seeds will float away to new areas using their silken hairs to catch the wind.

You can purchase packets of seed from vendors, or harvest them yourself to sprinkle in your garden this or next year. Wait for the seed to ripen on the plants and then collect the seed heads into a paper bag. You will know that they are ready to harvest when the seed capsules crack open and the seeds change in color, often turning brown. Leave the collected seeds to fully dry before storing them in glass jars in a cool, dry place. Seeds are amazing in that some can survive, alive but in suspended animation, for years, decades, or even longer if the storage conditions are correct.

Some seed is best grown outside by sprinkling or inserting them directly into the soil. Others are better started indoors before they are planted out as seedlings. Annuals are often the easiest, but you can also start biennials and perennials in the same way. Direct sowing outside is the easiest way to start hardy annual flowers. The seeds can be sown in regular garden soil in the fall or early spring to flower by summer. Half-hardy annuals cannot survive frosty weather, so they are best sown directly when the soil begins to warm up in mid or late spring. Biennial plants are started in summer to bloom the following spring. You can also grow perennials, but they may take a year or more to flower. Some hardy plants will not germinate without a period of freezing and thawing, so they should be sown outdoors in the fall. Self-sowing or volunteer seedlings come from seeds directly sown from a ripe seed head. They are a fabulous way to add some extra flower power to your bed and unify a border. Tie a piece of colored string around the stems of flower specimens you like so you can find them in later months after the seed has ripened. As you remove annual plants or deadhead perennials, you can sprinkle seeds back into the bed where you want them to flower.

Tender seeds that must be started indoors are sown in clean pots with drainage holes filled with seed starting mix. Follow the directions on the seed packet as to where, when, and how to sow your seeds. Count back by the specified number of weeks before your last frost date to calculate when seed should be started. Sow seeds thinly to avoid crowding, or be vigilant about thinning closely spaced seedlings. When they germinate, they will need as much light as possible to make sturdy plants, so consider acquiring a grow light even if you have sunny windowsills. Turn the plants regularly to stop them leaning over. Keep them well watered but not wet during their early growth so they do not succumb to a fungal disease called damping off. In the weeks before they are to be planted out, start acclimatizing them to outdoor conditions, a process known as hardening off. Bring them outside each day for a few hours if the weather is mild, and return them inside at night, gradually increasing the time spent outside. To transplant the seedlings into outdoor soil, gently remove the root ball from its container, holding the leaves and not the stem to avoid accidental damage, and place into a prepared hole.

Cool-Season Annuals Easy to Grow from Seed

from left This white borage is a reliable cool-season annual.

Hardy annuals like larkspur are easy from seed if they receive a period of cold weather, which helps them to germinate.

Borago officinalis, borage

Calendula officinalis, pot marigold

Centaurea cyanus, cornflower

Cerinthe major, honeywort

Consolida ajacis, larkspur

Eschscholzia californica, California poppy

Lobularia maritima, sweet alyssum

Nigella damascena, love-in-a-mist

Orlaya grandiflora, white lace flower

Papaver rhoeas, corn poppy

Warm-Season Annuals Easy to Grow from Seed

from left Cosmos are warm-season annuals that are simple to grow from seed directly sown after your last frost or started indoors earlier.

Mexican sunflower and amaranth are large annuals that do well in warm weather and grow easily from seed.

Amaranthus cruentus, red amaranth

Celosia argentea, celosia

Cleome hassleriana, spider flower

Cosmos bipinnatus, cosmos

Helianthus annus, annual sunflower

Nicotiana alata, flowering tobacco

Tagetes patula, French marigold

Tithonia rotundifolia, Mexican sunflower

Tropaeolum majus, nasturtium

Zinnia elegans, zinnia

Self-Sowing Biennials and Short-Lived Perennials

from left Biennial dame's rocket and short-lived perennial feverfew may both self-sow in your garden.

Biennial or short-lived perennial clary sage, *Salvia sclarea*, can be grown from seed sown the summer before it is to flower.

Digitalis purpurea, common foxglove

Eryngium giganteum, Miss Willmott's ghost

Knautia macedonica, Macedonian scabious

Lychnis coronaria, rose campion

Myosotis sylvatica, forget-me-not

Papaver atlanticum, Atlas poppy

Patrinia scabiosifolia, golden lace

Salvia coccinea, scarlet sage

Silene armeria, garden catchfly

Verbascum chaixii, nettle-leaved mullein

A FLOWER GARDEN IN CONTAINERS

Container plantings are a wonderfully flexible way to grow flowers. The pots can be clustered together for instant impact and then changed out and rearranged to bring seasonal interest. Containers are an excellent way to grow flowers if your access to in-ground gardening is limited. You can have a flower garden in pots anywhere there is enough sun: on your porch, windowsill, or patio, by your door, or on any sunny paved area. If you garden on a roof, balcony, or deck, find out if there are any weight limits before you plan your potted flower garden. You might use containers as a focal point, at the end of the garden, on either side of a path, or clustered near a bench. If you rent a house or anticipate moving, your whole garden might be in containers so that it can move with you.

When you choose containers, it is important to think about how they will function as well as what they look like. Possible containers include hanging baskets, window boxes, and any pot or recycled object as long as it has drainage holes in the bottom, is clean, and is free from pests or diseases. You can use wooden boxes, metal, resin, and plastic containers too. Large pots give the greatest impact and will require watering less often than smaller ones. Traditional terracotta pots are aesthetically pleasing and work well for drought-tolerant plants and silver-leaved herbs like lavender. Glazed ceramic pottery comes in many colors, shapes, and sizes, and doesn't lose water as quickly as unglazed terracotta.

Consider where you will put them and then choose colors, textures, sizes, and shapes that relate to their surroundings and will coordinate with the flowers that you love. If in doubt, choose a neutral color and buy several similar pots to help coordinate your compositions. If you are an eclectic gardener, you can use containers to create your own garden look by mixing and matching materials. The pots should provide an attractive frame for your plants without predominating.

A container is a mini flower garden, and many of the same design principles apply. You will want a bold flower as the centerpiece of your display and a few coordinating smaller-scale bloomers. Ideally, your central flower will be at least as tall as the pot it is growing in and have a striking flower shape, color, or interesting leaf form or texture. The supporting cast of flowers should have contrasting forms, different heights, and pleasing coloration. Add one or two little treasures toward the edge of the pot that have a billowing or trailing habit and will cascade down to soften the pot rim.

Design your container collection to include at least one plant to give height, like this canna, and then others with different flower shapes and habits like geranium, petunia, agapanthus, and dahlia.

Annuals, tender perennials, and bulbs are most often used in container plantings, but there is no reason to exclude perennials from your creations. Perennials and bulbs have a set period when they bloom, so it is important to consider their plant presence and leaf quality when you include them in your design. You can plant up mixed containers that have different plants in them, or you can plant each type in its own container and then cluster the pots in varying combinations to get the look you want. Rearrange your pots every few weeks to bring featured flowers to the front. If you want to, you can change out annuals and bulbs each season to keep the plantings interesting and fresh. Use upside-down pots, bricks, or blocks to raise up shorter pots and create the effect you want.

The container garden year begins with the flowers of hardy annuals and bulbs. Bulbs are planted up into pots in autumn and stored in a slightly protected area for the winter. I put my planted pots in an unheated garage to let the bulbs get their required period of cold and also protect the pot itself from cracking. Some pots are labeled frost resistant but will eventually crack after a few years of freezing and thawing in very cold wet weather. If the pot is too large to move inside for the winter, cover it with a waterproof layer before the first heavy frosts and then plant it up with prepotted bulbs and hardy annuals in spring. As the season changes into summer, replace the bulbs and hardy annuals with warm-season annuals and perennials. These plants should last you through the rest of the growing year until your first frost, but you can perk it up by adding in fresh cold-weather annuals for fall display.

Putting together a container flower garden is a chance for you to show your creative side. Make sure all the plants in one pot have the same water and sunlight requirements. Choose your bold beauties and supporting cast for each season before you go to the store, making sure to include some alternates in case your local nursery doesn't have one of your options. Container-grown flowers are planted more closely together than they would be if they were grown in the ground. Space the plants about a third to a half of the suggested distance that it says on the plant label to give a full, lush look. Consider this when planning how many plants to grow yourself or buy.

It is easier to assemble container plantings in place, so bring your materials to the site. To improve drainage, add a layer of broken terracotta pots, stones, or large gravel to the bottom of your containers before adding the potting mix. Choose a good-quality peat-free potting mix to fill the container. If you are growing flowers that need especially free-draining soil, mix in horticultural grit, coarse sand, or gravel. Any of these additions give extra weight to the potting mix to reduce the chance that your pots will blow over on a windy site. For a uniform look, mulch the top of container plantings with the same material.

These are some of my favorite container flowers, along with their growing season. Use them as a start and bring your own taste and creativity to your new container flower garden.

Cool-Season Container Plants

from left Bright orange tulip 'Ballerina' makes a colorful splash in this spring container under-planted with blue grape hyacinths.

This cool-season yellow viola picks up the colors in the glazed container. Plants like pansies can be used both in the spring and the fall to prolong your container show.

Calendula officinalis, pot marigold

Dianthus barbatus, sweet William

Erysimum cheiri, common wallflower

Lobelia erinus, trailing lobelia

Lobularia maritima, sweet alyssum

Narcissus, daffodil

Muscari, grape hyacinth

Scilla, squill

Tulipa, tulip

Viola ×*wittrockiana*, pansy

Warm-Season Container Plants

from left Use warm-season plants like million bells that have a trailing habit in hanging containers or around the edges of pots.

Group your containers together to create a show. This combination of blue mealycup sage and pale petunias has contrasting shapes and coordinating colors.

Angelonia angustifolia, angelonia

Calibrachoa, million bells

Dahlia, dahlia, especially dwarf cultivars

Euphorbia hypericifolia, baby's breath spurge

Gomphrena globosa, globe amaranth

Pelargonium, geranium

Pentas lanceolata, Egyptian starcluster

Petunia, petunia

Salvia farinacea, mealycup sage

Tagetes patula, French marigold

Maintaining

When you look after your garden, you are close to your flowers and can really enjoy being with them. Maintaining a flower garden is based on observations, gardening priorities, and common sense. If you have chosen healthy plants that suit your conditions and planted them carefully, they will be off to a good start. The first few weeks in the life of an annual plant and the first few months of a perennial's life are the most important, as the plants haven't had a chance to get their roots into the new soil. During this time, pay special attention to their basic needs, particularly watering. Most plants need a lower level of care once they are established. After that, you will need to do some occasional trimming, dead-heading, weeding, mulching, and watering as needed.

WATERING

All plants need water to live. It is a vital element that comes into the plant through its tiniest roots and from there travels up through the stems and to the leaves and flowers. Water hydrates their cells and keeps plants standing upright. It is also the vehicle for moving nutrients into the plants and cooling them down when they release water vapor through their leaf surfaces. If you live in a dry climate or one with erratic rainfall, you need to think carefully about water use. Human overuse of potable water in gardens puts a strain on the wider environment. If you live in a climate with plentiful rain throughout the year, watering your plants may be less of an issue. In any climate, you have the choice as to how much water you use in your garden. Your plants' watering needs depend on their species, how they are grown, the ambient temperature, humidity, and wind currents. Think of the windy, sunny, low-humidity days that most quickly air dry your laundry if you hang it outside. The same conditions that dry your washing also dry out plants, especially those with large leaf surface areas. If these conditions persist for days at a time, the soil will dry out, and eventually your plants will wilt and then need to be watered. Soil with a high humus content can hold on to and then release moisture to your plants over a period of time.

Different plant types and situations require different watering strategies. The goal of watering should be to water the soil and your plants' roots, not their leaves and flowers. It is especially important to fully soak your perennial plants when watering them in the first year or two but to do so infrequently. What you are trying to do is "train" the plants to look for water deep in the soil. Roots will grow in the direction of water, so if you water often and only provide a small volume of water each time, the roots will grow up to the soil surface and the plants will be unable to fend for themselves in times of drought. Some plants are better adapted to search for water down in the soil. Look for naturally deep-rooted plants or anything with a tap root, such as many prairie plants, desert plants and a lot of Mediterranean plants.

One of the least wasteful ways to water your plants is to use a watering can. Assembled together, they make a cute garden collection.

Annual plants, with their short life spans, do not have time to grow extensive root systems, so they may need more frequent watering. Annuals sown directly in the ground, either self-sown or hand sown, are typically more drought tolerant than transplants. Some tender perennials that come from water-rich environments are likely to need regular supplemental watering.

When you need to water, the least wasteful way is to hand water the plants as they need it with a watering can or a hose. Group your plants by how much water they need. Put the most moisture-loving plants together near your water source. You can capture rainwater by attaching rain barrels or water butts to your house's downspouts to collect water for later use.

When you water, add it until it has soaked down through the upper layers of topsoil and reached the deep roots of the plants. To check how deeply the water has penetrated, poke your finger into the soil to see if it feels dry. You can even dig a small hole and see where the layer of wetness stops. The two best times to water are early in the morning or late afternoon into evening when the sun is not beating down. If you prefer, you can use an oscillating sprinkler system to water your plants or install an automated system like soaker hoses or drip irrigation. For plants prone to fungal diseases like powdery mildew, it is best to keep water off their leaves. Standing water caused by poor drainage or excessive irrigation can cause roots to rot. Water-loving plants will grow in soggy soil, but most garden plants will not.

Any plants that you grow in a container can't seek out water in the ground and so will need frequent watering. You may need to water your containers every day in the heat of summer. Some pot types, like the unglazed terracotta pots that I love, dry out faster than others. When you water containers, keep going until it runs through the drainage hole to make sure that you have thoroughly soaked the roots. It is essential that every container have a hole in the bottom. If you have a tray or saucer under the pot, don't let water sit there for extended periods or the roots can rot. Cluster your pots together to make watering easier.

MULCHING

Adding mulch to your garden beds helps keep moisture in the soil and insulates it. There are two main mulch categories: organic and inorganic. Organic mulch is made from shredded wood, leaf mold, or compost that breaks down and assimilates into the soil, providing some nutrients and eventually improving the soil structure. A thick layer of organic mulch may be applied to prevent the germination of weed seeds, but this will stop wanted volunteer seeds from growing too. Be aware that some wood mulches have a tendency to form mats that can repel water and may provide cover for burrowing creatures. Chunky wood chips take a long time to integrate into the soil and can overwhelm delicate flowering plants. I like to use well-broken-down leaf mold or compost as a mulch in my flower beds. No matter what type of mulch you choose, only add it when needed and pull it away from the crowns of the plants.

Inorganic materials such as stone, gravel, or rock also cover the soil surface to keep roots moist but do not provide any extra nutrients. Stone absorbs heat from the sun, making the ambient temperature in a gravel-mulched bed warmer than the surrounding ones. It also improves drainage around the crown of your flowering plants and reduces frost heaving. Gravel mulch is not for every flower bed but looks fabulous for Mediterranean plantings and rock gardens.

COMPOSTING AND FERTILIZING

In my garden, most of the nutrition that my very healthy plants get comes from the action of organisms and microorganisms as they break down organic matter in the soil. I do use some bagged slow-release organic fertilizers, but I think of these additions as an occasional supplement. If you look after your soil by regularly adding doses of compost or leaf mold, you may not need to add fertilizer at all. If you garden on sandy soil, you are more likely to have to apply some than if you have clay. Every soil type benefits from the addition of organic matter. All dead plant matter naturally breaks down through the action of decomposers. The sticky brown humus that they ultimately produce is an essential component of healthy soil. To grow strong plants, you need to replenish the soil every year by adding decaying plant matter to the tops of your flower beds. Composting is an easy and free way of reusing and recycling old plant material and kitchen waste.

Gather fallen leaves, herbaceous plant remains, vegetable peelings, eggshells, coffee grounds, and biodegradable tea bags into a compost bin or a simple heap.

Don't add diseased plant parts, meat, dairy products, weed seeds, or weeds with big tap roots like dandelions that may start growing in your heap. You will need to add air and water to activate the process. Chopping up plant parts will accelerate the composting. Making leaf mold is even simpler than compost. Take fall leaves, shred them into pieces by running over them on the lawn with a lawn mower, and then pile them in their own place. Leave the pile to break down for about a year. Leaf mold and compost are wonderful soil conditioners or mulches on top of a flower bed. They quickly incorporate into the soil, enriching it.

If you cannot produce enough of your own compost, you can buy some. Look for local sources of green waste like mushroom compost, aged manure, or cocoa hulls. Check the acidity or alkalinity of any potential additions to make sure they don't alter your soil's pH (percentage of hydrogen). Plants take up nutrients from the soil when they absorb water through their roots. Different plants can only access certain nutrients within a particular pH range. Most flower garden plants grow best in soil that is neither too acidic nor too alkaline. You can send your soil away to be tested or buy an at-home pH kit if you want to check.

Annuals and cutting garden flowers need more fertilizer than perennials. Their fast growth rate and the number of flowers they produce during the season requires a rich soil. A good time to fertilize them is right as they are setting flower buds. Before I use bagged fertilizers, I look at a plant carefully and see if it is growing well. I assess the leaves to make sure they are the correct color and that there is fresh growth at the end of each stem. I also evaluate the flowers, checking their numbers and colors. If everything looks normal, I do not fertilize. Plants may need to be fertilized when they are in active growth in the spring if their leaves are yellowing or the plant is stunted.

One of my compost heaps is contained in a structure made of slatted wood to allow air circulation. It is located in the back corner of a fenced garden.

Overfertilized plants produce lots of soft and fleshy leafy growth, which is very attractive to pests like aphids that love to feast on the sappy shoot tips. Another reason not to overdo fertilizer is that plants fed with lots of nitrogen quickly put on extensive growth that flops over and will need staking or pruning. Too much fertilizer can injure, burn, or kill a plant, especially if applied during a drought. If in doubt, underfertilize rather than overfertilize. Use half or a quarter of the recommended amount and then assess the plant in a week or two to see how it is growing. If your plant is not growing well, it may lack one of three main plant nutrients: nitrogen (N), phosphorous (P), or potassium (K). These nutrients will be listed by percentage in this order as NPK on the side of commercially produced fertilizers. Nitrogen is used to help the plant make good green leaves, phosphorus promotes healthy roots, shoots, and flowers, and potassium stimulates good overall growth.

If you do add fertilizer, the type you use is important. The ideal is a slow-release organic fertilizer that can be gradually broken down in the soil. To encourage flowering, I tend to sprinkle a little bone meal around the base of my plants, which has an NPK of 3-15-0. Additionally, I add my own cooled wood ashes (approximately 0-1-5) to provide potassium if needed. This is alkaline, so keep it away from any plants that require acidic soil. Blood meal (12-0-0) is a good organic addition

This plant-packed container with canna, heliotrope, petunia, and marigold will need more regular fertilizing than the same plants would if grown in the ground.

Fertilizing Container-Grown Plants

Container-grown plants are dependent on the limited nutrients available in the potting mix and what you then add. Flowers growing in containers are often packed together for aesthetic reasons, so they compete for limited resources. Check your potting mix and see if it has added fertilizer. If it does, it will give you an approximate number of weeks that it should last. If there are no added nutrients, don't apply fertilizer right away. Instead, let the plants acclimatize to their new environment first. It is time to fertilize them when they start to show signs of new growth. Mix up a dilute-strength fertilizer, maybe using a liquid feed like a seaweed-based or fish emulsion product, and then water or spray the plants as well as the roots. Liquid fertilizers can be absorbed through the leaves as a foliar feed as well as from the soil. It is best to apply fertilizer when the plant is fully hydrated and the soil is not dry. Choose a time when the plant is not in full sun and the temperature is moderate.

if you want high nitrogen, and it will make your soil slightly more acidic. In addition to the three main nutrients, organic fertilizers contain various other micronutrients. Add only what fertilizer is needed, otherwise you will disturb the soil microbes that support your plants' growth. Excess fertilizer is not retained in the soil but washes downstream and can pollute the environment.

STAKING

Staking is a way to support your plants and hold up their stems and flowers. This is especially important in gardens that are windy, near large bodies of water, or shaded. The gold standard is unobtrusive staking that highlights the plant without drawing attention to the supports. Another approach is to use staking systems that are an attractive part of your garden design. No matter which method you use, put them in before the plant flowers.

Even if you don't grow in extreme conditions, you may still find it necessary to provide support for the tallest plants you grow. Some tall flowering plants have a natural tendency toward floppiness, and others can fall over if they are grown in overly rich or loose soil conditions. I am a fan of tall plants in my garden, and I don't mind too much if they sprawl into each other, but I take care to place them away from paths, and I use my fences as partial support. There are also a few medium-height plants that will need supporting. As you garden, you will discover which ones need this treatment in your conditions. One person may be able to grow yarrows without support, but another may need to underpin them. Shorter plants are likely to self-support or use their neighbors to keep themselves upright. Other plants, like hardy geraniums, have a desirably sprawling habit so should not be tied up.

There are several ways to hold plants upright. The easiest is to insert a circle of bamboo or other stakes around the base of the plant, carefully avoiding the roots. Tie biodegradable string like jute or hemp twine to these uprights, encircling the plant within. There is a fine line between holding up your plants with twine and making them look like trussed turkeys. If in doubt, tie the plant loosely, then stand back and look before making final adjustments. For added internal support, you can weave a star shape of twine from stake to stake. This will corral stems as they grow and make them less likely to splay apart. If the plant has stiff stems, you can use this same method, using the exterior stems in place of stakes. I do this to hold up my sweet coneflower, taking care not to make the knots too tight.

To support top-heavy flowers with substantial stems like dahlias and lilies, insert one large wooden or bamboo stake into the ground behind the plant. Tie the twine to the stake and run a figure-eight-shaped loop around the plant stem and then back to the stake. This gives the plant a chance to wiggle in the wind without the string cutting into the stem. You can also tie your plants to an

next page A summer border may need supports to hold up taller plants like delphinium, sneezeweed, and beebalm.

What to Do When Visitors are Coming

If you have visitors coming to see your garden, there are several strategies to use to give the flower bed its best face forward. The first is to give it a neat frame. If lawn abuts the bed, cut a clean edge with a sharp shovel. If the bed overspills a path, trim the plants back so that you can walk along. It doesn't have to be a precise line, as it is a lovely experience to brush against plants, especially if they are fragrant. Then work on the mid-border. Pull out or trim back any plants that are browned or past their prime, remove obvious weeds, and fluff up flowers so that they face the path. You may need a few natural sticks and twine to tie up floppy plants but, if possible, keep drastic intervention to a minimum because it often looks contrived. Stand back and scan the whole bed. If you have large gaps, a quick trip to the garden center may yield a couple of plants already in flower that can be tucked in among other leafy occupants. Sometimes you don't even have to plant them. Drop them into the border and hide the pot with surrounding leaves. After the guests have left, take a longer look and see what your bed was missing at this time of year and what you really want to add for next year.

adjacent fence. There are commercially available plant supports of different sizes that are held up on metal legs. Look for peony rings, tripods, or half-circles for full plants, or a loop of wire for single-stemmed plants like lilies.

Another way to support plants as they grow is to insert freshly cut twiggy sticks around them in spring. Twigs are brown in color, so they don't stand out and can be bent and tied to the correct height. The earlier in the growing season you can do this, the better, as then the plant stems grow through the crossing branches, covering them. You can make a shape like an upside-down basket, a pyramid, or any other creative form that you want. You can either design supports to be concealed as the foliage grows through them or be part of the artistic show in the bed. I grow dahlias, and I hammer heavy wooden stakes into the ground as I plant the tubers. Because the stakes need to be so large, they cannot be hidden and so I have chosen to make them a feature in my garden. They are painted lilac pink to go with the colors of the flowers that I am growing. I have also seen painted rebar, wire sculptures, and found objects used to fun effect. You can be as creative as you like as you design methods of plant support.

I have made a feature of the pink poles that I use to support the flowers in my cutting garden like the coordinating *Dahlia* 'Vassio Meggos'.

DEADHEADING AND TRIMMING

One of the most enjoyable ways to interact with your flowers is to do a regular walk along your flower bed with a little pair of snips in your hand. Trim off any brown or floppy parts. You may also want to deadhead spent flowers before the plant turns its energy to making seed. Take the old blooms off just above the set of leaves below the flowers to encourage plants to rebloom later in the year. Leave flower heads alone if you want to save their seeds. While you are in your garden, cut yourself a little posy of flowers (I like to think of this as preemptive deadheading).

Beyond deadheading, you may need to trim the stems of your plants to control their overall size or alter the flowering time. Removing the growing tips of some plants will encourage side shoots to develop, producing smaller though more numerous flowers that bloom later. If you cut the front part of the clump, the back half will flower first, followed by the section that you cut. I like to do this with my border phlox, nipping down bits to stagger their flowering times. You can choose to partially or completely "Chelsea chop" (cut back by a third to a half) late-blooming perennials that form multiple flowering stems, delaying bloom and reducing height. Some perennials will rebloom if they are thoroughly dead-headed, but the second flush will not be as spectacular as the first. Late-spring or early-summer perennials like hardy salvias can be cut back to their basal foliage. Water and care for them well during the next few weeks.

Hardy chrysanthemums are some of the last garden flowers to bloom, and the plants can get leggy and splay open in the center if they are not pinched. Cut back the ends of the longest shoots two or three times before midsummer. Look

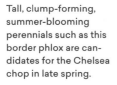

Tall, clump-forming, summer-blooming perennials such as this border phlox are candidates for the Chelsea chop in late spring.

from left Goldfinches and other birds consume the seeds of many flowers, like this New England aster, if you leave them standing in your garden in the fall.

These flower beds have been planted to provide food and shelter for a wide range of wildlife.

at how the plant performs in the fall and see if you pinched it enough. If not, change your regime next year. The easiest way to remove the tiny tips are when they are still soft. Use your thumb and forefinger to pinch off the end. For a larger group that has lots of small flowers, use sharp clippers or even hedge shears. If what you take off is healthy, it can go straight into your compost heap. If you see any dead or diseased parts, do not compost them.

I manage my garden differently than I was brought up to do in the gardens of my childhood. We were raised with the idea that you "put the garden to bed" after the frosts of autumn killed the tops of plants. Now I leave stems and seed heads standing over winter to provide food for birds, and deliberately create habitat where insects and other creatures can live and proliferate. This is what happens in nature; no one comes in and takes away old stems, so they are left in situ to become safe winter resting places for insects and other little creatures, especially if they are hollow. There is no need to buy bug hotels if you have the natural places they need.

There are aesthetic reasons to leave seed heads standing over winter too. Some plants look great in their winter forms, especially when outlined by frost or snow. In autumn I cut off any plant stems that have fallen over paths or that look mushy or ugly and compost them. The rest are left standing through the cold months, and the top growth is not cleared away until early spring before flowering bulbs emerge. Depending on your winter climate and the look that you want for your garden, you can decide how many plants you leave. If you are leery of leaving old plant growth throughout your garden, you could choose a quiet corner to try this method. Keep stems at a few feet over the cold months and let the new growth come in between the old. The stems will act like natural stakes to hold up next year's flowers. The seed heads of coneflowers, rudbeckias, beebalms, evening primroses, sedums, Jerusalem sage, sea hollies, Joe-Pye weed, mountain mints, and blue false indigos all add structure, shape, and interest to the winter landscape while acting as natural bird feeders.

Daylilies are clump-forming perennials that are easy to dig and divide after a few years of growth.

MOVING AND DIVIDING PERENNIALS

One of the ways you can make your garden more to your liking is to grow plenty of your favorite plants. You can make more from existing clump-forming perennials by digging up large plants and dividing them. The new plants are free; they just take a little time and effort. I had a gardening mentor who filled her garden with the classic fragrant daylily 'Hyperion' in this way. She had moved them around in her flower beds over the years, and when they were in bloom it was a lovely sight that helped to coordinate her garden.

To move or divide a perennial, dig around the outside of the whole plant deeply enough to allow for a significant root ball. You can then either place it into a similarly sized new hole or divide it. If your perennial has a tap root or a single stem, you are unlikely to be able to divide it successfully. If the perennial has multiple stems arising from its roots, like catmint or yarrow, it should be easy to split it into at least two parts. Once the plant is out of the ground, look where it might naturally break apart and use any sharp garden tool to cut it into sections. Try not to make them too small. Water them in thoroughly after planting and keep them moist in the following months.

WEEDING

Plants that you do not want growing in your garden are considered weeds. Weedy plants rob your chosen flowers of needed light, water, and nutrients, take up valuable space, and make your garden look less beautiful. They may already

from left My way of weeding is to pull a few weeds whenever I get a chance. I throw them into one of my strategically placed "weed buckets."

Get to know what your flowers and weeds look like as seedlings. These are young annual poppies grown from scattered seed.

exist in your soil as seeds or plants or may blow in or be introduced with plants you bring into your garden.

I started weeding at a young age in my parents' garden and did not enjoy it. Once I had my own garden, my mindset changed as I came to understand its importance to the survival of my baby plants. By removing unwanted competitors, I gave my precious seedlings the best chance of success. I now love weeding in the same way that you might enjoy ironing a tablecloth or spring cleaning your house. When I look at a flower bed that I have weeded, I feel a real sense of accomplishment. When I weed my garden, I enjoy being down near the soil and swaying flower heads, where I can pay attention to the activities of insects and birds. When I have finished my weeding, I can look back at the completed bed with satisfaction and return to other pressing needs with a calmer frame of mind. Even a few stolen moments down on your knees in a flower bed can be remarkably restorative.

Learning to identify weeds when they are in their juvenile stages is vital to the success of your flower garden. Young weeds are easy to remove, as their roots are small and they are not shooting seeds all over the bed as you pull them out. If you have a purely perennial and bulb garden, it is fairly obvious which plants are weeds and which are not. It is trickier when you have a mixed bed that relies on self-sown or directly seeded flowers because newly germinated seeds look different from the adult plants they will become. If you are growing your flower garden from seed, you need to identify which seedlings are ones that you planted and which are interloping weeds so you don't pull out desirable ones by accident. I have done that, and it is maddening! Some seed packets have a little picture that shows you what the seedlings look like, but you can also search for images in books or on the internet. If you are not sure whether they are weeds, let them grow until they get big enough to have recognizable leaves.

Begin weeding by removing obvious ones like this dandelion, whose yellow flowers produce many seeds.

One way to figure out what the seedlings of your desirable plants look like is to grow one or two in a labeled pot and watch them as they develop. In the garden, try sowing seeds in a distinctive shape such as an X or a triangle, or outline the perimeter of the sown area with a ring of sand or small stakes. The seedlings will be obvious when they emerge, and you will know that everything else is a weed.

Be diligent about weeding. Weeding often, a little at a time, is a much better approach than once-a-month megaweeding. It becomes part of the rhythm of gardening to scan a bed as you walk along and spot the unwelcome plants. Make it a game to find the odd plant out. It takes a while to get your eye adjusted, but once you get used to finding them it becomes quite fun. If you need to clear a large area, start at the same place each time and work your way along systematically. Eventually, the first section will become better and better, and then you can expand the well-weeded part.

Hand weeding is easiest when the soil is moist, like the day after a rain. Grab the undesirable plant at its base and pull firmly upward to remove the whole thing, including its roots, if possible. If you know that it has a taproot, like a dandelion, use your trowel or other narrow tool to dig down and extricate the root. Keep soil disturbance to a minimum. Turning over the soil will bring further weed seeds to the surface where they can germinate. If you have no time to pull out weeds properly but see that some are about to flower or set seed, cut off their heads to prevent one weed from making hundreds of new ones.

If you are gardening in rows or blocks—for example, in a cutting garden— use a sharp-edged hoe to cultivate between the rows regularly. Run the hoe through the soil to chop the weeds off at their roots. Any seedlings that pop up will be unearthed and dry out. You can also hoe between perennials in a mixed bed if you haven't sown any seeds directly into the ground. If you have sown flower seeds directly, you need to remove weed seedlings by hand. At the same

Invasive Weeds

There is a difference between an everyday weed that is merely a garden nuisance and the terrible introduced weeds that are wreaking havoc in our natural ecosystems. These plants are the worst of the worst and take over wild places with their aggressive growth, excessive seeding, and ability to thrive in inhospitable areas. Look for lists by country or state that tell you which plants are considered to be invasive in your area. They vary from place to place, and something invasive in your region might be a desirable wildflower elsewhere.

time, you can thin out your desirable seedlings so each one has enough space to grow strongly.

When you begin a new bed that has pernicious weeds, take the time to clear it before you plant the permanent occupants. Use the method outlined earlier: smother the chopped-down weeds with thick layers of newspaper or cardboard covered in mulch. You can plant annuals right into this upper layer for a temporary display as the weeds beneath rot down. The annuals can be replaced by perennials in a couple of years when you have removed as much of the dreadful weed as you can.

DON'T BRING IN WEEDS

Some of my worst weeds are ones I inadvertently brought into my garden myself. Plants purchased in containers may have little weeds or weed seeds residing in the same pot. When you bring new plants home from the nursery, discard the top layer of potting compost along with any weed sprouts. Perennials in large pots may need a couple of inches removed. Pay special attention around the base of newly added plants in case you missed some weeds. Gardening is one occasion where you do want to "look a gift horse in the mouth." If you acquire a plant that you suspect or are told has been grown alongside weeds, get rid of the soil around the plant and carefully wash off its roots before you plant it in your own garden.

HERBIVORES, PESTS, AND DISEASES

Plants' unique ability to make energy from sunlight means they are the target of a whole range of animals and microorganisms. Garden plants are grown in ideal conditions, so they are lush and therefore especially tempting for herbivores. Small plants that you have just set out are particularly vulnerable, as their soft new foliage is a tasty treat. To defend themselves against damage, plants have developed all kinds of mechanisms against being eaten, including spines and thorns, fragrant oils, and toxic chemicals that are produced within their cells. Each garden has its own set of challenging pests and diseases. You will learn which of your flowering plants are susceptible and how to deal with them.

Gardening with herbivores, like one of my resident rabbits, can be a challenge, so choose plants they do not prefer and exclude them from certain areas if possible.

BROWSING HERBIVORES I have a whole menagerie of animals that live in or pass through my garden. I deal with deer, rabbits, and voles that seem to do the most damage, squirrels that dig up every bulb I plant, plus groundhogs, skunks, raccoons, and a resident snapping turtle. I even once had an escaped wallaby that bounced in to eat my roses! My husband is convinced that the more I pay for a plant, the faster it gets eaten. He took to describing one particular border favored by the deer as my "salad bar," and it wasn't just lettuce.

I love seeing all the wildlife that uses my garden, but it can be frustrating to see big holes bitten out of leaves and flowers eaten off. Over the years I have sequestered my most vulnerable plants in fenced or hidden places where they are protected from most herbivorous animal visitors. In more open areas, I choose plants that are less likely to be eaten. The types and population sizes of browsing herbivores vary regionally. Before you can decide on a plan for dealing with them, you need to find out what your garden is prone to and how much browsing you can live with.

Identify which animals are causing the most destruction so that you can work on your coping strategies. Ask local gardeners for help or take note of the kind of damage herbivores inflict. Deer do not have upper front teeth, so when they bite into a plant, they leave a torn stem behind. They eat a lot of food and can mow down a whole bed in a night. Their eyesight is not very good, and they tend to feed using their sense of smell, so you can use plants with fragrant foliage to confuse them. Rabbits nip through shoots cleanly, and the damage is usually close to the ground.

One of the most comprehensive ways to keep out larger animals is to install a fence around all or part of your garden. If you have rabbits or groundhogs, your fence needs to be solid, or you can add closely spaced mesh like chicken wire along it, with at least a foot buried into the soil. Be sure you don't have any gaps. To keep out deer, your fence needs to be at least eight feet high, or you can use several lower perimeter fences separated by about four feet.

Smaller creatures like voles, field mice, and chipmunks live at ground level or underground, where they can eat roots and bulbs hidden in the soil. We use sharp chicken grit around vulnerable bulbs when we plant them to dissuade burrowers from digging there for a while. You can also plant appetizing bulbs, like tulips and crocus, in little chicken wire cages that you bury. Voles and mice are particularly damaging during a snowy winter when they live and tunnel under the snow, eating whatever plants they can find.

Another method of dissuading munching herbivores is to use repellents that are sprayed or sprinkled on or around plants. Some gardeners make their own repellents using garlic, old eggs, chili peppers, and other stinky ingredients, but there are also plenty of premade versions for sale. Whatever you choose, reapply them regularly, especially after rain. Some herbivore repellents can smell so appalling that they dissuade you from being out in your garden! Change the type of repellent that you use every now and then because you don't want the animals to get used to the scent. I don't spray anything, but I do use some of the natural shake-on repellents that contain blood meal and other ingredients that dissuade herbivores. Repellents do not completely eliminate damage, and a very hungry

from left Rabbits rarely eat strongly scented plants, like this summer-blooming allium 'Windy City'.

Both the coral pink hummingbird mint and the yellow Carolina lupine behind it are typically left alone by rabbits.

animal or a curious young one may still try your plants. Losing some leaves or plants is part of gardening alongside multiple critters.

As you experiment with different plants in your own garden, try one or more of these typically deer-resistant flowers: *Aquilegia vulgaris*, common columbine; *Baptisia australis*, blue false indigo; *Eutrochium purpureum*, sweet-scented Joe-Pye weed; *Monarda didyma*, scarlet beebalm; *Narcissus*, daffodil; *Nepeta ×faassenii*, garden catmint; *Salvia yangii*, Russian sage; *Stachys byzantina*, lamb's ears; *Verbena bonariensis*, tall verbena; and many fragrant herbs.

Some rabbit-resistant plants to grow include *Agastache*, giant hyssop; *Allium*, allium; *Calamintha nepeta*, lesser calamint; *Chrysanthemum*, chrysanthemum; *Digitalis*, foxglove; *Galanthus*, snowdrop; *Iris reticulata*, rock garden iris; *Lavandula*, lavender; *Nicotiana*, flowering tobacco; and *Symphyotrichum novae-angliae*, New England aster.

Slugs and snails are some of the most reviled garden herbivores. If you garden in a damp climate, they may be a particular problem, as these wet-footed mollusks require moisture to move, live, and breed. Look for their telltale silvery slime trails meandering across stones after a night of feeding. Their bites have characteristic jagged edges because slugs and snails do not have teeth, instead using rasping mouthparts to take off layers of the leaves. The best long-term solution if slugs and snails are an issue is to encourage their predators.

from left Encourage
wildlife like this frog
to act as a natural pest
control in your garden.

This pansy has been nib-
bled by a slug or a snail.

I am lucky to have a large toad and frog population that seems to keep mollusks under control. Some birds also find snails to be delicious.

You can also manage slugs and snails by sinking shallow cans into the ground and filling them with beer. The yeasty odor is attractive, and they fall in and drown. Upside-down grapefruit or orange halves are also slug and snail magnets. The mollusks are mostly active at night, so each morning, check and empty the traps. Slugs and snails are loath to cross copper barriers, sharp grit, or crushed eggshells, so use these to surround your favorite flowers. Another way is to grow vulnerable plants in elevated containers to reduce damage.

Insect pests The vast majority of garden insects are benign or beneficial in spite of a common misconception that they are all pests. As gardeners, we should be supporting insects for their essential roles in pollination and as a food source for other animals. There are comparatively few insects that are true pests in your garden, and these vary from region to region. Before you act, make sure you are correct that it is really a problem insect and not a similar-looking beneficial one. Actual pests multiply, quickly defoliating leaves and decimating flowers if they have no natural predators in your area.

Appreciating Insects in Your Garden

Late-flowering plants like this chrysanthemum provide pollen and nectar for a wide range of insects.

One day in late October, I observed one of the last groups of chrysanthemums in bloom in my fall garden. I watched for about half an hour and was astounded at the variety and numbers of insects that visited the flowers. We keep honeybees, so they were there, along with various large bumblebees,

ants, wasps, flies, and beetles. There was one little creature with white legs I had never seen before and a little sweat bee with a shiny yellow-green body that looked like mirrored sunglass lenses. It was truly fascinating to see what turned up just because I had planted a patch of flowers. How many insects use my garden during the course of the year? Many of them I know I do not see, as they are out in my garden at night. If you are curious about the insect visitors in your garden, set aside some time to watch one patch of flowers, and take photos if you like. You will not know what insects, animals, or birds might use your garden until you plant it for them.

I know that some of my insect visitors are getting their food by eating holes in my leaves, but there is an ever-growing body of evidence about the widespread harm that pesticides and herbicides cause within ecosystems. As gardeners, we can do our part by reducing or eliminating their use in our gardens. I am not trying to produce a "perfect" home garden, and I care more about making sure that my birds have safe insects to eat. It is not that I don't get rid of unwanted pests, but I do it in a nontoxic and selective way. If there are flowers you want to keep pristine, take a page from vegetable management practices and throw a lightweight cloth, like a floating cover, over the buds as they are opening to protect the flower. And once you have tackled the occasional pests, appreciate how the diversity of your flower garden benefits the local insect population.

A simple way to dispose of problem insects is to knock them into a bucket or jar of soapy water in the cool of the morning when they are sluggish. This works if they are immobile or slow, but not if they hop or fly too quickly to be caught. You could resort to a net, a hand-held vacuum, a fly swat, squashing by hand, or whatever other ingenious method you come up with. If you are not sure about the insect, wear gloves before you touch them. I will not spray pesticides, as they are indiscriminate killers with terrible continuing effects for the environment. I am very targeted in what I remove. Pests tend to emerge at certain times of year that coincide with the plants they feed on. Once you know their life cycles, you can be prepared to deal with them. Some beetles are voracious munching herbivores with the propensity to multiply rapidly. Get to know the problem beetles in your area. I have particular trouble with the bright red lily beetle, the iridescent brown Japanese beetle, and the spotted or striped cucumber beetle. I stagger the sowing times of some flowering plants to avoid peak emergence of these beetles and regularly hand pick them off my plants. You will have your own cast of nasties that you will gradually begin to recognize and work out coping strategies that suit you. Most problematic insects are ones that have been introduced from other ecosystems and have few or no natural predators to keep their population in check.

Some problems are caused by the larval phase of an insect, like that of vine weevils, which eat the roots of plants, especially those grown in containers. Always use fresh potting compost and check the soil around new plants for C-shaped white grubs. If you see them, spread out the soil and let the birds pick through and eat them, or dispose of the soil in the trash. If you grow bearded iris, look out for iris borers that will eat into the tasty rhizomes. These are moth

from left Check your plants regularly for insect damage so you can take action before it becomes a bigger problem. These aphids are on the bottom of a prairie cup plant leaf. I squirt some off with the hose, squish some, and let ladybugs eat the rest.

Before you remove a caterpillar that is eating a flowering plant in your garden, try to identify it and figure out whether it is a pest or if it will become a favored moth or butterfly.

larvae that overwinter in old foliage, so remove and dispose of last year's leaves in early spring before the new ones start to grow. Another example are the leaf miners, which are usually species-specific fly larvae that produce strange wiggly lines inside leaves. The larvae burrow and eat their way between the upper and lower leaf layers before emerging as an adult later in the season. Take a few moments to hand pluck affected leaves from susceptible plants like columbines.

Sap-sucking aphids are another category of insect pest. They feed on fresh new growth by sticking their stylet, a sharp tubular mouthpart, right into the plant to suck out sugars. They are messy feeders, so some of what they eat emerges from their rear and drips down onto plants below. The first sign of aphid feeding may be the sooty mold that develops on this sticky residue. Look up into the plants and see where the aphids are feeding. You can hand squash them or spray them off with a hose, but make sure not to kill the black larval stage of the ladybug beetles that might be there eating the aphids.

Caterpillars, the larval stage of butterflies and moths, gnaw on your plants before making a chrysalis and then transforming into their adult form. There are some pest caterpillars, but they tend to be more of a problem in vegetable rather than flower gardens. If you are gardening to encourage insects that will in turn feed birds, learn which plants are caterpillar host plants to ensure you are providing food sources. Plant enough flowers so you won't notice a little nibbling, and then, when they emerge as adults, you can enjoy having them in your garden.

Plant diseases are afflictions caused by organisms too small to be seen with the naked eye. They are spread by air and by insects such as leaf hoppers. Diseases rob plants of some of their energy and may cause physical damage. Most of them are fungal, with a few caused by bacteria or viruses. It is easy to grow healthy flowers if you make smart plant choices and quickly intervene if a problem arises. Look for disease-resistant plants, and be sure to choose species that will do well in your conditions. Good gardening practices encourage the growth of healthy plants. Keep your fertilizer levels to a minimum, as excess fertilizer pushes new, soft growth, which is more susceptible to attack. Grow a wide variety of plants in the bed rather than a vast swath of one kind. This way, even if one plant succumbs to a disease, the rest of your garden will look fine.

If you suspect that a plant has a disease problem, you can cut off the infected leaves. If the whole plant is affected, remove and dispose of it entirely into the trash. Check around the plant after you are finished to make sure you have thoroughly cleaned up all diseased parts, including any bits that fell off, because pathogens can linger in dead leaves on the ground. Make sure to clean your clippers or pruners with a spray of rubbing alcohol after cutting each plant. Let the tools dry off before trimming the next one.

There are a couple of common garden plants that are regularly afflicted by plant diseases. For example, I grow border phlox, which is prone to powdery mildew, a fungus that looks like a dusting of flour on leaf surfaces. As the mildew

Some plants, like this zinnia, are prone to powdery mildew. To help reduce problems, choose resistant cultivars, provide good air circulation, and water the soil and not the leaves.

grows, it robs the plant of nutrients. The disease is particularly prevalent in humid summers, which are common where I garden, but I still choose to grow phlox for its fragrant summer blooms in delicious pinky purples or whites. I look for varieties bred to be disease resistant and spread them out in the bed to promote good air flow. I still see some powdery mildew, but most years it does not detract from the flowery display. There are different types of powdery mildew that affect beebalms, peonies, and other flowers. Provide adequate air movement through your flower bed to reduce its occurrence, and make sure your plants are regularly watered at the root zone for optimal growth.

Another garden plant disease you may see is called rust, which appears as circles of orangey brown on the leaves, like rust on an old car. These are caused by host-specific fungi, so rust on one plant will not spread to a different neighboring species. Rusts are often found in the flower garden on common hollyhocks. There is little you can do about this disease. If you want to grow hollyhocks, they will have a certain amount of rust on their foliage. Remove affected leaves and do not compost them. If rust troubles you, grow resistant varieties or other similarly flowered tall spires, like hardy hibiscus.

There are a few other plant diseases you might see in your flower bed. If you are not sure, and a plant is looking wilted or you can see odd leaf spots, streaks, or fuzzy, cottony growth, they are probably fungal or bacterial diseases. Remove the afflicted leaves and throw them away. Any flowering plant that gets affected year after year in your garden should probably be moved to a different place or removed entirely and replaced with another lovely flowering plant.

Epilogue

Into the Future

A flower garden is never static. Your garden will change week by week, season by season, and year by year as buds open to reveal new and beautiful floral combinations. This evolution is central to the enjoyment of flower gardening.

Developing a flower garden requires a combination of learned knowledge, practical experience, and some creative flair. The beginning of your flower gardening love affair starts with the initial plant selection, sowing seeds, nurturing seedlings, preparing the planting area, and then combining the plants to create a pleasing overall picture. Your relationship with your garden then continues and changes over time as you learn more about how to make your plants grow well, what flowers you really love, and which ones go well together.

When you open up a gardening magazine and see photos of smiling gardeners with their lovely garden compositions, remember that the flower beds you see are the result of thousands of small decisions that led to this one specific moment in time. If that same garden is photographed in a couple of years, it will look different. Your garden will develop and morph in the same way, as you play with the inflorescence shapes in your beds, choose to place a plant here and not there, shift the seasonal color palette, or even select a scarlet red cultivar instead of a crimson one. Once you realize that making your flower garden does not happen all at once, some of the pressure is off. You can then treat it as a fun occupation for the long haul, and not something that has to be finished right now.

As you spend time in your garden, you will get to know your plants. You will find out their needs, what they look like when they are growing healthily, and how to tell if they are not. You will learn which plants thrive in your soil and climate. As each year passes, you develop an increasing body of knowledge to inform your garden making next year. You will gradually realize which plants are your "happy" plants: the ones you long to see bloom each year. Grow more of these favorites and seek out other plants that like the same conditions and will look good together. Even flower failures are just hiccups that give you more information about your garden. Everyone kills a plant or two in the course of gardening! Perhaps it wasn't right for your conditions, you may have animals that eat it, or the plant was weak to begin with. Also, don't be afraid to get rid of plants you don't like. Take the duds to a plant swap. Someone might love to give that plant a new home. Replace it with a sturdier plant from your flower wish list.

opposite An abundance of pink poppies glowing in late evening light.

As we close out this exploration of flower gardening, my final words to you are to get stuck in and get started. All gardeners have to begin somewhere. It is easy to get bogged down in the weeds. Just have a go. If I look back at some of my early gardens, I was so proud of the little patch of pot marigolds outside my back door and the tubs of geraniums in bright and cheerful colors. Those early successes were just as meaningful to me when I began gardening as my full flower beds are today. Gardening has been one of the greatest joys in my life. It gives me solace when I am sad, and it has taught me patience and resilience when the deer run through the garden or a summer hailstorm hits. It has made me a great problem solver and given me the ability to laugh at myself. Over the years my garden has been my escape and my way to destress. Nothing in my life seems as bad when I am down on my knees in the garden listening to the hum of the bees, the singing of the birds, smelling fresh earth and my favorite flowers. My wish for you is that this book encourages you to find inspiration to grow your own glorious flower garden.

Suggested Reading

General Flower Gardening Books

Armitage, Allan M. *Herbaceous Perennial Plants: A Treatise on their Identification, Culture, and Garden Attributes*. 4th ed. Champaign, IL: Stipes, 2020.

Carey, Jenny Rose. *Glorious Shade: Dazzling Plants, Design Ideas, and Proven Techniques for Your Shady Garden*. Portland, OR: Timber Press, 2017.

Chatto, Beth. *Drought-Resistant Planting: Lessons from Beth Chatto's Gravel Garden*. London: Frances Lincoln, 2016.

Harper, Pamela. *Time-Tested Plants: Thirty Years in a Four-Season Garden*, Portland, OR: Timber Press, 2005.

Hitchmough, James. *Sowing Beauty: Designing Flowering Meadows from Seed*. Portland, OR: Timber Press, 2017.

Hobhouse, Penelope. *Flower Gardens*. New York: New Line Books, 2001.

Loades, Greg. *The Modern Cottage Garden: A Fresh Approach to a Classic Style*. Portland, OR: Timber Press, 2020.

Jekyll, Gertrude. *Color Schemes for the Flower Garden*. Salem, NH: Ayer Company, 1983.

Lloyd, Christopher. *Color for Adventurous Gardeners*. London: Penguin Random House, 2004.

Monheim, Eva. *Shrubs and Hedges: Discover, Grow, and Care for the World's Most Popular Plants*. Beverly, MA: Cool Springs Press, 2020.

Oudolf, Piet, and Henk Gerritsen. *Planting the Natural Garden*. Portland, OR: Timber Press, 2019.

Tallamy, Douglas W. *Nature's Best Hope: A New Approach to Conservation That Starts in Your Yard*. Portland, OR: Timber Press, 2020.

Specific Flowers

Eastoe, Jane. *Peonies: Beautiful Varieties for Home and Garden*. Kaysville, UT: Gibbs Smith, 2018.

Heath, Brent, and Becky Heath. *Daffodils for North American Gardens*. Houston, TX: Bright Sky Press, 2001.

Parer, Robin. *The Plant Lover's Guide to Hardy Geraniums*. Portland, OR: Timber Press, 2016.

Pavord, Anna. *The Tulip: The Story of a Flower That Has Made Men Mad*. London: Bloomsbury, 2019.

Vernon, Andy. *The Plant Lover's Guide to Dahlias*. Portland, OR: Timber Press. 2014.

Whittlesey, John. *The Plant Lover's Guide to Salvias*. Portland, OR: Timber Press, 2014.

Wilford, Richard. *The Plant Lover's Guide to Tulips*. Portland, OR: Timber Press, 2015.

Garden and Photography Credits

Garden Credits

Tony, Madge, and Glenn Ashton garden, Trevose, Pennsylvania

Jane and Nick Baker, Pembury House, West Sussex, United Kingdom

Carol and Richard Bushell garden, Upway, Oxfordshire, United Kingdom

Jenny Rose and Gus Carey garden, Northview, Ambler, Pennsylvania

Chanticleer public garden, Wayne, Pennsylvania

Alex and John Dodge garden, Broadway, Worcestershire, United Kingdom

Becky and Brent Heath, Brent and Becky's Bulbs, Gloucester, Virginia

Pamela and Duane Hubbard garden, Effort, Pennsylvania

Kathleen Gagan, Peony's Envy, Bernardsville, New Jersey

Jane and Dick Kettler garden, Biddeford Pool, Maine

Meadowbrook Farm, Pennsylvania Horticultural Society, Jenkintown, Pennsylvania

Photography Credits

All photographs are by the author except for the following:

Pages 19, 30 (left), 32 (right), 42, 60 (top right), 69 (top left), 69 (top right), 80 (left), 122 (left), 154 (middle), 177 (left), 181 (right), 242 (bottom), 245, and 260 by Hanna von Schlegell

Page 207 (right) by Rob Cardillo

NOTE

This book was written with the help and advice of many people and is based on decades of practical gardening experience. The information is true and complete to the best of my knowledge, but I accept that all mistakes are my own. Please note that while some advice has been given about edible flowers, it is imperative that you check the correct identification of all plants before consuming them, as many garden plants are not suitable for eating and may be poisonous. If in doubt, do not consume plants or plant parts from your garden. All recommendations are made without guarantee on the part of the author or Timber Press.

Acknowledgments

Creating a book is a collaborative process, so a huge thank-you to all the people on the team at Timber Press who have helped bring this book to fruition, especially Tom Fischer. I wish you all the best in your retirement. To Laura Whittemore and Mike Dempsey for their brilliant editing.

Thank you to all the garden clubs, horticultural societies, and public gardens around the country who have invited me to speak and then taken me to see your lovely gardens. This book is the result of your many requests for a sunny companion book to *Glorious Shade*.

Thanks to all the garden owners who have allowed me to stroll around and photograph your gardens. I have appreciated sharing your creativity and passion.

Special thanks to the directors and staff at the public gardens that make up the Greater Philadelphia Gardens group, especially Bill Thomas and Maitreyi Roy, who have ably led the group. I have enjoyed our collaborations over the years and am thankful to you for allowing me access after hours to photograph your beautiful gardens. I am lucky to have over thirty high-quality public gardens right at my doorstep, including some of the world's best.

Thank you to the wonderful staff and board at the Pennsylvania Horticultural Society (PHS) for their enduring support, especially President Matt Rader. To the staff at PHS Meadowbrook Farm, whom I loved working with, thank you for your friendship and knowledgeable gardening advice.

Great big thanks to my understanding family, who have helped me with moral support, food, and words of encouragement. To my English family, for coming with me on endless garden visits and having tea and cake while waiting for me to finish my photography. To my dad, John Dodge, and stepmother, Alex, my sisters, Katy, Rosie, and Lizzie, my brother-in-law, Terry, and my lovely nieces.

To my husband, Gus, for his unfailing support and love, my three lovely daughters, Meade, Janet, and Emily, my super sons-in-law, David and Anastas, and my grandson, Oliver, who loves to dig in the garden.

To my Northview crew, who have helped me create my lovely garden. To Joe Giampa Jr. for his creativity, for mending the many things that break and chasing Oscar the groundhog. I know that you really love all flowers, not just the blue ones.

Finally, I extend my heartfelt thanks to Hanna von Schlegell, my head gardener. Thank you for leading garden tours, keeping the garden looking beautiful, and maintaining plant records. Most importantly, thank you for reading, rereading, and editing the book manuscript, and changing all of my commas! It is wonderful to have you as my gardening conspirator, especially when we order way too many plants and seeds for the garden.

Index

ROB CARDILLO

JENNY ROSE CAREY is a renowned gardener, educator, historian, and author, and the former senior director at the Pennsylvania Horticultural Society's Meadowbrook Farm in Jenkintown. She previously worked at Temple University for over a decade, first as an adjunct professor in the Department of Landscape Architecture and Horticulture and then as director of the Ambler Arboretum. Jenny Rose has been lecturing nationally and internationally for many years. She is an avid hands-on gardener who has gardened in both England and the United States. Her Victorian property, Northview, contains diverse garden spaces, including a cutting garden, an herb garden, a dry garden, and various mixed flower beds. Jenny Rose and her gardens have been featured on the PBS series *The Victory Garden*, in the *Wall Street Journal*, the *Washington Post*, the *Philadelphia Inquirer*, *GROW* magazine, and the *Pennsylvania Gardener*.